Susie's
SUN SIGNS

Susie's
SUN SIGNS

How to Truly Understand Your Lover, Family,
Friends, Pets, and Yourself Using Astrology

Susie Cox

STERLING

New York / London
www.sterlingpublishing.com

This book is dedicated to my only two astrology teachers, whom I will always love:

Carl Payne Tobey and Sydney Omarr.

STERLING and the distinctive Sterling logo are registered trademarks
of Sterling Publishing Co., Inc.

Library of Congress Cataloging-in-Publication Data

Cox, Susie.
  Susie's sun signs : how to truly understand your lover, family, friends, pets, and
yourself using astrology / Susie Cox.
    p. cm.
  Includes bibliographical references.
  ISBN 978-1-4027-7495-9
  1. Astrology. I. Title. II. Title: Sun signs.
  BF1708.1.C694 2010
  133.5'2--dc22
                            2010017916

10 9 8 7 6 5 4 3 2 1

Published by Sterling Publishing Co., Inc.
387 Park Avenue South, New York, NY 10016
© 2011 by Susie Cox
Distributed in Canada by Sterling Publishing
c/o Canadian Manda Group, 165 Dufferin Street
Toronto, Ontario, Canada M6K 3H6
Distributed in the United Kingdom by GMC Distribution Services
Castle Place, 166 High Street, Lewes, East Sussex, England BN7 1XU
Distributed in Australia by Capricorn Link (Australia) Pty. Ltd.
P.O. Box 704, Windsor, NSW 2756, Australia

Illustrated by Ron Tanovitz

Sterling ISBN 978-1-4027-7495-9

For information about custom editions, special sales, premium and
corporate purchases, please contact Sterling Special Sales
Department at 800-805-5489 or specialsales@sterlingpublishing.com.

Acknowledgments

At five years old, my earliest memories of astrology were from conversations with one of my great aunts, named Rosemary, who had a profound interest in metaphysics and astrology. She had her chart done in 1929 by the famous astrologer Evangeline Adams; I still have and cherish that chart. I am so grateful to both Rosemary and Evangeline for giving me such a remarkable start to my career as an astrologer.

I also want to thank:

Creativity
Susan Day and her brilliant son, Patrick: who inspired the artist in me to blossom.
Carolyn Crawford: for being there for me, no matter what the Virgo task.
Leslie Sieveke: whose strong opinions changed my direction, luckily.
Tina Tuttle: for helping me find the perfect celebrities.

Edits
Tom Whatley and Diana Hunter: who have been my editors for over three decades, so why change now?
Wafah Dufour: my Gemini buddy, for her clever ideas.
Michael Lutin: my streetwise brother who always watches out for me.
Jason Fleming-El: my best astrology student ever, who also ended up being the best editor ever, too.
Michael Munkasey: for valuable keyword advice and his comprehensive book, *The Astrological Thesaurus*.

Support

Clients: for their loyalty and commitment to me and to astrology.

Friend: Jeannine Smith, who made sure my food and TV shows nourished me.

Agent: William Gladstone, for his confidence in me that made this book possible.

PostNet: Jill, Tina, and Joe, for being friends as well as my print and mail gurus.

Canyon Ranch: Enid and Mel Zuckerman, who helped make astrology mainstream.

Sisters: Cathy and Nancy, for laughing, crying, and traveling with me.

Parents: Bill and Jackie Cox, who always believed in me as an astrologer.

Dearest Great Aunt: Katherine Cox, who will love me forever.

Contents

Author's Note

As a professional astrologer, I see a wave of change happening with humanity. It's a new level of awareness. We are experiencing nothing less than a sweeping evolution in consciousness. The motivating force behind this evolution is the drive for self-understanding. We are now entering the 2,000-year Age of Aquarius, which occurs approximately every 25,000 years, as we end the 2,000-year Age of Pisces. The Age of Pisces was about spirituality and our push to understand how we fit into the bigger picture. The Age of Aquarius is about personal independence and the pursuit of self-knowledge. The purpose of this book is to help you get to know yourself and your loved ones using the wonderful language of astrology. It is written for all of you who are curious about the deeper meaning and purpose in your life.

The East is going west and the West is headed east. Thirty years ago I produced a magazine called the *Aquarian Almanac Monthly*, which was full of spiritual and metaphysical curiosities, astrology, meditations, yoga, crystals, and organic food. These were considered fringe elements at the time. Many years later, these subjects are mainstream.

Susie's Sun Signs is part of this shift in consciousness—reaching for self-actualization. Astrology is an ancient method of divination, a way of connecting with the universe. I see it as the perfect clock in the sky, which holds up a mirror to our soul. Astrology has been practiced for over five thousand years and was used before the genesis of the written word. Now is the time to make this ancient, symbolic language modern, starting with *Susie's Sun Signs*.

Astrology is the ideal code for understanding our place in the universe, but it is at the mercy of humans to interpret it correctly.

Introduction:
Sun Signs

t is said that "Happy Birthday" is the most played song of all time. I would venture to say that "What is your sign?" is one of the most commonly asked questions. These two are forever connected, because they both honor the importance of your birth. The sun's position on the day of your birth explains your personality as well as your direction in life. Astrology is a method of interpreting your destiny and this book will show you how to discover that precious knowledge.

Astrology is a tool for self-understanding. Not only does it help us get to know ourselves, it also gives us amazing insight into others. The very first thing I do when I meet someone is to ask for her birth information, which allows me to get to know her quite well—immediately. Of course, the entire birth chart, including all the planets, tells the most about someone. But the best place to start is with the sun.

Astrology is a language of symbols, and each symbol offers volumes of information. Hidden in the sun sign is a detailed explanation of a person's likes and dislikes, personality traits, occupational leanings, overall attitude, and natural talents. It even shows us the most challenging parts of the personality, those that people typically hide—and that's certainly a handy thing to know about someone. It's like shorthand or a secret code. This book reveals the secret code that astrologers have known for thousands of years. Now you have the key that will unlock your innermost mysteries. If you know someone's birthday, you can easily ferret out his secrets, too.

This will be a reference book that you will dip into often. I'm already picturing it with dog-eared pages sitting next to your bed because you will use it so much. Look up your family, friends, even your employer. Once you understand their inner motivations and true natures, you will be able to develop tolerance for even disagreeable people much more easily. After you read this book, you'll realize that everyone has quirky habits. When you realize that these habits can be traced to their signs, how can you hold them against the people around you any more? These characteristics are part of their core natures and need to be viewed with compassion.

I have written this book using true stories in each of the scenarios. Throughout my years as a professional astrologer, I've collected some wonderful experiences involving each sign. So these are real stories about my friends, family, and clients. To protect their privacy, I have changed most of the names in this book, although not all of them. I know my friends and clients will recognize their own stories. But for the rest of you, this will be reality TV astrology because the best way to learn astrology is through real-life stories from other people. Have fun looking into the lives of some of the most interesting people on the planet today!

HOW TO USE THIS BOOK

Susie's Sun Signs is divided into twelve chapters, starting with the sign of Aries and ending with the sign of Pisces. The signs have categories to help you understand different sides of each sun sign. The categories include: male partner, female partner, father figure, mother figure, child, employer, lover, and your pet. If you want to look up your Gemini boyfriend, partner, or husband, go to the Gemini chapter, look up Gemini male partner, and read about him. If you have an Aries newborn son, go to the Aries chapter and read about the Aries child. You just got a new job and want to get to know your Capricorn boss. Go to the Capricorn chapter and look up Capricorn employer. You will instantly know each of them better than you can imagine.

Another way to use this book is to read it from cover to cover. Even though you have your sun in a certain sign, your personal birth chart contains nine other planets in various signs. Luckily, none of us are 100 percent our sun sign. That's impossible, and that's a good thing. If I were 100 percent Gemini, you'd be pulling me off the ceiling. We all have a necessary balance inherent in our birth charts. For example, my Capricorn rising balances all my planets in Gemini and makes me much more focused than many Gemini. Your sun sign will always represent your core nature, but you will definitely have personality traits of the other signs, too. The more planets you have in one sign, the more you act like that sign. If you have your sun in Libra but have several planets in Scorpio, your personality will have a definite Scorpio leaning. So you will enjoy reading this entire book to learn about all the facets of your personality. In addition, I encourage all of you to have your complete chart interpreted by a professional astrologer. Learning the sun signs will only enhance your consultation and give you a deeper understanding of yourself through astrology.

KEYWORDS AND IMAGES

The beginning of each sign starts with the sign's image on the left, and a page of keywords and sign information on the right. Some people learn better with words and others with visuals. Each sign has at least nine keywords. The top five or six keywords are the positive personality traits of each sign. The bottom three or four keywords are "caution" keywords. These words show the challenges of that sign. To modernize astrology, I have taken out all the old illustrations and designed these new images that capture the deep meaning of the signs. These two opening pages summarize the essence of each sign.

INFORMATION

Every chapter has an information box that contains bits and pieces of useful information on each sign. Here is the explanation of the list of information:

Glyph: Each sign has a character called a glyph. Astrology uses these figures instead of writing the words. (For example, Aries = ♈ and Taurus = ♉.

Planet: Each sign is associated with a particular planet. Because their styles are similar, getting to know each sign's planet adds another level of understanding to the sign. For example, Aries is linked with the planet Mars. Taurus is connected to the planet Venus.

Symbol: These are the traditional symbols connected with each sign. For example, Aries = the ram, Taurus = the bull, and Gemini = the twins.

Element: There are four elements in Western astrology: fire, earth, air, and water. Fire = enthusiasm, earth = stability, air = communication, and water = compassion. The twelve signs are divided up into the elements with three per element. The fire signs are Aries, Leo, and Sagittarius. The earth signs are Taurus, Virgo, and Capricorn. The air signs are Gemini, Libra, and Aquarius. The water signs are Cancer, Scorpio, and Pisces.

Mode, or the energetic divisions of the signs. There are three modes in astrology: cardinal, fixed, and mutable. Cardinal = "go"; fixed = "stop"; and mutable = "maybe." The cardinal cross is made up of Aries, Cancer, Libra, and Capricorn. It is quite famous, because these signs begin each season. The first degree of Aries is the first day of spring—March 21—which is also the beginning of each astrological year. The sign of Cancer starts summer, falling as it does at the summer solstice. Virgo begins the fall, and Capricorn starts the winter. Following the lead of Aries, all the signs start from approximately the nineteenth to the twenty-third of each month. When someone is born "on the cusp," or this dividing line, their Sun might be in either sign depending on the date, time, and location of birth.

Number of the sign: Since there are twelve signs of the zodiac, each sign has a number. Aries is number one with Pisces being number twelve.

Color: Each sign is linked to one of more colors. For example, Aries = red.

Gemstone: Each sign is also associated with one or more gemstones. For example, Aries = ruby and sapphire.

Metal: Each sign is associated with a metal. For example, Aries = copper.

Body Part: Each sign is linked to one or more body parts. For example, Aries = the head and adrenals, and Pisces = the feet.

WHAT IS A SUN SIGN?

I'm a Gemini, so when I was born, the sun was traveling through the section in the sky called Gemini. So I'm called sun in Gemini. If you were born with the sun moving through the part of the sky called Leo, you would be called sun in Leo. Thousands of years ago, astrologers divided the sky into twelve sections and named them the signs of the zodiac. These sections were named: Aries, Taurus, Gemini, Cancer, Leo, Virgo, Libra, Scorpio, Sagittarius, Capricorn, Aquarius, and Pisces. Basically, they form a circle around the earth called the zodiac, which is Greek for "circle of animals." It's a reference system—if we all want to point to one part of the sky, we can all call it the same name.

Our individual sun sign explains most of our personality. Each sign has definite traits and tendencies that are obvious when we know the person's sign. Our sun sign shows our inner essence—our basic core nature and how we identify ourselves in society. For example, Leos are natural leaders and Pisces often see themselves as healers.

MORE ON ASTROLOGY

Astrology is the study of the solar system and how it connects with each of us individually through our birth chart. The personal birth chart is a picture of the planets in the sky when a person was born. It is the divine clock in the sky that explains everything—if you know how to read the clock. Your birth chart describes your childhood and your relationship with your parents. It illuminates the type of partner who would be perfect for you. My clients always ask me about the Big Three Questions. What does everyone want to know about? Health, love, and money! Your chart specifically clarifies your karma and your destiny, which is priceless information. Why are we here on earth? Some would say that we are here to get to know who we are so that we can be the very best version of ourselves during this lifetime. Your astrology birth chart is the blueprint that reveals your lifetime patterns.

When you go to a professional astrologer to have your birth chart read, the astrologer will use your entire chart and not just your sun sign. The information you will need to have a complete birth chart interpreted includes the date, time, and location of your birth. Your sun sign describes your personality and lifestyle tendencies, but the entire chart explains everything about your life. You are learning about sun signs, but I also want to give you a peek into the larger world of astrology. The most important parts of the chart are your sun, moon, and rising signs. The sun represents your inner essence. The moon represents your emotions. The rising sign represents your outer personality. My sun is in Gemini, my rising sign is Capricorn, with my moon in Pisces. The Gemini sun is the communicator in me, the Capricorn rising is my dedicated businessperson, and the Pisces moon is my spirituality.

Remember the zodiac and how astrologers divided up the sky into the twelve signs? When I say my moon is in Pisces, it means that the moon was moving through the part of the sky named Pisces when I was born. The moon shows the emotions and feelings in my personality. The rising sign is the astrology sign that was rising in the east when I was born. When I was born, the sign of Capricorn was rising, which gives my outside personality a steady, determined style.

Throughout this book, when I discuss the different scenarios, I describe some people as a double Gemini or a triple Virgo or a mega-Aquarius. Referring to the sun, moon, and rising sign again, you are a double if you have both your sun and moon in one sign, therefore making you a double Gemini (or Taurus or Sagittarius or whatever the case may be). That only happens once a month at the new moon. Or, you can have your sun and rising in the same sign; that also makes you a double. That happens when a person is born at sunrise. A triple is when a person has all three—sun, moon, and rising—in the same sign. Triples are not very common because it means the person is born on a new moon, right at sunrise. That only happens one day a month. But the mega is the rarest of all. I'm defining a mega as a person who has at least five planets in one sign. Since there are only ten planets to go around, five planets is a full 50 percent of the personality, which is huge. That means that megas get the extremes—the best and the worst of the sign.

PETS

Animals have birth charts, just like humans. But unless you have a show dog or a prize racehorse, most of the time you don't know your pet's birth date. But it is easy to find your precious pet's sun sign, since the sun is in a sign for one entire month. And even if you don't know the sign of your current animal friend, when you decide to get a new puppy, kitty, parrot, or chinchilla one day, with the help of this book, you can choose a pet with a compatible sign for your family. (Yes, this works for all the animals.) If you have three Aries little boys who are running around a lot, maybe an Aries dog would be good for your family so the pooch can keep up with the children. In the same way, the Aries boys would make a little Virgo Chihuahua nervous, so when you choose the right sign in your dog, you can make sure it will match your family.

I have chosen one breed of a dog as an example for each of the sun signs, just for fun. For example, I picked a Doberman for Aries and a Basset Hound for Taurus. Your Aries dog doesn't have to be a Doberman, of course. Certain dogs were just good examples of that sign. I also included other animals that are associated with each sign. Maybe Scorpios will prefer a snake to a fluffy little doggie.

Have fun with the pets. One of my friends is a Taurus sun with a Cancer rising. She told me, "Now with your system, I'm a Basset Hound with a Cocker Spaniel rising. At least I'm real cute." The funny thing is that if I were guessing what dogs she looked like, those would be the ones.

SUMMARY

Enjoy reading this book; look up your loved ones to find out what makes them tick; gather some friends together and have a party to look up everyone's astrological traits. You will be truly amazed at how much better you'll know them after reading about their sign. Enjoy learning about yourself and others. Now you'll be able to see why astrology has been used and loved for over five thousand years. It works.

THE 12 SIGNS OF THE ZODIAC

SIGN	DATES	PRIME TRAIT
Aries	March 21–April 20	Dynamic
Taurus	April 21–May 21	Stable
Gemini	May 22–June 21	Talkative
Cancer	June 22–July 23	Nurturing
Leo	July 24–August 23	Confident
Virgo	August 24–September 23	Detail-oriented
Libra	September 24–October 23	Refined
Scorpio	October 24–November 22	Mysterious
Sagittarius	November 23–December 21	Adventurous
Capricorn	December 22–January 20	Determined
Aquarius	January 21–February 19	Inventive
Pisces	February 20–March 20	Compassionate

ARIES

March 21–April 20

KEYWORDS

POSITIVE KEYWORDS

Fast

Courageous

Eager

Emphatic

Self-starter

Energetic

CAUTION KEYWORDS

Pushy

Impulsive

Rude

INFORMATION

FIRST SIGN OF THE ZODIAC

Glyph: ♈

Planet: Mars

Symbol: Ram

Mode: Cardinal

Color: Red

Gemstones: Ruby, Sapphire

Metal: Iron

Body Parts: Head, Adrenals

ARIES: THE PIONEER

Aries are the warriors, and one of my clients—I'll call him Anthony—is a huge action star. He's an Academy Award–winning actor and stars in blockbuster movies. His face and love life are splashed on the cover of tabloids everywhere. Anthony is a double Aries with a strong Mars, so he lives the action star image, even in his private life. Known for his temper, I smile when I see him in a fight scene in a movie as I think of his chart. He is living out his Aries bully in fantasy instead of in reality . . . at least most of the time.

Aries, the first sign of the zodiac, starts on March 21, and marks the beginning of spring. I compare the Aries personality to a sprout just popping up through the ground. That little sprout somehow knows it will one day be a huge, magnificent oak tree, but today it's just a little sprout. And Aries only think about themselves, just as the sprout does. Nothing else really matters in the Aries mind except his survival and success. But just as we can't fault the sprout for wanting to thrive, we need to honor the Aries for his self-focus. Aries is the first of the three fire signs; the others are Leo and Sagittarius. Aries' fire can be compared to the wooden match as it strikes a hard surface, suddenly bursting into a bright flame. But just like Aries, the flame burns out very quickly while searching for another source of fuel. Aries are great initiators, but get bored when the project is up and running. I would advise them to delegate it to a Virgo to ensure long-term success.

The ram, along with its rugged horns, is the symbol for Aries. *Headstrong* is an appropriate word for Aries. Mars, the planet of war, belongs to Aries. And, yes, Aries, like Anthony, are known for their hot temper. Aries forget fast and never hold grudges. Aries live in the moment and not in the past at all. What you see is what you get with an Aries. There are no hidden agendas or ulterior motives. In fact, they are incapable of intrigue. Save that for the Scorpios. Even though Aries are outspoken, courageous, aggressive, and fearless, they also have an optimistic innocence that saves them from their worst tendencies. They can't even imagine failure, even if it's staring them in the face. This is the way of the Aries warrior.

IF YOU'RE AN ARIES, READ THIS!

Aries is the sign of bravery, and you are probably proud of that in yourself. Since you love a challenge, you will never shy away from something because it's too hard. Why do you love a challenge? Because you know you can succeed at anything. The question is this: How passionate are you about the object of your desire? You know that you can't just go through the motions—a goal has to grab you deeply for you to even want to begin your pursuit. If it's not totally exciting, it's a waste of your precious time, since so many other projects are calling you, too. Don't compromise yourself for anyone else. The only way you will fail is if you are not in charge of yourself. Since Mars is your planet, you need to keep physically active. Pass on that meditation retreat and indulge in martial arts instead!

WHAT MAKES YOU HAPPY?

Physical Activity

Every day needs to be different, and you must have something new to discover all the time. Since you are skilled at making quick decisions, situations are often presented to you in which you are in charge of the outcome. Aries are good at scouting locations and love being outdoors. Make time for camping, but forget about hanging out in a folding chair watching the trees grow. Take a hike or even do some rock climbing. Extreme sports were made for Aries—the scarier the better. Bungee jumping or white-water rafting, anyone? The Pisces are hiding right now, but the Aries are saying, "Yes!"

You will be happier when you are the first in line. Aries drive fast, drink coffee, and love stimulants of all kinds. I've asked my Aries clients how they relax and so often they have told me, "I get on my motorcycle and drive really fast!" So I've named that the "Aries motorcycle meditation."

The Ideal Aries Lifestyle

Since you don't take direction well, you own your own business and therefore can run it as you please, without interference. You are a fitness coach and lead your clients on wilderness journeys. You have hiked the

Grand Canyon, jumped out of airplanes, and built campfires with just a flint and a knife. Aries are the pied pipers of the zodiac, who innocently lead people into precarious situations with pure joy. Danger translates into excitement for Aries. They are like the fearless five-year-old boy climbing a tree just to prove he can do it. Leave the closed-in office cubicles for Virgos and Capricorns—Aries need plenty of space and action.

Your Ultimate Dream

To have unlimited freedom to act as you want. You will never have a boss or a partner who even hints at telling you what to do. Every day is full of exciting events that others would see as commotion. You love it and see these events as evidence that you are living life to the very fullest in every moment.

ARIES STRENGTH

Aries are the courageous warriors of the zodiac. They are fast, decisive, energetic, outspoken, and honest. They are natural leaders and are successful because of their innocence. Everything is current, easy, and exciting for the dynamic Aries. Leos are also leaders, but their leadership is related more to politics and business. The typical opinionated Aries doesn't necessarily fare well in these realms, due to her fiercely individual nature. The Aries leadership style is spontaneous and not preplanned. One of the primary strengths of Aries is the ability to think on the fly. It's no wonder that martial artists, members of the military, and surgeons are all strong Aries-type professions. Aries are experts at weaponry, knives, and scalpels. Aries are lovers of masculine sports, such as football, boxing, and car racing. You probably won't catch many Aries watching golf on TV. Just a bet.

ARIES CHALLENGE

Selfishness is the primary challenge for Aries to overcome. Admitting their selfishness can be a tough pill to swallow because they are clearly the best and they know it. They can do anything well if they want to. Aries are the fastest, the strongest, and the bravest of all the zodiac signs. Why can't others see that? They can be incredibly impulsive, arrogant, impetuous, and brash at times. Patience is definitely not their virtue. Especially when Aries defends himself against oppression, his assertiveness often turns into aggression or even anger. Aries outbursts can be quite intense while they're in progress. However, the good news is that these outbursts are short-lived. Daredevils with a reckless style and a cocky attitude are classic Aries. This is the sign of the soldier, the martial artist, and the bully. The word *macho* comes to mind when describing the challenge side of Aries.

MENTAL CHARACTERISTICS

The style of the Aries mind is quick and lively. They think and talk fast. I've noticed that they tend to talk quite a bit and have a habit of interrupting others. Aries see this as enthusiasm, while others might see it as arrogance. The Aries mind is the most decisive of the zodiac. They are experts at initiating but absolutely the worst at completion. As soon as a project is up and running, the enterprising Aries wants to start something new. As soon as routine or boredom creeps in, it's guaranteed that the end is near. *Think before I speak* would be a good mantra for Aries. Impulsive choices could potentially result in disaster for the hard-driving Aries. However, in the end, the Aries capacity for dauntless valor ensures their success. They always get what they want, even though it might take a while.

EMOTIONAL MAKEUP

Even though Aries can act bold and brave, that doesn't mean they can't connect with their emotions. Underneath the strong exterior is quite a sensitive person. Remember the little sprout? Emotionally, Aries is like a small child, often acting out to get what she wants. But the acting out is covering up the more vulnerable emotions of the inner Aries. However, although Aries might feel vulnerable, she never begins to feel helpless or weak. Aries would just hate the thought of being weak, so she shows the world a tough exterior instead. You don't have to worry about Aries hiding her emotions or using them to manipulate anyone. The fiery Aries is pure expression. An Aries will let you know when she is mad and let you know when she is happy. You will never have to guess how an Aries is feeling because she truly wears her emotions on the outside, like a shirt of many colors.

PHYSICAL CHARACTERISTICS

Appearance

As you would expect with the associated planet of Mars around, the typical Aries body is very muscular. They walk fast wherever they are going. Where is the fire? Their facial features are often sharp and angular, with high cheekbones. The most distinguishing feature of Aries is their prominent head and bold eyebrows. Some Aries even have a unibrow. Since red is the color of Aries, many have a ruddy complexion or a reddish hue to their hair. Isn't red hair associated with passion, fire, and intensity? It seems to fit the dynamic Aries.

Fashion Sense

Aries are very sure of themselves and that translates into meticulous care for their appearance. They are usually smartly dressed. Aries can handle bold or dramatic styles with panache. Red, which is dominant in their wardrobe, empowers the warrior energy within them. Female Aries can be the perfect power exec in the black suit with a red silk blouse. Not prone to ultrafeminine details, like frilly ruffles and lace, a more modern and streamlined all-business style would be much more effective. Many of my female Aries clients are prosecuting attorneys who sport sharp Aries power suits in the courtroom.

Health Type

The head and adrenals are associated with the sign of Aries, and that sign usually carries a scar or two to prove it. They are notorious for jumping up quickly and not noticing that tree branch in their path. Aries can easily get over-stimulated with too much activity, coffee, or both. When I have Aries clients, they predictably walk in with coffee in hand. They love their coffee. It's their drug of choice.

Exercise Approach

The very physical Aries needs to sweat. A restorative yoga class would be torture for Aries. They thrive on fast and competitive sports like tennis or racquetball. Aries are much better sprinters than long-distance runners. Martial arts is the perfect kind of exercise for Aries, and not slow forms of exercise, like tai chi. They need to punch something. Buy a punching bag or find a sparring partner. Also, try to stick with the class long enough to get to the weapons part. Now that would be fun for an Aries!

PROFESSIONAL LIFE

Since Aries is the warrior of the zodiac, comfortable occupations include firefighting, police work, mining, engineering, professional sports, and the military. They love working with sharp instruments and make good barbers, aestheticians, dentists, and surgeons. One Aries I know is an emergency room doctor, who loves the fast pace. He uses astrology with his patients and responds to them according to their sign. He shows the charts and all the details to the Virgos, but holds hands with the Pisces. He told me that he only has thirty seconds to bond with a patient in an emergency situation and uses astrology to accelerate the doctor-patient bonding process and speed the patient's healing.

Aries Employer

Your Aries boss, whether male or female, has boundless energy, and you had better be able to keep up with this fire sign. An Aries boss will expect you to have the same enthusiasm and drive as he does. If you want to slide by and coast under the radar, you won't last long. Your Aries boss will be as fast to hire you as he is to fire you. And if you ever do get fired by an Aries, no energy is wasted on sentiment. You're gone in a flash. But if you are truly excited to do what you're told, the Aries employer will be flexible and very generous with you financially. As long as you get your work done with drive and passion, he usually doesn't care if you come in late or take a long lunch. Your Aries employer will be open to your ideas because it shows that you care about your job.

ARIES IN THE BEDROOM

Aries are impulsive and often fall in love at first sight. They have a tendency to act quickly in the bedroom if they really feel passionate about their partner. Being the rough-and-tumble type in the bedroom, almost anything goes. The best way to turn on your Aries lover is to let the compliments flow freely. Let Aries take the lead—they like that. They are wonderful lovers, very sexy, and quite attentive to your needs. Once Aries know you are totally there for them, they are very generous, romantic, and inventive. Take a massage class, rub your partner's head and neck, and he or she will be yours forever.

ARIES MALE PARTNER

Cindy went to a NASCAR race with her brother. They met some other friends there and they all had a wild time yelling encouragement to the drivers. Her brother knew one of the star racecar drivers, who was named Sam, and invited him over to their group. He said he was a double Aries. His energy was strong and masculine, but so much fun. They talked and laughed the entire evening. Afterward, they all went to a sports bar and had even more fun. In fact, they closed the place with a wild party. Cindy was exhausted the next day, but wanted more of Sam. He was the life of the party, so she wondered if she could keep up with him. "Oh, it was probably just the excitement of the race. I'm sure he's more relaxed other times."

After six crazy months of dating Sam, it was just too much for Cindy. She always wanted to be with a man who was the epitome of masculinity. A male Aries is the most manly of all the signs. If you want excitement, choose an Aries. Even though NASCAR isn't my sport, I laugh when I watch Sam on TV, thinking of how fast a double Aries can drive. If you want to laugh, and never quite know what's coming up next, choose an Aries. If you want to go to athletic events and sports parties, choose an Aries. However, if you want security and a calm life, this is not the man for you. You will always be on your toes, running just to keep up with him. Cindy is a Cancer and needs security, so she decided to go with a more stable man and pass on the excitement. Although she will always miss Sam and his thrilling style, her yearning for security meant that she ultimately couldn't handle him. The Aries male needs a partner who can run as fast as he does. Could she have the four children she wants with Sam?

Actually, she could have a family with an Aries. Once they totally fall in love, Aries are very romantic partners. They will stand up, be real men, and take care of their families with integrity and honesty. Aries are very straightforward and can't pretend. The truth just shows through and they can't fake love. Let an Aries pursue you because it makes him feel like a man. If you chase him, he'll run away. But when he is in love, he will give his heart fully and passionately until the very end. Remember, Aries are winners, and they have a very difficult time dealing with failure. It just isn't in their vocabulary. They will work, trying and trying until they succeed. This is true in their careers as well as in their love lives. So if you capture an Aries, you have a real man on your hands. The question is this: Can you handle him?

Because Mars is the planet associated with Aries, pure raw energy runs through the male Aries like electricity through a live wire. They are exciting but can be sizzling to the touch. Listen to me on this one—they need to be in charge. It's the right of the male Aries. He is first in line of all the astrology signs and he takes that position seriously. If your Aries knows he's in charge and his family honors his authority, he's a happy man. If he has to fight to maintain his position of leadership, you'll meet the angry side of an Aries—not a pretty sight. He has a quick and hot temper. But remember: It doesn't last long! He can intimidate everyone when he gives free rein to that part of his personality. But this only happens when his authority is being challenged. If you love him, just let him be the boss.

So what kind of a woman could handle an Aries? You have to be a combination of the perfectly feminine woman, who loves her manly man, and one who also is strong in her own right. The Aries male doesn't just want a woman who sits there waiting for him to tell her what to do. He wants a bold woman who can be his true partner. Are you part diva and part tomboy? Can you dress up in that sexy strapless number for his birthday? Can you go out camping and really enjoy the outdoors thing? Can you drink beer and yell with him at the game? Can you tell him when he's a bit out of control? If you can stand up to him without allowing him to intimidate you, he will respect you and treat you like his precious lady.

ARIES FEMALE PARTNER

Roberta is a successful business owner. She is a headhunter for corporate executives. Her assertiveness serves her very well. Everyone knows her as a tough negotiator who always gets what she wants. Although she's quite feminine, she can hold her own with men in her field. Roberta was the firstborn in her family and was named after her father, Robert. Her father wanted a son, but she is just as strong and successful as any son he could have had. Her peers listen to her when she speaks because of her dynamic style of leadership. Roberta is independent, very bright, and wears red silk when she's in the mood.

If you are interested in a female Aries, you need to read this and understand it well. You have a wildcat on your hands! Sometimes you will get scratched for no apparent reason and other times she'll purr while resting her head in your lap. Which one is the real Aries? Both are . . . it just depends on her frame of mind at the time. She is as tough as nails on the outside and a sweetheart on the inside. I think female Aries act tough to protect their inner sensitivity, but they'll never tell you that. Roberta always puts on a strong front, even with me. The worst thing that can happen to an Aries—male or female—is to appear weak. They are natural leaders—no way can they be soft or feel taken advantage of by anyone. It just won't happen, because they won't let it happen. So what is the best way to deal with your Aries partner? Gently—or you'll get scratched again.

What are some tricks to stay on the good side of your Aries partner so you won't see the wildcat (much)? Aries need to be number one, always. Being number two will never, ever do. They lean toward the selfish side because of their fiery, first-day-of-spring sense of entitlement. Don't even think of playing around or even flirting with other women. Your Aries is one of the most possessive and jealous signs of the zodiac. The only sign that surpasses the Aries jealousy is the notorious Scorpio woman. Scorpio will give you the cold shoulder forever, but your Aries will have red-hot fits of temper. If she ever does catch you with another woman, I feel sorry for you. You are in so much trouble, and if she does stay with you, which is quite doubtful, from then on she will be totally in charge.

Now that you know how to stay out of trouble, how can you bond with your Aries wildcat? Connect with her amazing mind. Aries have one of the quickest minds of the zodiac. Gemini is the only other sign that can outthink the Aries mind. This is the most important bit of information to have if you want to keep your Aries! You *must* have a mind that can not only keep up with her, but that can also engage her in fascinating conversations about a wide variety of subjects. Are you interesting enough to keep her attention? You need to look at her as if she were the only one in the world when you talk with her. Don't even think about answering your cell phone when you're talking with her, or else you will definitely see the wildcat.

The most endearing part of Aries is their positivity. They always think that everything will work out. No, they *know* that everything will be exactly the way they want it to be. Aries are fabulous at easily accomplishing enormous feats that would be daunting or impossible for other signs. They just *will* it done. Their biggest talent is their incredible combination of having a not-taking-no-for-an-answer style enhanced by unbridled positivity. Aries are just not wired for failure. Once your Aries decides that she can be totally herself and be with you, too, she's yours. When she applies her winning attitude to your relationship, you'll have an exciting, romantic, smart, bold, and driven partner. She won't be the easiest sign to be with, but she will be one of the most exciting and, ultimately, rewarding.

ARIES FATHER FIGURE

Frank is a triple Aries and he's a football coach. This Aries is not just any coach; he's an NFL Super Bowl–winning coach. I love watching his fiery aggression on TV during one of his games. What a great outlet for his Mars! As a father, his boys love him but they know they all need to stay in line, because their Aries dad will take no funny business from them—ever. He goes from exciting dad to controlling, loud dad in a flash if anyone gets out of line. The Aries dad is only tough if he feels as if he needs to put out a fire somewhere.

If there is one alpha male of the entire zodiac, it's the Aries father. Good thing Charlie is into sports, because Aries is the sign of the athlete. Not only are Aries naturally coordinated, but their aggression has a positive outlet in sports. They need to punch or kick something regularly, and it might as well be a ball. After a number of fights as a kid, Charlie's parents luckily recognized his aggressive tendencies early in his life and directed him toward athletics. Great choice! Instead of fighting, Aries can become experts at boxing or martial arts. The speed and decisiveness of Aries make for the perfect athlete. Charlie's fire sign energy makes him energetic and fearless, so he can enjoy being rough-and-tumble.

Since Aries is the first sign of the zodiac, they always need to be first. They think of their needs first, like the little sprout of spring. It's not their fault—they just can't help it. This trait definitely shows up in your Aries father. He is the dad who rules with an iron fist. You must have wanted a very strong, masculine, and headstrong father for some reason. Do *you* want to be powerful? He will definitely want you to be as strong as he is . . . eventually. But don't think he wants to see power in his children yet; remember, he is the only one who gives the orders now.

Just watch the sparks fly if you even try to challenge his authority. He is totally in charge and when you realize that, your life will be much easier.

Even if you think that everything is going smoothly, your Aries dad will occasionally have his fiery outbursts. He has to run the entire household by his rules. Aries rules! Your mother will have to obey the rules, too, if the house is going to be peaceful at all. He likes a more traditional style of parenting, one in which the man definitely wears the pants in the family. One thing that can always set off your father's temper is when anyone in his family challenges him in public. His image of being the man in charge is especially important to his reputation. So when the alpha male Aries father does get mad, things get pretty intense. He has a loud voice anyway, but when he yells, the walls shake. He is brutally honest and he won't stand for cheating in others. Remember, the Aries temper is like the wooden match that ignites quickly but also flares out just as fast. Just stay out of his way, because it will be over as quickly as it began.

Once your Aries father knows that everyone understands the pecking order, he will be one of the most generous and exciting fathers in the zodiac. He is uncomplicated and has no hidden agenda or sneaky side, so he will always be easy to read. Your father will take his family on cool, active, and memorable vacations. If nothing else, he is true to himself. He feels that his job as a father is to raise his children to be true to themselves, just as he is. Always be honest and up front with him, because he will find out if you're hiding something anyway. You definitely don't want to get caught with your hand in the cookie jar with an Aries father.

ARIES MOTHER FIGURE

Ann is the mother of two boys and is so glad she had sons. She's been a tomboy since she was a child and always wanted boys. She is the type of mother who invites the entire baseball team over after the big game. She doesn't even mind if all the players run around the backyard yelling happily at the top of their lungs. She's happiest when there is commotion and activity in her home all the time. After all, your Aries mother is one of the guys. She is your biggest fan and will always be on the sidelines at your games, cheering your team on to success.

If your mother is an Aries, you can be assured that there will be lots of activity in your home. Since she is a fire sign and full of energy, your home will be very lively. A Pisces mother would see your home as being in chaos, but the Aries mother sees it as evidence of life being lived to the fullest. Your mother is friendly, outspoken, and honest. She talks loudly and gestures wildly at times. She has as much energy as you have, even though she is your mother. Aries is the Energizer Bunny of the zodiac. Typically, she gets up early and expects the entire house to get up with her, and everyone will get up because of all the ruckus and noise she makes. Aries are never known for being quiet. Remember that Aries lives in the moment and won't reflect on the past, like a Cancer mother. There are simply too many fun things to do today to dwell on yesterday.

Your Aries mother is the type who will wear the pants in your family. Unless your father is also an Aries or a Leo, she will be in charge of the household. If both your parents are Aries—a rare occurrence—they will have to figure out which one will be in charge. My hunch is that she will win. The sign of Aries is prominent in businesswomen, so, in addition, you could have a powerhouse professional mother. It doesn't matter if she is gone during the day; she will still be in charge. While she is at work, it would be easy for her to check on you and know exactly what is happening with everyone. Don't ever think you can get away with anything around her because somehow she always knows.

Every now and then, your Aries mother will do too much and get tired. Help her when she needs your help, because you want a rested, happy Aries mother. When she is tired or upset, watch out! Your fun-loving, enthusiastic mother can quickly turn into an angry shrew. I know those are strong words, but if you have an Aries mother, I'm sure you know what I mean. She will be quick to anger and will lash out intensely at times. Your mother will always be honest with you and she expects—no, she demands—the same honesty from you. Yes, let's face it: Your mother has a temper. But the upside is that, although it's severe while she is yelling at you, it doesn't last long at all. Aries have short-term memories when it comes to their temper. In just a few minutes, you will have your loving mom back again. Whew!

Pushy. Is that a good word for your Aries mom? Sharp and impatient also come to mind. But she has a reason for her pushy attitude—she wants to inspire you. The Aries mom is a tough love kind of a mother. She wants you to be strong and succeed in your life and her style is to give you not-so-gentle nudges. She might not be the most domestic mom of the zodiac, knitting you sweaters and baking cookies. She might rule the roost with a strong hand. But she'll play ball with you in the backyard. She'll take you and your friends to the beach for a vacation and learn how to surf with you. Even though you might not realize it now, you are lucky to have your Aries mother. Not many other mothers will always say, "You can do it! You can do anything if you want it badly enough. Go for it!"

ARIES CHILD

Tyler is a nine-year-old Aries boy. His Libra mother, Sharon, had her hands full with him as a baby. She couldn't wait for him to get a little older, so he would be easier. She now sees that that was wishful thinking on her part, because he didn't outgrow his temper tantrums. They are just getting more sophisticated. Sharon thinks he's going to be the king of the debate team when he grows up, and she could be right. One thing that she has learned is that the key to his happiness is to keep him active.

If you were blessed with an Aries child, put on your running shoes right now. You are so going to need them just to keep up with your little fire baby. Aries children have the highest energy level of all the signs of the zodiac. Your little one is guaranteed to keep you young. Those born under this fire sign are impetuous and defiant if they feel controlled. They want to do what they want to do when they want to do it. Since Aries is the first sign of the zodiac, they are often born leaders. As children, those leadership skills aren't developed yet. But they don't know that. Aries are born with a sense of entitlement that only gets stronger as they mature.

The Aries baby is one of the most restless of the zodiac. Don't take it personally if your little fire baby doesn't snuggle for hours. You'll be lucky to get snuggles for a few minutes. If your little one gets fidgety, take her for a stroller ride in the park. As long as your Aries is active, you will have a happy baby on your hands.

When your Aries is old enough for school, put her in sports or dancing as soon as you can. Aries are rough-and-tumble. It is the sign that will climb trees and yes, you will go to the doctor for occasional stitches to be sewn up. Fast-moving martial arts, like karate, are perfect classes for the Aries child.

Aries are hardwired to go fast. Just get used to it, because that's not going to change. I have a huge concern about Aries children and the trend to give schoolchildren drugs to slow them down. Don't think your Aries has Attention Deficit Disorder (ADD) because more than likely you can blame it on the typical healthy Aries energy. Read as much as you can about Aries before you give your little one drugs to slow him down. Your Aries child goes fast and is *supposed* to go fast.

You might have your hands full with your Aries teenager. It is not the best sign to automatically do their homework, as a little Virgo does. You will have learned by the time your Aries is a teenager that telling her what to do simply does not work! The best way to talk your Aries teenager into doing something is to present it as a game or a challenge. They are natural competitors so, for Aries, competing in a contest is great fun. Aries have plenty of energy, but the trick is not to demand anything of them, but to coax them into it.

The best talent of Aries children is their innate sense of leadership. You might want to enlist them in a leadership class. As they grow up, they will go through different stages, from being selfish to being the bully to eventually growing into their full power as a leader. As their parent, you will just need to be patient to watch that Aries evolution occur. It will all be worth the effort when you see your little Aries mature into an amazing and powerful person.

ARIES PET

Is your household wild and wooly? Are your kids running out to the backyard while they slam the screen door? Is one or more of your children an Aries? Then you have a perfect family for an Aries pet. Using a Doberman as an example of an Aries pet, it will always have lots of energy, whether it's a puppy or a grown dog. Get an Aries dog if you have a big backyard and have lots of room for the dog to run. Do not get an Aries pet if you can't give it plenty of attention. The Aries dog needs you to focus on it, just as the Aries human does. Take your Aries dog on long runs to the park or out camping in the wilderness. It will be much happier when things are busy and active. Aries dogs are the ones who are obsessed with chasing a ball. Some of them always have that grungy, wet ball in their mouths, just in case.

ANIMALS FOR ARIES
Anteater
Ape
Badger
Boar
Chimpanzee
Grizzly Bear
Polar Bear
Ram
Rooster

PERFECT GIFTS FOR ARIES

It will be fun and easy to buy the perfect gift for your Aries, since that sign is so active. Their main interests are games, sports, accessories, and keeping stimulated. Here are some suggestions for the present any Aries will love!

Games

- How-to DVD for a new game or hobby
- High-adventure computer games

Sports

- Season tickets to a favorite sports team
- Workout equipment
- Skydiving lessons
- A very nice sweatsuit

Accessories

- Cool sunglasses
- Red hat or scarf
- Earrings
- High-tech shaving kit
- Makeover or facial
- Lighter
- Fireplace tools
- Pocket knife

Stimulants

- Gift card to Starbucks
- Cappuccino or espresso maker
- A year's supply of vitamins and supplements
- Aries coffee cup
- Stopwatch

ARIES CELEBRITIES AND THEIR BIRTH DATES

Matthew Broderick	March 21
Reese Witherspoon	March 22
William Shatner	March 22
Sarah Jessica Parker	March 25
Sir Elton John	March 25
Sandra Day O'Connor	March 26
Reba McEntire	March 28
Eric Clapton	March 30
Christopher Walken	March 31
Ewan McGregor	March 31
Al Gore	March 31
Debbie Reynolds	April 1
Alec Baldwin	April 3
Eddie Murphy	April 3
Robert Downey Jr.	April 4
Heath Ledger	April 4
Colin Powell	April 5
Russell Crowe	April 7
Robin Wright	April 8
Dennis Quaid	April 9
Joss Stone	April 11
David Letterman	April 12
Andy Garcia	April 12
Abigail Breslin	April 14
Emma Thompson	April 15
Charlie Chaplin	April 16
Victoria "Posh" Beckham	April 17
Jennifer Garner	April 17
Kate Hudson	April 19
Ashley Judd	April 19

TAURUS

April 21–May 21

KEYWORDS

POSITIVE KEYWORDS

Calm

Stable

Deliberate

Leisurely

Laid back

Realistic

CAUTION KEYWORDS

Stubborn

Materialistic

Passive

INFORMATION

SECOND SIGN OF THE ZODIAC

Glyph: ♉

Planet: Venus

Symbol: Bull

Element: Earth

Mode: Fixed

Colors: Blue, Sea Green

Gemstones: Azurite, Malachite

Metal: Copper

Body Parts: Neck, Throat

TAURUS: THE BANKER

Kenneth, a double Taurus, has owned a real estate business for twenty years. He loves luxury so much that he only handles high-end properties. This stable Taurus is a money magnet and always seems to smell the good deals. He is very hardworking, but his success is mostly attributed to his calm and steady attitude. His clients trust him and he would never let them down. But, of course, even among the swanky properties that he sells, Kenneth's home is the nicest of them all.

Taurus loves luxury. I call it the sign of creature comforts. Their planet is Venus, the planet of indulgence. Being true to their element, they love the sensual feeling of the earth and are never very far from it, whether it's a garden, a hike in natural surroundings, or a barbecue in the backyard. In fact, Taurus is the earthiest sign in the zodiac. You can easily recognize a Taurus by her incredibly steady and calm inner strength. It's quiet power. Geminis will chatter on when they talk. Taureans answer deliberately and with far fewer words. They have a sense of authority when they speak. People listen. My sister is a Taurus and she usually is right when a situation arises. She told me, "I'm always right, and when people realize that, my life will be much easier." She makes people say, "Yes, you are right and I am wrong."

Like the bull that symbolizes their sign, slow and steady is Taurus' style. They are peace-loving and not prone to being nervous or worried. The typical Taurus is stable and knows exactly where he is going. While some signs, like Leos, enjoy closing the blockbuster deal, Taurus saves steadily over the years to accumulate his fortune. And, yes, most Taureans do have fortunes. Although Taurus is the sign of luxury, they are actually quite frugal. You will never see a Taurus being extravagant or wasteful. *Quality not quantity* is their mantra.

You are lucky indeed if you are close to a Taurus. They are one of the most loyal of all the signs. Even though they are frugal, they are never stingy. If loved ones need money, they are always there for them. But they had better pay it back, sooner or later. The Taurus won't forget. Most Taureans are homebodies and would rather entertain at home than go out to busy, noisy venues. They don't like loud noises. So, save the flash for the Leos . . . Taureans like peaceful gatherings with family and close friends. By the way, make sure to bring a nice bouquet of flowers and a bottle of good wine.

IF YOU'RE A TAURUS, READ THIS!

I'll bet you're glad that you're a Taurus. Did you know that Taurus is the sign of money? Personal money, not other people's money (like Scorpio), but your money! That is why most Taureans are successful in business. You have the strongest tendency of all the signs to focus until you get what you want. It doesn't matter how long it takes; you are in no rush. Patience is one of your finest virtues. You naturally know that good things might take a while to accomplish, but it will be worth it when you look at all the beautiful things you have acquired. Your planet is luxurious Venus, the planet of love and beauty. Venus wouldn't waste itself on a sign that doesn't appreciate beauty. So don't think that luxury is an indulgence—for you it's a necessity. Always surround yourself with the most sumptuous fabrics and the finest works of art. You love it; you need it. Luxury feeds your soul.

WHAT MAKES YOU HAPPY?

Financial Security

You must have a life of comfort and beauty; otherwise, you aren't living up to the fine Taurus lifestyle. While other signs can struggle or live in a bohemian world, you have amazing earning power. Success comes easily to you. If any sign has the golden touch, it's Taurus. Oh, it's not that you haven't worked hard and earned your lifestyle. But you see that all your hard work pays off in aces.

Nature

Nature is very important to you, with your earth sign of Taurus. Make sure that you absolutely take time to go outdoors and appreciate this beautiful world of ours. Try taking a class in gardening or flower arranging. How about going hiking with friends? Is your home landscaped beautifully? I'm sure it is! But you can always make it more appealing. Invest in that garden sculpture you want—you know you have to have it. Won't it look great in your garden?

Usually the most important thing for a Taurus is to have a peaceful life. You crave comfort and tranquility and are willing to work hard to get what you want. But at some point, hopefully sooner rather than later, you want to live the life you have been working so hard to achieve. Make sure you don't get caught up in your career so much that you aren't living the life you want—one of peaceful abundance.

The Ideal Taurus Lifestyle

Early retirement. Because of frugal spending and good planning, you now can live the lifestyle others envy. Some days you sleep late, other days you get up early to plant your garden, still other days you just lounge around on the sofa with a good book. But you always have time to get together with your best friends and family. Call up your buddy, get a bit dressed up, and go out to that new, upscale restaurant. You have saved up, and now you can buy that Jaguar you always dreamed of driving. The Taurus in you isn't showing off or you'd be driving a huge Cadillac. You just like quality, that's all. You are a Taurus . . . you deserve it!

Your Ultimate Dream

To work hard and retire from your respectable career with enough money so that you can buy or have anything you want, within reason. You always have the time to be with your loved ones as much as you want. You have achieved your goal of financial security and now you can relax into a life of comfort, luxury, and for you, bliss.

TAURUS STRENGTH

Taureans are fabulous at anything dealing with the material world. They are industrious, sensible, deliberate, and, almost always, very successful at their endeavors. With fortunate Venus as their planet, how can they go wrong? Venus offers a keen sense of beauty with a natural talent for color and design. Many Taureans are creative artists or interior designers. They make everything more beautiful than it was before.

But I think the best talent of Taureans is their steadfast attitude. They are not easily discouraged when they have a goal in mind. They act with purpose instead of just running around looking busy. Their deliberate and focused mind can accomplish more than almost any other sign. Taureans are so good at endurance that they could bottle it and sell it. They are excellent money managers, and with all that ability to focus, no wonder they drive Jags.

TAURUS CHALLENGE

Plain and simple, Taureans are stubborn. They are resistant to change and tend to be more conservative than other signs. Their opinions are firm and they don't appreciate people trying to change their minds. Don't even try, Aquarius—it won't work. Flexibility is definitely not their forte. Since they love possessions and can be materialistic, some Taureans have a tendency toward overindulgence. They might overeat, overdrink, and love the life of excess, so some Taureans have issues with excess weight. Do they have a temper? You bet they do! It takes a lot to make a Taurus mad, but when they get backed into a corner—watch out! They will surprise you with an amazing temper. Don't think that all their sweetness dilutes their strength. Guess what? A Taurus can be sweet and tough at the same time.

MENTAL CHARACTERISTICS

This earth sign is more set mentally than other signs. They are conservative, structured, determined, and always have a plan. Taurus is the sign that saves a nice chunk from each of their paychecks faithfully for their entire career. Save the risky investment schemes for Aquarius, because Taurus plays it safe and steady. They have a strong sense of self-worth that grows as they mature. Since their planet is Venus, a sweet kindness and thoughtfulness also characterize almost all Taureans. My sister is a Taurus. She is always the one to pull the siblings together for family events. She is the glue that keeps us connected—so typical of a stable Taurus. If you want to know about financial security and how to achieve it, just ask a Taurus. They are the masters of the material world.

EMOTIONAL MAKEUP

Taurus is one of the most stable signs emotionally. They are warm-hearted to their loved ones as well as to strangers. Taurus will be kind to a waitress without even thinking about it. That is just their way. They seldom worry, fret, or even get irritated. If they are living the peaceful, comfortable, and luxurious life they want, there is no need for upset. They seem to have the natural wisdom to know that all is well, all the time. It really takes a lot to throw the secure Taurus off his game, but don't think they don't feel deeply. Although Venus is the planet of beauty and creativity, it is also the planet of love. Taurus gives unconditional love to her loved ones. This sign has one of the biggest hearts and truly wants to assist people. But also because of their kindness, they have a tendency to get entangled in the situations of others in an effort to help. Sometimes with the loving style of Venus, they almost care too much.

PHYSICAL CHARACTERISTICS
Appearance

The Taurus body is compact, muscular with a low center of gravity. The classic body style would be somewhat like a wrestler's body. Taureans typically have short necks and a broad or heart-shaped face with large eyes and full, sensuous lips. Their neck is short and matches their compact body. Oftentimes, the women shop in the Petites section of the store. Their gait is slow and deliberate.

You won't find Taurus running around in circles out of control over anything. There is no rush with this earthy sign of the zodiac. Often the hair, eyes, and overall coloring are dark. Taurus could be called sturdy with a solid structure, but some of the more indulgent types of Taurus could be called round or plump.

Fashion Sense

Classic with a twist would be the most common style for a Taurus. I've named it the sign of cashmere—no rough, scratchy wool for the very tactile Taurus. The texture of the fabric is extremely important. It must—*must*—be soft for the delicate Taurus. Plus, they are not at all prone to the trendy, hip, changeable fashion trends of the season. They would see it as a waste of money to buy something that will be out of style next season. The true Taurus buys high-quality clothing at very expensive stores . . . on sale! The frugal part of the Taurus just loves a good deal but is unwilling to compromise on quality. Their closet is filled with classic pieces that will last forever and never go out of style. They always look stylish and sophisticated.

Health Type

The parts of the body that is associated with Taurus are the neck and throat. I have also seen the teeth connected with Taurus, so floss every day and get your teeth cleaned often to ensure good dental health. Since this is an earth sign and prone to being stiff, they need to do exercises that promote flexibility. Taureans would probably be more comfortable buying a yoga or stretching DVD and using it in their home than going to a gym. They don't like loud noises, and all the banging of the exercise equipment, along with people's voices, just wouldn't be cozy enough for this peaceful sign.

Exercise Approach

This steady earth sign usually has the greatest endurance of all the signs of the zodiac. Since they savor nature, great exercises for them need to be done outdoors. They love to take long walks in the morning with their dog. Hiking in the cool mountains with friends is always a joy for them. Gardening serves two purposes: It's good exercise and it also makes their yard more beautiful. Great combo for a Taurus! Weight training would feel comfortable for the compact, strong Taurus. Pass on the fast, competitive racquetball . . . save that for Aries.

PROFESSIONAL LIFE

Since Taurus needs to feel financially secure, the most important thing in a Taurean's career is stability. They will set up their 401k plan early and will get the best benefits possible. Some Taureans will settle for a career that may not be their dream job but that will offer them security instead. An obvious career path is a bank teller, financial advisor, or financier. The more creative Taurus types do well as clothing designers, artists, musicians, perfumers, aestheticians, or makeup artists. The outdoorsy types might go into biology, horticulture, or landscape design.

Taurus Employer

You are lucky indeed to have a kind Taurus boss—if you play by his or her rules, that is. As an earth sign, the Taurean boss puts in place definite procedures with an old-fashioned style of operation. Save the high-tech stuff for Gemini and Aquarius. Typical Taureans get dragged kicking and screaming into cyberspace, yet never really understand it. But they are very hardworking and expect the same from you. The Taurus needs a peaceful working environment . . . no drama for them, please. They are fair and understanding and will listen to you when you have a special need. But this kindness will end abruptly with a loud voice if they realize you are taking advantage of their caring nature. Yes, Taurus has a temper if they get pushed far enough. Remember, they are in it for the money. So if you are not holding up your end, you will be gone soon. If you show your Taurus employer loyalty and dedication, the two of you will have a long and successful career together.

TAURUS IN THE BEDROOM

If you have a Taurus lover, you are one of the lucky ones. This sign simply owns sensuality. If you like cuddling, being massaged, and getting hours of gentle lovemaking regularly, then you are with the right sign. Since their planet is Venus, how could they be any other way? Romance, flowers, epicurean snacks, and good sex . . . who wouldn't want that? And remember: They have the greatest endurance of all the signs. That translates into being a wonder in the bedroom. If you want unpredictable excitement, choose an Aquarius. If you want fast and furious, choose an Aries. But if you want to be satisfied and contented, choose a sweet, sweet Taurus.

TAURUS MALE PARTNER

Mike is an investment banker. He loves helping people get a solid start in their new business. People listen when he talks because of his calm, positive attitude. He not only speaks from a wealth of experience, but also has amazing common sense. His advice is rock-solid and will prove the test of time. No shaky, high-risk, scary deals here. Since this sign is the master of the material world, what a perfect sign to turn to for money advice. Listen to him. Like all Taureans, he has a love of the nicer things in life and attracts abundance easily. No wonder he has a smile on his face. It's the smile of success.

If you want a relaxed, comfortable, stable life, choose a Taurus man. Just like Mike, he will always be there for you, although that is hard to figure out at first. You must have patience with your Taurus because in romance he doesn't move quickly. The speedy Aries often falls in love at first sight, but does it last? The slow and steady Taurus needs to make absolutely sure about his feelings first—and that might take a while. Let him take the lead and don't rush him or he will get scared off. Taureans have their own rhythm and just can't go any faster and still feel comfortable. Mike told me that he wants love, but at the right time, and with the right person. If you need drama or want life in the fast lane, this is definitely not the sign for you. If you want emotional security and are willing to have set routines in your life, he might be the one.

Venus is the planet of love and is proudly associated with Taurus. Once your Taurus man finally knows you are the one for him, the romance begins and never ends. You can expect devotion, loyalty, honesty, and a total consideration of your needs. He is the perfect provider, and not just of money. He will protect you and give you unconditional love in addition to lovely presents. Another added plus is that there is hardly another sign that is better in the bedroom. You will find a rose under your pillow . . . for no reason at all except that he loves you. He is the type you can call at 2:00 a.m. with a flat tire and he'd be there in a flash . . . and with a little snack for you in case you haven't eaten. Parents love this kind of a man because they know you are in good hands. Others might like the excitement of the bad boys, but you are one of the smart ones and got the purity of one of the good boys.

So why doesn't everyone choose a Taurus if they are so perfect? Well, like all signs, there is always a challenging side. The challenge side of Taureans is their stability, which can turn rigid at times. *Stubborn* is the word that belongs to this sign. They are absolutely attached to their routines and have strong, set opinions about almost everything. They are resistant to change, so keep the furniture where it is without surprising him. The Taurus male likes to be in charge. He is a manly man. He doesn't have the bravado of Aries, but he is very masculine indeed. He loves sports. However, being an earth sign, he likes nature, too, and his quiet life. He is not comfortable with loud, wild, and crazy people or lifestyles. Your Taurus can have a temper, but it takes a lot to rile him. He will take it and take it and then one day just explode over it. Then you see his loud, grand temper . . . not a pretty sight.

Taureans are attracted to women who are both strong and feminine. You need to be able to stand up and say what you want in life. He needs to respect his woman for her confidence. But the most important thing for him to know is that you are totally there for him. Since he doesn't commit himself easily to a relationship, he needs to know that it's for keeps. Can you embrace his love of structure and routine? If you can, you are halfway there. Then you can be assured of a stable, calm, and comfortable life. Beauty, love, and romance are all yours with your lovely Taurus. So if you are lucky enough to have a Taurus partner, you will have the promise of sensual happiness. What could be better than that?

TAURUS FEMALE PARTNER

Cathy is a famous clothing designer whose clothes are on runways in New York, Milan, and Paris. Since Taureans are very tactile, the feel of the fabric is the most important element to her design. She uses mostly silk, velvet, and cashmere. Her mantra is shiny, sparkly, soft, and furry. Her style leans toward the classic with a hint of luxury and a little edge. Cathy's favorite design piece is the simple, yet elegant, little black dress. She knows that all women want to feel feminine and sexy, but they also want clothes that are flattering yet not too revealing. So her clothes offer the clean lines and feminine style of the perfect woman. She is very dedicated, ambitious, and successful. The question is this: Are you man enough for her?

A Taurus woman is a strong woman. She is the perfect combination of strength and femininity. This earth sign makes her as solid as the rich ground. The beautiful Venus influence in her brings all the birds, butterflies, and hummingbirds to her quiet field of flowers. If one sign of the zodiac could personify Mother Nature, it is the female Taurus. She is a lover and protector of animals and takes her passion for all creatures quite seriously. The Taurus woman is also a guardian of the earth. Nature is her home and where she feels the most at ease. She is incredibly loyal, stable, and easily creates a beautiful home. She is a one-man woman and will have a comfortable, cozy lifestyle. It's her destiny. Can you give her the lifestyle she deserves? If you can't, just walk away now. It will never work.

Luxury is what makes a Taurus woman happy. Not gaudy and glitzy, but genuine quality. She isn't a show-off with her possessions. It's not about other people. It's about her own sense of entitlement. She's worth it and she's going to get what she wants. A Taurus woman doesn't want to be *taken care of*. She wants to be *cared for* by her mate. She likes to have her own money to spend on that outrageous pair of shoes without having to ask permission from anyone. She is willing to work hard to earn her luxurious lifestyle. No prima donna or lazy taker here. What is the ultimate present for your Taurus partner? A holiday at the spa. Being pampered with facials, pedicures, a new haircut, and a makeup session to top it off? Yes, then you have a happy Taurus in your arms.

Your Taurus partner is easygoing, peace-loving, and gentle. She will go along with most of your plans with just a friendly nod. But, as they say, you don't ever want to mess around with Mother Nature. Since she is not prone to making demands or engaging in inane chatter, when she does talk, please listen. She doesn't ask for much, but when she does, she absolutely needs you to pay attention to her. If you fail to listen to her, you will feel the wrath of nothing less your own version of Mother Nature. Although it is quite rare, the house will shake, the animals will run for cover, and you will wonder what got unleashed. Her fury will amaze you and will make even the strongest Capricorn quiver. If you are an intelligent person, it won't take more than one time to learn that valuable lesson. Don't ever underestimate a Taurus woman or you will be in trouble.

Now that you know how to stay out of trouble, how do you keep your Taurus beauty? Treat her with the respect and kindness that she deserves. She doesn't accept criticism well at all. She takes it to heart and it hurts her feelings. Oh, she might accept it for a while, but you will eventually find out that you need to treat her like a lady or else you will suffer. Believe me, you will suffer. What makes her shine is emotional security, a good home, a solid family, and old friends. Oh yes, and also luxury. One Taurus I know says that she would much rather have a one-carat diamond ring in the blue Tiffany box than a flawed three-carat diamond. Maybe no one else will know, but the Taurus can definitely tell the difference. So see your radiant Taurus partner as a perfect diamond. She is hard as a rock and at the same time the most beautiful jewel in the world.

TAURUS FATHER FIGURE

Stephen, a biologist, is a double Taurus. He has three children and is the typical traditional father. He loves nature and takes the family camping quite often. He has his favorite overstuffed chair, likes to read the paper as soon as he gets home, and does it exactly the same way every night. No one bothers him during his evening ritual. They don't even cause a lot of ruckus when he wants to be quiet. It's not that they are afraid of him—they aren't at all. They just have a healthy respect for his habits, since they are so important to him. Once he gets his own time, then he's ready for dinner and to be with his whole family. His children love him, even with his stubborn ways. He is the most loving dad of all.

If you have a Taurus dad, this will help you understand him better, since he's not the easiest to figure out. Do you think he's being hard on you? Do you feel that other kids can get away with more than you can? You might not realize it now, but your Taurus dad is one of the best fathers in the zodiac. You are going to be very grateful for your Taurus dad when you grow up. They are a bit tough on their children, because of their deep love for them. Your dad wants you to be strong enough to be able to support yourself well. Remember, Taurus is the sign of financial security. He feels that discipline and hard work will be good for you, since you will get that in the real world. So it might as well start at home. But he will always be a great role model for you—look at his work ethic.

You will not want for anything, because your father will see to it that his family is well taken care of, financially as well as emotionally. Your home will be nice, but you'll have to do some chores. Your father loves nice possessions and is here to teach his children how to take care of these nice things. You will have to mow the lawn, take out the garbage, help your mother with the dishes, and generally need to be held accountable. Your appearance and the look of your home are very important to him. Why work so hard and have things in shambles? When you are old enough for a car, he will pay half the cost, but will make you save up and pay the other half. But that's not fair—your friends are getting cars just for turning sixteen! But your father wants you to appreciate your car and never take possessions for granted.

I see the Taurus father as a big bear. He is either the cuddly teddy bear or sometimes he turns into the grumpy bear with a thorn in his paw. You will know which bear comes home from work; he won't hide his feelings. If he's tired, leave him alone to his paper. He just needs to rest and regroup. See it as the bear hibernating, seeking out a little rest. Taureans don't like too much disruption, so temper tantrums or noisy running around won't do. You don't want to see the grumpy bear's temper, that's for sure. He's not the best communicator when he's in a good mood, but when he's not in a good mood, his barely grunts instead of talking. Don't expect anything more. He can't do it.

The Taurean dad likes a calm and quiet home. He also likes a beautiful home. Try doing family projects together. What if you plant a family vegetable garden with everyone helping out? Or maybe the family can go to a baseball game together? Taurus dads love sports. To make your dad really happy with you, take care of your possessions properly. Wash your new car regularly so it looks shiny and clean. Get that summer job so you can start saving some money for college. He'll pay for most of it, but he will want you to help. Why? Because you are learning to be self-sufficient and that means he's doing his job. If you remember that your Taurus father is in charge and follow his guidelines, you will have a happy household.

TAURUS MOTHER FIGURE

Susan has five children and four grandchildren. Her entire life revolves around her family. They live just outside the city and their home is surrounded by lush plants, flowers, gardens, and pristine nature. Her sweet backyard has a playhouse for the girls and a sandbox and toy trucks for the boys. It's the perfect comfy family home with at least three doggies running around wagging their happy doggy tails. Oh, did I tell you about the two horses in the barn? She's an artist and an author who writes children's books about animals who talk to each other, just as humans do. Susan loves being a mother and it shows. You can usually smell homemade soup on the stove when you visit her. There is so much love in the home that you can feel it when you walk through her colorful front door.

If you have a Taurus mother, I'm sure Susan's life feels very familiar to you. How many animals do you have? The Taurus mother is the classic matriarch of the zodiac. Only a Cancer mother is as domestic as this earth sign. The Taurus mother is the glue who holds everyone closely together. In fact, she makes her home so comfortable and inviting that she entertains her family as well as her many friends on holidays. The place to be on Christmas Eve is Susan's party. I look forward to it each year. Everyone is there and dressed in their best red, green, and gold holiday attire. People are walking around the big central dining table talking to each other and piling all kinds of food on their plates. Taureans like comfort food: a roast, ham, mashed potatoes, veggies, bread, and many colorful salads. Be sure to save some room for dessert. There is an entire room devoted to desserts, of course.

The female Taurus personality really does embody Mother Nature. You can see it easily if your mother is a Taurus. Your mother has an earthiness about her in that she loves animals, plants, food, and nature. She really loves nature and wants to take care of the environment. Often Taurus mothers are involved with community gardens, recycling, and green practices. Some take the care of the earth so seriously that they are instrumental in helping pass legislation that protects animals or preserves the land. This maternal earth sign has a mission to protect what she loves.

Your mother likes it when people are busy. She enjoys seeing everyone happily creating beautiful things. Taureans surround themselves with art and beautiful objects. So what throws your calm Taurus mother off her game? Disruption. If the children are not getting along or they're fighting with each other, she just can't handle it. That's when she'll take control. What will your earth mother make you do? Work! She will organize a family workday and get everyone working together. "Let's move that fence and make the horse corral larger," she bellows. "But, Mom, I want to go out to the mall with my friends!" Your Taurus mother has the last word, and says, "Oh, no, you don't—not until your work is done." Of course, all the children moved the fence, had a lovely lunch, and ended up laughing and having a grand time.

Even though your mother makes you do chores and holds you accountable for what you say you're going to do, you are fortunate to have her. She gives you unconditional love and tells you she loves you often. The Taurus mother is affectionate, demonstrative, and thoughtful. She will never forget your birthday and even makes a big deal of her dear friends' birthdays, too. You can always count on her to help you when you need help. And she helps you with a big smile, as if she had all the time in the world. Nothing else matters except you. Your mother has one of the biggest hearts of all the signs of the zodiac. So now can you see how lucky you are to have your Taurus mother?

TAURUS CHILD

Tiffany is a pretty little eight-year-old Taurus. She loves to dress up in her fancy party dresses all the time. Her mother, Margaret, is a Virgo and wants her to be more practical and save her party dresses for parties. But Tiffany must see every day as a special day, because she *has* to wear her pink dress, and it *has* to be today! Tiffany is very strong-willed when she wants something. Stubborn? Yes—and quite set in her desires. Margaret thinks she always wants something! But that is the destiny of a Taurus child—to get what she wants. Taurus is the sign of luxury and you can even see it at eight years old.

Security is the reason your little Taurus came to you. This sign needs both emotional and financial security. If you haven't already done so, open a bank account for your little one. Being a Taurus, he will need it. Since this is the sign associated with the planet Venus, you have a sweetie pie in your life. A Taurus loves to cuddle, needs affection, and is comfortable with a close family. As long as your little one feels secure, you will have a happy child.

You have no idea how lucky you are to have little Taurus. They are just about the easiest children to raise of all the astrology signs. A Taurus baby is calm, contented, and almost always in a good mood. If she gets irritable, there is something that is causing discomfort. Taureans must be cozy and comfortable and if they aren't, you will know it right away. Here is a nice trick to ensure your baby's comfort: very soft fabric. Every Taurus has delicate skin and can't handle anything even slightly rough or scratchy. Make sure everything that touches the skin of your little Taurus is velvety soft.

As a child, Taurus will have a steady rhythm that might be a little slower than that of the other kids. Taurus is an earth sign and is not speedy, like Aries or even Gemini. Do not compare your Taurus to fire sign children, because the fire kids will always start things early and run fast. That does not mean that your Taurus is lagging behind. It is just the nature of earth to be more deliberate and pensive. They need to process things for a while before they act on something. I compare it to the fable of the Tortoise and the Hare. Taurus plays the role of the Tortoise. If you remember, the Hare gets a huge head start in a race with the Tortoise, but because of perseverance and tenacity, the Tortoise wins. Steady and stable, your Taurus will always win in the long run.

The teenage Taurus might be a handful for you. The natural stubbornness of this sign usually crops up around that time in life. Your Taurus needs structure to feel secure. But the trick is to give your Taurus enough guidelines to offer security, but not so many that he will rebel. He won't throw temper tantrums like Aries or show defiance like Aquarius. Instead, the Taurus rebel will become withdrawn. They have a tendency to pout quietly if they don't get what they want. They might spend a lot of time alone in their room or away with their friends as their teenage style of defiance. One suggestion is to help them find a summer job. Once your Taurus is working, he is in his element and will flourish.

The challenge for Taurus is the set attitude and quiet obstinacy. They are hardwired to get what they want. It's the Venus influence that gives them a sense of entitlement. As adults, they are hardworking, ambitious, and usually very successful. The biggest Taurus asset is their easygoing personality: In nearly all their interactions, they exude love and caring. Kindness belongs to Taurus.

TAURUS PET

Is your household calm and fairly quiet? Are there family members who are the earth signs of Taurus, Virgo, and Capricorn? Are you looking for a pet for your grandmother? Find a nice pet that was born during the sign of Taurus and it might be just perfect for your family. Even though you can find Taurus pets in any breed, I'm using a Basset Hound as an example for Taurus. Hounds remind me of earth signs. My family had a couple of dogs that were Basset Hounds when I was a child, and they were wonderful with our family. The loving Taurus personality will come through a pet, just as it does in people. A Taurus puppy will be easier to live with than other signs, so if you want a calm, easygoing, affectionate pet, look for a Taurus. Your grandmother will thank you.

ANIMALS FOR TAURUS
Bear
Bee
Bull
Insects
Mule
Ox
Rabbit
Sloth

TAURUS CELEBRITIES AND THEIR BIRTH DATES

Jessica Lange	April 20
Andie MacDowell	April 21
Jack Nicholson	April 22
Valerie Bertinelli	April 23
Leonardo Da Vinci	April 23
Shirley MacLaine	April 24
Barbra Streisand	April 24
Al Pacino	April 25
Renée Zellweger	April 25
Jay Leno	April 28
Penélope Cruz Sánchez	April 28
Jerry Seinfeld	April 29
Michelle Pfeiffer	April 29
Uma Thurman	April 29
Willie Nelson	April 30
David Beckham	May 2
James Brown	May 3
Audrey Hepburn	May 4
George Clooney	May 6
Tony Blair	May 6
Eva Perón	May 7
Billy Joel	May 9
Candice Bergen	May 9
Bono	May 10
Fred Astaire	May 10
Katharine Hepburn	May 12
Stevie Wonder	May 13
Cate Blanchett	May 14
George Lucas	May 14
Pierce Brosnan	May 16

PERFECT GIFTS FOR TAURUS

Taureans are very easy to buy for because of their love of luxury. Make sure these items are of good quality: You might have to spend a chunk of money on this sign. Here are some suggestions to make your Taurus feel pampered!

Money
- Cash
- Stocks and bonds
- A nice leather wallet
- A gift certificate to the most expensive store you can find

Art
- Garden sculpture
- Paintings

Softies
- Anything in cashmere—hat, scarf, socks, sweater, blanket
- Down pillows
- 1,000-thread-count Egyptian cotton bedding and comforter

Jewelry

- Two-carat diamond stud earrings
- A matching necklace
- A money clip

Spa Treatments

- Facial
- Massage
- Manicure
- Pedicure
- Haircut
- Makeup session

GEMINI

May 22–June 21

KEYWORDS

POSITIVE KEYWORDS

Talkative

Curious

Articulate

Flexible

Versatile

Animated

CAUTION KEYWORDS

Restless

Chatty

Gossipy

INFORMATION

THIRD SIGN OF THE ZODIAC

Glyph: ♊

Planet: Mercury

Symbol: Twins

Element: Air

Mode: Mutable

Colors: Orange, Pink

Gemstones: Rhodolite, Andradite

Metal: Mercury

Body Parts: Lungs, Nerves, Brain

GEMINI: THE STUDENT TEACHER

Julia, a triple Gemini, is searching through her favorite place, the biggest bookstore in town. She's been wandering for a while, happily breezing through a variety of books. But she suddenly gets impatient and wants *that* book. She quickly finds the information booth and now has the friendly book geek helping her. "What book did you want?" Well, actually, Julia has quite a list of books. They end up chatting nonstop, laughing and having a grand old time finding all her books. Ahhh, now Gemini is happy.

The purpose of Gemini is to learn. Once Gemini learns something, it is absolutely necessary for her to share her knowledge with others. For Gemini it's not a choice, but a mission. Gemini is an air sign with its planet Mercury, which is why so many Gemini are in the communications industry. They are the teachers and communicators of the zodiac. They are also one of the easiest signs to recognize in public. Just spot the one talking the fastest with arms gesticulating wildly. They will probably have a group of people around them listening intently in between regular, unbridled bursts of laughter from the entire happy group. Gemini is one of the best public speakers. Their lecture opens by getting everyone to laugh. But don't think that the lecture will be lightweight, as Gemini is a master at making complex subjects easy. Their innocent appearance is a façade, because they are brilliant, concise, and can impart huge volumes of information in a very short period.

The symbol for Gemini is the Twins, who work together as the perfect multitaskers. Being a Gemini myself, I know this sign intimately. Many talk of Gemini as being two-faced, and I want to set that myth aside. See us instead as chameleons with the ability to change when our surroundings change. I'm one person with my clients, another person with my friends, another with my family, and yet another when I'm by myself. It's not a good side or a bad side, but lots of different sides, like a prism. How many hats can a Gemini wear? Gemini are great friends to have, since they are connected with interesting and unusual people. Their social calendar is filled with wild and wonderful events. Gemini's life is always full of excitement!

IF YOU'RE A GEMINI, READ THIS!

Did you know that Gemini is the sign of youth? A Gemini looks *much* younger than her actual age! You are here to live life to the fullest at every moment, which is why you love to multitask. If you could eat, read, or watch TV while you answer a quick e-mail—hey, you're in heaven. I have a friend with several planets in Gemini who is the perfect example of his sign. As he watches a movie, he has his laptop at his fingertips and searches the Internet for information on the actors. Now that's Gemini! Boredom isn't in your vocabulary and never will be. In fact, you don't even understand the concept of boredom when there are so many wonderful things to investigate in this wide, wide world. Patience is not your virtue, especially with slow, negative people. Don't even try—stay with the fun, mentally stimulating types.

WHAT MAKES YOU HAPPY?
Mental Freedom

Your lifestyle must offer you freedom. Sometimes you are so excited about a project that you stay with it until 2:00 a.m., but that means you might not get up early the next day. Being a Gemini, you know how important it is to follow your own rhythm; otherwise, you are nervous and irritable. And every day might have a different rhythm—you never know.

You will be happiest when you are challenging yourself mentally. Write that book that's been on your mind. All Gemini have a book in their head and their destiny is to get it out to the world. Many Gemini are artists, so instead of a book, it might be a work of art. It doesn't matter where their creativity leads them: Since Gemini is the sign of the inventor, the process of creating is the most important part. Take a class to learn a new subject often—it will feed your mind and your soul.

Travel is very important to you, so travel as much as possible. Always have an overnight bag packed, just in case the opportunity for a spontaneous trip comes your way. Travel to somewhere new and different to feed that hunger for experiencing life to the fullest. The biggest fear for a Gemini is feeling that you might be missing something, somewhere. There is a bit of "The grass is greener . . ." in Gemini.

The Ideal Gemini Lifestyle

Working out of your home as an independent consultant, talking on the phone a lot, with just the right amount of travel mixed in. Each day is a little different, with your work always balanced with fun. You incorporate breaks often to exercise or run an errand or two. You are respected for your creative ideas and the ability to get them done. Why is that? Because you are easy to get along with, people like you. Gemini is one of the most popular and social signs of the zodiac and attracts fantastic situations. Other people live their lives vicariously through Gemini's adventures.

Your Ultimate Dream

To have a winter home and another location for the summer. The second one isn't another home you own—that would hold you down too much. You want to be able to travel at will. Your twin nature would love two distinctly different lives.

GEMINI STRENGTH

Gemini excel at anything mental. They are quick, clever, and very witty. With a strong Mars, they can be the masters of debate. They are the student/teacher and love to share new ideas with the world. Languages come so easily to Gemini that they usually speak several of them. I know a Gemini who teaches herself new languages just for fun. Many are great orators, interpreters, or translators. Gemini is one of the very best travel companions since they are excellent at reading maps and have one on their lap during the trip, just to check where they are at any moment. Their very best travel toy would be the newest little phone, music, and GPS–combination gadget for navigation. Plus Gemini love adventure, so if the train is late, they will happily talk to the stranger they just met at the train station.

GEMINI CHALLENGE

Overstimulation is the biggest challenge for Gemini. Since they have such a pressing desire to do it all, they may have a frenzied walk with a sense of rushing for no reason. Oftentimes, Gemini think that they are so busy that they can't take time for themselves. It's crucial to calm the Gemini monkey mind that jumps all over the place. But anger doesn't come naturally to Gemini, who see it as a waste of mental energy. Sometimes they have nervous chatter and truly don't know when to shut up. They are blessed with the gift of enthusiasm gone wild that often needs to be curbed. Since Gemini is an air sign, it helps to go out in nature and sit on a rock and just breathe. Deep breathing is the Gemini style of meditation and no amount of mental calming would be too much for Gemini. Breathe, breathe, and breathe! Can a Gemini reach a state of calmness? Maybe not, but they can at least try.

MENTAL CHARACTERISTICS

Gemini rules! The mental arena is home for Gemini. They excel in school and usually take classes throughout their lives just for fun. Gemini is always the teacher's pet. Although Gemini love to learn, they rapidly get their fill of a subject. Their rational minds are like trapdoors, learning easily, but they get bored just as easily. They have a tendency to get mentally satisfied and move on to the next exciting subject of study quickly. Gemini are voracious readers of nonfiction and reference books. Those born under that sign can read *Webster's Dictionary* from cover to cover. Actually, they probably will make it to the Ss or Ts and then get bored and not finish—at least that's what happened to me. Poetry is too fluffy; save it for a less logical sign, like Pisces. When you see Gemini focus their wonderful minds, they can accomplish anything.

EMOTIONAL MAKEUP

Oh, no! Emotions?! Gemini don't know how to express emotion at all. They are so mental that emotions are totally out of their comfort zone. If you want someone to hold your hand, cry, and commiserate with you over anything more serious than a broken fingernail, please don't turn to a Gemini! It will be unsatisfying for you and awkward for Gemini. Save them for the fun times. They will go with you to a movie—a comedy, of course—or brainstorm with you about all the projects that would be cool for you to do now that you feel better. A Gemini is just too darned perky to be around when you feel depressed.

On a personal level, it is very easy to see when Gemini is uncomfortable: They will be quiet. That never happens to a Gemini unless something is wrong. Pay attention when Gemini is quiet, because they are either sick or not happy with their immediate situation. If Gemini are at a dinner party and don't like the scene, they will be very quiet and will leave quickly. You turn around to get a drink and whissshhh . . . they're gone. By themselves, Gemini have an almost childlike innocence and joy of discovery.

PHYSICAL CHARACTERISTICS
Appearance
The Gemini body is slender and a bit taller than average. The forehead is broad with a long neck and sharp, chiseled features. They are very flexible, agile, and extremely well-coordinated. Their hand/eye coordination is astounding—the best of all the signs of the zodiac. But the defining features of Gemini are the eyes—the darting, restless-to-nervous eyes. The overall Gemini look is fast, smooth-talking, witty, fun, but a bit manic at times.

Fashion Sense
The youthful Gemini is always up for the current style, if it's relaxed, that is. They are too active for tall, uncomfortable shoes or confining clothes. Their style is sporty/artsy with fun, useful accessories. Their favorite colors are often in the yellow/orange/brown spectrum, or bright and multicolored. If one sign could wear neon, it's Gemini. The experienced traveler in Gemini can leave for a few days with one roller carry-on and a gold oversized travel bag—in just a few minutes he's ready to go!

Health Type

The lungs are associated with the sign of Gemini and I've found that that sign needs even more air movement than other signs. When the room is closed up with little circulating air, Gemini gets claustrophobic. It's not claustrophobia in terms of small spaces, but lack of air movement. I personally travel with a fold-out fan in my purse at all times. This sign doesn't need stimulants like caffeine, because it is already overstimulated by just being a Gemini. This sign of the zodiac needs more sleep than most signs, except maybe Pisces. Since Gemini move at 150 miles per hour during the day, when they do sleep, it's a long, sound sleep.

Exercise Approach

The very mental Gemini needs a sport or exercise that holds her interest and is not boring. The classic Gemini exercise is noncompetitive and fun, like power walking through her neighborhood, roller skating, cross-country skiing, or dancing wildly when no one is around. That yoga class at 2:00 p.m. becomes too much of a routine after the first class. Since the lungs are associated with this sign of the zodiac, aerobic movements with deep breathing are essential. Gemini is the master at manual dexterity and might love juggling.

PROFESSIONAL LIFE

A brilliant Gemini mind devoted to anything other than a career is a total waste. Gemini absolutely need to work at their passion, which is the love of the word. The classic Gemini excels as a journalist, teacher, permanent student, author, public speaker, or linguist—often traveling with his work. Many Gemini work at a variety of jobs just for the different experiences, but their real focus is on teaching themselves new things. Their sign is also common in the communications industry, such as radio and TV, advertising, sales, and PR. Gemini is the sign of the artist and inventor, and is one of the best entrepreneurs of the entire zodiac.

Gemini Employer

The Gemini boss is one of the friendliest authority figures of the zodiac, whether man or woman. But don't count on her being there from 9 to 5; it's just not her style. Gemini are quick and learn so fast that they assume everyone has the same kind of rapid learning curve. Gemini love high-tech stuff, so computer skills are a must. They are fair, don't hold grudges, and look for the best in each of their employees. You'll notice immediately that patience is definitely not their virtue. Even though the Gemini is open to dialogue, don't let that nice façade fool you. The root side of Gemini is brilliant and extremely efficient, and they demand productivity. With an amazing power of persuasion, the work environment is usually comfortable as well as filled with amazing accomplishments.

GEMINI IN THE BEDROOM

Gemini are wonderful lovers, if you can engage their mind. What turns on a Gemini? Sexy words . . . the sexier and naughtier the better. Save the visuals for other signs; your Gemini needs to hear your voice. If you can speak a foreign language, you will be irresistible to your Gemini lover. Maybe read a sensual novel like *Lady Chatterley's Lover*—together, of course. The multiple personality of the Gemini is perfect for costumes and role-playing. Your Gemini is part friend and part lover, and remember that the words are just as important as the touch. Gemini need relationships with people who like to communicate, so they have no use for the silent, mysterious type.

GEMINI MALE PARTNER

Sally's been dating Joe, her exciting Gemini boyfriend, for about six months. She wrote *excitement* on her wish list for the perfect man, and, well, she sure got it with Joe. He's an entrepreneur in the communications industry. They met at an art opening, instantly connected, and started talking nonstop for hours as they walked arm and arm through the city. He seemed to be able to finish her sentences; he actually understood her. They laughed and talked well into the night. She found him to be charming, well-mannered, clever, and a great conversationalist. Never been married? "I'm sure he just hasn't found the right woman. He'll call me tomorrow . . ." But Joe didn't call, did he? He didn't call the next day or the day after that, either. And then, after Sally went through feelings of abandonment, anger, and finally acceptance, guess what? Gemini Joe calls with that sweet, charming voice she loves. Yes, she melted. He just got back from a quick trip out of town. Does this sound familiar with your Gemini guy? You'd better get used to it if you want a Gemini partner. Just like Sally, you will always be on your toes with your Gemini. He's not intentionally standing you up—something important just happened. Gemini have their own fast rhythm and usually have so much going on at the same time that things get rearranged constantly. They are masters at being in the flow effortlessly, but not many people can keep up with their pace. Can you? Or do you want to?

If you want a white picket fence with 2.5 children, run as fast as you can! This is not the sign for you!

Once you can get used to his restlessness and see it as pure, exciting energy, then you can embrace him. If you accept this in him, you are also embracing change. The Gemini lifestyle will be exciting, unusual, and unpredictable, with lots of travel. Your friends and family will love your Gemini partner. He always seems to have the right thing to say and is knowledgeable about many different subjects. His charm and friendliness win everyone over easily. Not only is he brilliant, but his clever one-liners are even more memorable. People will be talking about him and quoting him the next day!

Remember the Gemini twins? If you think your guy has two personalities, you're wrong. He has multiple personalities. Just pretend you are dating five guys and not just one. If you want a stable, predictable man who always eats at the same restaurant, you are definitely with the wrong person. Your life with a Gemini will constantly be young, new, and fresh. Last weekend, the two of you took a short road trip up the coast in his little red sports car with the top down. After that, he asked you to go to that new movie that just came out. Of course, wandering for hours at the bookstore is always fun. He's loves texting you throughout the day, which is so great when you want a guy who actually communicates.

But drop in on him for a surprise visit and you'll find that he's another person entirely. He could easily be aloof, withdrawn, nervous, and unusually scattered! He'll seem not-at-all-excited to see you. You interrupted him while he was working on an important writing project. It seems as if he hasn't left the house for quite a while by the way he looks: disheveled, with books and papers everywhere, laptop open on the couch, snacks scattered around. Yuck, peanuts crunched into the carpet! If you're a Virgo, just leave now. Please, do not even be tempted to do a quick little cleanup; he likes it exactly the way it is! The worst thing you could say now is that you want to talk about your future together. Watch him disappear before your eyes. He hates confrontation or drama. The Gemini man, unless there are some planets in Cancer in his chart, is not at all the domestic type. He wants a friend/lover, not a mother. Mothering him would be like smothering him.

GEMINI FEMALE PARTNER

Frank met Elaine in an anthropology class and they became fast friends. He loves her quick mind and her curiosity about almost everything. She's a sociologist and is writing a book on new patterns of social interaction relative to the Internet. Frank and Elaine started dating and tonight is the big night when he introduces her to his closest group of friends. As Frank and Elaine walk into the friends' living room, all of a sudden everyone laughs and gives hugs like they have known each other forever. Actually his Gemini girlfriend knows almost everyone there, and quite well. They whisk her away, laughing and talking wildly . . . and

maybe, flirting. Frank stands there stunned, and feels left in the dust.

Of course, Frank stayed with Elaine because she's so adorable. But he realized that night that he has more than a sweet, bouncy cheerleader on his hands. Under that naive exterior is a worldly and streetwise woman with lots of savvy. She thrives on excitement and needs a partner who offers that on a silver platter. If she senses even a hint of boredom, she's gone. She adores Renaissance men. Are you exciting enough to keep her satisfied?

The Gemini woman is perfect for the man who thinks he can't live with just one woman for the rest of his life. Being with a Gemini is like having five girlfriends/wives at the same time, all wrapped up in one neat little package. The only trick is that you will never know which one will show up to surprise you. Which Gemini face pops in and when—that is the big question. If you're up for an exciting and unpredictable life, she is the best one for you!

Gemini #1: She's your best friend, confidant, and wise advisor to whom you can tell absolutely everything and at any time. She likes to text you five times a day and wants a reply each time. No jealousy in the Gemini vocabulary, because she has so much confidence in herself. This face is the author, public speaker, and sharp communications exec.

Gemini #2: Your Gemini partner is absolutely the best travel companion of the entire zodiac. She lives for great adventures and is usually athletic and can keep up with or surpass most men. Since Gemini are amazing linguists, she most likely can even speak the language. Be prepared to have a fast-paced journey. Can you keep up with your high-energy Gemini?

Gemini #3: Welcome to the nervous side of your Gemini partner. The dog chasing its own tail is very much the overwhelmed Gemini. This side of her is the sharp-tongued robot, prone to sarcasm and curt, one-word answers. No time for you, that's for sure. Just stay out of her way when she's wearing this Gemini face. Come back in a few hours and she'll be happy.

Gemini #4: Say hello to the Gemini escape artist. When things get just too much for Gemini, she escapes. It could be a short road trip, a hike to get some fresh air, or just a dark matinee movie alone in the middle of the day. Sometimes she will need to sleep for a couple of days. Just let her sleep because when she is truly rested, the happy Gemini emerges again.

Gemini #5: Finally, the gracious hostess and loving mother is at the root of your Gemini prize. She is the life of any party and is fabulous at entertaining. Everyone likes her and she has lots of interesting friends from many different walks of life. Gemini is equally comfortable with a rock star and the gardener. She is kind to them all.

To make your Gemini happy, the main thing to remember is this: Listen to her and respect her words. She needs to communicate with you often. You do know that she is the best thing that ever happened to you. From now on, you are going to be spoiled and think other women are not exciting enough for you. If you can keep your Gemini interested in your clever mind and fascinating lifestyle, you might have a chance with her. If she's intellectually bored, she's gone like the wind.

GEMINI FATHER FIGURE

Don loves his four kids—he really does. But it's hard with him traveling so much. He's a successful self-help author, who's often away on speaking tours and teaching seminars. He's well-known and loved by everyone. But sometimes his children feel like they know him better through his books than through their personal interactions with him. They crave time with him and when they are together, it truly is magical. They really have fun with him, too. He's so funny; he makes everyone laugh all the time. He almost feels more like a buddy or a friend than a father. "Why is the suitcase out? Oh, Daddy's going away again . . ."

Although Don isn't very domestic, he's the cool father who always has plans for outrageous adventures. Remember when he took his family out camping and they learned about the stars in the nighttime sky? Then there was the hot-air balloon birthday party last month. The vacation last summer was full of adventure when he took the entire family on a train and bike trip across Europe. But when they were finished, he had all the children write essays on their experiences. He makes homework and learning so much fun that it turns education into a game. He passes on his love of learning to his four children, who are excelling in school with his encouragement.

Don't worry about Don or his four children, because the Gemini father is smart enough to do it all. None of his children will be in therapy as an adult over a father who abandoned them. In fact, they seem to be taking after him, as they are creating very interesting lives for themselves. One of them is going to be a teacher, one owns a bookstore, one is an author, and the other is an artist. All are very happy and are glad that they have a Gemini father who understands them. Even now that they are all adults, their Gemini father is one of their best brainstorming buddies. He is always excited about their new projects and often collaborates with them.

If you are lucky enough to have a father who is a Gemini, you can count your blessings. He will be open to your ideas, even if they are unusual or have uncertain outcomes. Remember that Gemini is the sign of the inventor, so he will always support your creativity. Some Gemini fathers get the entire family involved in art or writing projects. Since Gemini loves the high-tech world, try writing a family story and putting it on a DVD or on YouTube. Design a family website and produce a travel blog from all your exotic holidays. Always be in contact with each other through social networking sites. Twitter is the perfect medium for Gemini: short and tweet. Gemini fathers make sure the family gets together for family reunions regularly. He will keep the communications going between everyone.

The education of his children is a very high priority for the Gemini father. Take your homework to heart, as your Gemini father makes it fun and will be involved if he possibly can. Your father will support you in pursuing your dreams, even if they are unorthodox. The Gemini father loves you without smothering you and will give you plenty of space to grow on your own. He wants his children to be independent, just as he is.

Since Gemini is made up of multiple personalities, beware of the different sides of your father. When he's in his reading or Internet work mode, don't bother him. One of the personalities of Gemini can be short and to the point with one-word sentences. He can be prone to sarcasm if he's tired, pressured, or doesn't feel well. But your Gemini father can move from being detached and aloof to laughing in a matter of minutes. He's the quick-change artist. You just have to love all the different sides of your exciting Gemini father.

GEMINI MOTHER FIGURE

Shirley is the mother of three beautiful girls and she loves them dearly, but right now she's off to her pottery class. Everyone loves this bubbly, energetic Gemini. She has lots of friends from her many different interests and clubs. She takes a dance class as well as a conversational Spanish class. This summer she is taking her family to Mexico for a vacation. What a great way to teach another language to her girls! Oh, no! She just realized it is 7:30 p.m. and she hasn't even thought of dinner for her family. "No problem, I'll just pick something up on the way home . . ."

Is your mother a Gemini? Isn't it fun? Well, maybe it's not fun all the time, but it sure is an adventure. I hope you didn't want the kind of mother who bakes cookies and stays up worrying about you. Your Gemini mother is more of a friend than a domesticated mother. In fact, Gemini is one of the least domestic signs of the zodiac, unless she has planets in the homey sign of Cancer. The typical Gemini home is more like a dormitory, with people coming, going, and eating on the go. No formal dining rules here. Gemini mothers are more aligned with the free-spirit style of rough-and-tumble etiquette.

The Gemini mother has a plan in all this seeming chaos. She is fostering independence in her children. She will not be the controlling mother who puts you on a ridiculous curfew, like some other mothers. Your Gemini mother trusts you, because it is the innocent nature of a Gemini to see the best in everyone. So please, please don't betray her trust. You can tell her anything—*hear me*—anything! She's the type of mother who is going to push you to go on that weekend trip with your girlfriends. In fact, the Gemini mother spoils her children, so you are one of the lucky ones.

The one area where your mother is going to be relentless is with your education. She will not tolerate any funny business when it comes to learning. If you want her on your side, get good grades. Her intention is for you to be independent and be able to take care of yourself financially, and she's knows that a good education is the key.

Remember the multiple personalities of every Gemini? Your mother is no different. One mother is the fun, youthful, and joyous one. The perky Gemini mother looks and acts more like a big sister than a traditional mother. Mothers and daughters often share the same clothes and jewelry, due to the eternal youthfulness of Gemini. You are proud to say that your mother is named the "coolest mom on the block" by your friends. The next Gemini mother is busy with classes and clubs in the community. This is an important outlet for your mother. Support her outside activities because she will be much happier engaged in creative pursuits. If she feels caged and can't find her creative release—watch out! That's when the meanie Gemini mother emerges, the one you don't want to see very much. This mother is stressed out, unaffectionate, overwhelmed, and prone to harsh, quick answers.

A huge part of the equation in dealing with your Gemini mother requires you to develop a keen sense of timing. Which Gemini mother is home today? Is it the schoolmarm, the friend, the meanie, or the social director? The Gemini mother is up front, honest, and can't hide her feelings. You *know* which one is home, so you are becoming an expert in the art of timing. How lucky are you to have several mothers instead of just one normal mother like everyone else!

GEMINI CHILD

Jannette and Jeannine are twins as well as being Gemini. They are best friends and do everything together. In fact, they look so much alike that their teachers and even some of their friends can't tell them apart. Jeannine, the trickster, often pretends to be her sister and actually gets away with it. They don't get in trouble but like a little mischief just for the fun of it. These girls can handle it because they are straight-A students as well as being very popular. Their teachers love them, even their mischievous side.

Your Gemini child came to you for one main reason: education. They wanted to get all the information they could possibly squeeze into that fabulous mind. Please, please read to your Gemini child each and every day! The other reason Gemini chose you was for you to honor her independence. Gemini is like a delicate butterfly that, if caged, dies. Do not restrict your brilliant Gemini child physically or mentally, or you will have a cunning wildcat on your hands.

As a baby, Gemini are not usually as affectionate as other children. They are just too interested in all the activities in the world to focus on one thing for too long, even if it's a mother's hug. Gemini have a tendency toward claustrophobia, so the playpen is the last resort. Keep them entertained and they are happy babies.

The Gemini child will do everything quickly. They will crawl, walk, and talk early. One Gemini baby I know started speaking in full sentences as soon as he could say one word. Have a baby computer for the Gemini infant and a real computer for the Gemini toddler. They will be teaching you tricks on it in no time.

School is the favorite place of the Gemini because of their love of learning. They are usually the teacher's pet because they are excellent students. Gemini are natural at speaking foreign languages, so teach your Gemini child another language early on. Their clever wit feeds a very active imagination. Foster your Gemini child's fantasies, because Gemini are the artists, inventors, and entrepreneurs of the zodiac. Their remarkable manual dexterity might make them adept at musical instruments, juggling, or magic tricks.

The teenage Gemini will seem glued to his cell phone. Remember, Gemini is the sign of communication, so your Gemini is the perfect child for a permanent earbud. Gemini are very social and popular, so expect lots of parties and sleepovers. Since Gemini are the perfect multitaskers, believe your Gemini when he says he can do his homework and listen to his iPod at the same time. He learns better with other things happening—really!

Most Gemini like to have two different living situations. Often a great aunt will take in Gemini for weekends or summer vacations. Your Gemini child loves to travel, so give your little Gemini the freedom that is crucial for this air sign of the zodiac. This is the absolutely perfect sign for foreign exchange students.

The challenge for the Gemini child is boredom; he has a strong dislike of routines. Gemini are inherently restless and get distracted easily.

If they are bored in school, they will get in trouble for talking to their neighbor or just being fidgety or restless. That translates into impatience or scattered energy if they have no focus for their interest.

GEMINI PET

If you want a friendly family pet, then choose one born under the sign of Gemini. The Gemini pet will want to be around people all the time, just like the human Gemini does. Using the example of a Golden Retriever, when a Gemini dog is a puppy, it is a bundle of energy and a bit out of control. He will be very social and will want to spend time playing and rolling around with the children. Don't get a Gemini pet if you need to leave it alone for long periods. He will get nervous and anxious. But as your Gemini puppy matures, if he has plenty to do to keep him busy, he will settle down nicely and become an integral part of the family. The Gemini pet will be an excellent traveling companion and will love to ride in the car with his head out the window. Let him run outside often. Your Gemini pet will have an easy temperament and will get along very well with small children. You will be happy with your choice of a Gemini pet as he will provide your family with years of enjoyment.

ANIMALS FOR GEMINI
Chameleon
Coyote
Crow
Fox
Hare
Monkey
Octopus
Orangutan
Parrot
Raven
Weasel

PERFECT GIFTS FOR GEMINI

Gemini are easy to buy presents for because of their many activities. Their main areas of interest are media, communications, trendy fashion, and travel. So here are some presents that will definitely make any Gemini happy!

Media

- Miniature travel laptop computer
- Gift card to bookstores
- Diary, journal, or personalized stationery
- Nice pen-and-pencil set
- Magazine subscription

Communications

- The latest electronic gadgets
- The highest-tech smartphone
- Free long-distance calling cards

Trendy Fashion

- Gift card to a trendy clothing store
- Rings or bracelets (Gemini rules arms and hands)

Travel

- Luggage or cool tote bags
- Airline travel vouchers
- Foreign language CDs or software programs
- Hot-air balloon ride
- Bicycle or Porsche, depending on your budget

GEMINI CELEBRITIES AND THEIR BIRTH DATES

Sir Laurence Olivier	May 22
Jewel	May 23
Bob Dylan	May 24
Mike Myers	May 25
Lenny Kravitz	May 26
Joseph Fiennes	May 27
Annette Bening	May 29
John F. Kennedy	May 29
Joe Namath	May 31
Brooke Shields	May 31
Clint Eastwood	May 31
Colin Farrell	May 31
Prince Rainier III	May 31
Alanis Morissette	June 1
Angelina Jolie	June 4
Noah Wyle	June 4
Kenny G	June 5
Liam Neeson	June 7
Joan Rivers	June 8
Andrew Weil	June 8
Johnny Depp	June 9
Michael J. Fox	June 9
Natalie Portman	June 9
Mary-Kate and Ashley Olsen	June 13
Courtney Cox	June 15
Helen Hunt	June 15
Paul McCartney	June 18
Paula Abdul	June 19
Kathleen Turner	June 19
Nicole Kidman	June 20

CANCER

June 22–July 23

KEYWORDS

POSITIVE KEYWORDS

Emotional

Nurturing

Domestic

Traditional

Sentimental

Affectionate

CAUTION KEYWORDS

Hypersensitive

Clingy

Moody

INFORMATION

FOURTH SIGN OF THE ZODIAC

Glyph: ♋

Planet: Moon

Symbol: Crab

Element: Water

Mode: Cardinal

Colors: Aqua, Pearl, Silver

Gemstones: Pearl, Ivory, Coral

Metals: Platinum, Pewter

Body Parts: Stomach, Breasts

CANCER: THE CAREGIVER

Marie, an obstetrician, delivers babies for a living. What a perfect profession for a children-loving Cancer! She has three kids of her own in addition to having ushered into the world thousands of little ones throughout her career. Her nurturing instinct knows just what to do to make both the mother and the new infant feel safe and secure. Her patients love her so much that they wouldn't even consider switching doctors. Why would they? She really is part of the family.

The sign of Cancer is the perfect mother or father. This water sign is like the mother hen who cares for her many little chicks. Cancer's planet is the emotional moon. Marie sees every baby she delivers as an extension of her own family. She knows all their names, as well as their family histories, and is always there for them. Many times she has to get up at 2:00 a.m. for a delivery, but loves every minute of it. It's her purpose in life to serve others. And her choice is to serve the most vulnerable ones—the infants. Even though she seems like the loving, caring, and sympathetic mother all the time, there is another side to the Cancer mother. Just like the mother hen, when her chicks are threatened by a coyote, she will turn from the quiet, kind mother to a protective wild animal. No one had better mess with Marie's newborn babies or they will see a wrath unequaled by any other sign of the zodiac. You want the mother hen on your side and not against you. Her tenacity and perseverance will never let go—never.

The symbol for Cancer is the crab, and that is a great image for this sign. When the crab is poked at, what does it do? It retreats within the safety of the hard shell that it calls home. This is absolutely the most domestic of all the zodiac signs. A Cancerian needs to take care of others. They are the caregivers in the astrology world because of their natural instinct to nurture and protect. In fact, often their entire identity is shaped by their involvement with family and community. If they don't feel needed, it cuts to their core. Unfulfilled Cancerians are moody, intro-verted, and emotionally despondent. So if you see a sad Cancerian, ask him to help you and watch him perk up. When they are being supportive to others, they feel useful. We have to make the mother hens of the world happy, because then they will pass that joy on to their little chickies.

IF YOU'RE A CANCER, READ THIS!

I'm sure you realize this, but you are the most sensitive sign in the zodiac. It's not easy sometimes, I know. But if your emotions didn't run so deeply, you wouldn't have the compassion that you have for others. Also, did you know that Cancer is also the sign of bravery? You can handle just about anything that is thrown your way. If someone is hurt-ing, you are the first to come to her aid. Sometimes a kind word and a warm touch is all that is necessary. Plus, you help without any fanfare for yourself. A Cancerian will never say, "Hey, look how I'm helping the world!" You have a built-in humility and modesty and are helping just because it's the right thing to do. As a result, it lifts your spirits. As a Cancer, it is your destiny to help yourself as much as you help others. Typically, you think of yourself last. But you know what? You can take the last cookie . . . there will always be more cookies.

WHAT MAKES YOU HAPPY?
Emotional Security

You need to feel safe and comfortable in your home. Do you love where you live? Does your lifestyle give you a deep inner peace? If not, you need to make a change, because you know that it's not your chosen life. Being a Cancer, you intuitively know what makes you happy. You must have your family and loved ones close to you. Don't feel bad if you miss people you love—it's natural to your sign.

What happens if you don't have your loved ones around? You feel lonely and isolated. That is the opposite of what Cancerians want. You are the most domestic sign of the zodiac and must feel needed.

If you don't feel that you can help people, you could get moody and a bit depressed. Remember the crab who pulls into his shell if he feels uncomfortable? Unhappy Cancerians may become agoraphobic if they don't come out of their shell.

Since your sign of Cancer is the caregiver, find someone or something else to take care of if you don't have a family close to you. You can volunteer to visit people who are homebound and need help. You would make a great Big Brother or Big Sister for children who don't have a parent. Pets are wonderful for your sign. Get a kitten or puppy and you will have a little being totally dependent on you. Now that will make you happy!

The Ideal Cancer Lifestyle

You came from a divorced, dysfunctional family and your lifetime dream is to give love in a way you never received it as a child. So now you have a family of five children, three dogs, and a guinea pig. There is always a pot of soup on the stove, just in case anyone is hungry. Your home has a lived-in style, with comfortable, cozy pillows and a traditional feel. Even though there is a lot of commotion with all your children's friends over, you seem to thrive on the energy. You have a backyard with grass, a swing set, and a swimming pool. Saturday there's a barbecue and Sunday a family dinner. Everyone feels loved.

Your Ultimate Dream

To have lived with your spouse in your dream home for thirty years while raising your five children. Now you have been blessed with eight little angels as grandchildren. You're retired and financially secure, so you can babysit two days a week and have a big dinner for your family every Sunday. Thanksgiving is your favorite holiday because you are so very thankful.

CANCER STRENGTH

Cancerians know how to nurture. It is a water sign, connected with the moon, which represents emotions and family contentment. They are amazing hosts when entertaining due to their natural talent to make their home intimate and inviting. They also love food and are usually wonderful cooks. Cancer is the sign that is the best at unconditional love. Their watery moon just can't do it any other way.

Cancers are very sentimental and are experts at tracking down their heritage and ancestry. Genealogy, the study of their family tree, comes naturally to them. Give them the family photo albums to save and reorganize. They are prone to collecting. They will collect anything that makes them feel secure. Some would call it hoarding—Cancerians call it "collecting treasures." They love little boxes filled with treats. If you need a big hug, find a loving Cancer.

CANCER CHALLENGE

Feeling insecure and therefore needy is the biggest challenge for a Cancer. Their insecurity is based on the fear of not having enough money. That is the most important need—take care of that first. Then there is the need to take care of the world. If their purpose to nurture isn't fulfilled, they could cling to old situations. They have a very, very hard time letting go of the past. Often Cancerians live in the past more easily than they live in the present. Oh, yes—separation anxiety! This sign is extremely sensitive and emotional and gets their feelings hurt very easily. Don't ever yell at a Cancer or you will see tears immediately. They are sympathetic to everyone's needs, but people had better be there when they need some help. If not, watch them disappear into their hard shell. They might not leave their room for days and just want to be left alone and sleep. If you see them act out like that, they are desperately crying for your help. They need food in the cupboard and money in the bank to feel secure. Where is Santa Claus when you need him?

MENTAL CHARACTERISTICS

Cancerians are more emotional than cerebral. If it feels good to them, they will do it. No research like Virgos or common sense like Taureans. How does it feel to them? This doesn't mean that they aren't intelligent;

they just trust their intuition more. Gemini will chatter about anything. Cancerians talk about their family. They also love their country and are quite patriotic. Their country is the larger version of their family. Even though typical Cancerians are gentle and on the introverted side, they are amazingly brave and tenacious. They are modest and humble and almost always put others before themselves. Remember the mother hen with her chicks? She will protect and defend her little ones, if necessary, like a ferocious animal. I wouldn't mess around with her family if I were you.

EMOTIONAL MAKEUP

Aaahhh, finally home! This is the most comfortable world for the watery, affectionate sign of Cancer. Since intuition comes so easily to this sign, emotions are second nature. The moon is their planet, which is known for feelings. This is the sign that can cry at commercials, especially about children or animals. Cancerians will flow from one mood to the next like water in a stream. They don't see themselves as moody, just sensitive. To others, the moodiness is readily apparent. Emotional stability is not part of this sign. That would be stiff and unfeeling to them. They enjoy laughing, hugging, emoting . . . which includes crying. Typical Cancerians reach out and touch your arm when they talk to you. They have a great sense of touch and need a physical connection. This sign lives the emotional spectrum from top to bottom. They can be depressed today and then give a party for the neighborhood tomorrow. But since they are so full of love, you just have to return it fully, even if they aren't in a good mood. Oh, well . . .

PHYSICAL CHARACTERISTICS
Appearance
The typical Cancerian face is round, like their planet, the moon. They are expressive and sensitive when they talk. Their bodies are soft and their walk is gentle, like a rolling river. You won't see a Cancer running around too fast. They prefer to walk more slowly. Typically, the Cancer

eyes are broad and large, and they have a turned-up nose. With the Cancerian love of food, often their bodies are round as well. The full-figured grandmother is the perfect prototype of the Cancer body. If you want a warm, affectionate hug, isn't that the one you want a hug from?

Fashion Sense

The conservative Cancer likes more traditional dress. Not prone to flash, trendiness, or revealing clothing, they feel better in comfortable attire. Muted, softer colors and fabrics attract the domestic Cancerian. Often the women like small prints with flowing skirts or dresses and a small wrap around their shoulders. The men prefer an unassuming, clean style, like khaki trousers or blue jeans with a cotton shirt. The texture is essential: Soft is very important to the cozy Cancer.

Health Type

The body parts associated with this sign are the stomach and the breasts. If Cancer gets worried about loved ones, he could have digestive issues. So good nutrition is critical, since food is this sign's drug of choice. Often Cancerians need to watch their weight, as well as their love of rich, creamy foods. Fish is a good choice for this water sign. There is absolutely no correlation between the sign of Cancer and the disease of the same name.

Exercise Approach

Since Cancerians are homebodies, exercising in the privacy of their personal space is the best. This water sign likes gentle exercise—save the marathon running for Sagittarians. Cancers are lucky if they get in a stretch once a week. Buy a yoga DVD and set up a place in the bedroom for ultimate coziness. This water sign might love swimming or at least splashing around in the pool. Maybe working out with a sister or good friend will give her incentive. Dancing is also a good exercise for Cancerians. Then they can reward themselves with a snack afterwards. Hey, they worked out—they deserve it!

PROFESSIONAL LIFE

The loving Cancerian is perfect for social work or the helping professions, like medicine. If you are lucky enough to get a nurse who is a
Cancer when you get your appendix removed, you will remember her
with fondness as one of the best memories of your hospital stay. She
will sneak you in a treat late at night because she shares your love of
sweets. Of course, midwives fall into this category beautifully. Cancerians are good cooks and make great chefs, bakers, caterers, or restaurant owners. As lovers of the past, they make fabulous historians,
archeologists, and oceanographers. The ideal profession for a Cancer
just might be as an owner of a bed-and-breakfast. Imagine the smell of
the homemade biscuits and fresh coffee in the morning!

Cancer Employer

If you have a Cancerian boss, expect a hardworking professional atmosphere. Remember: Cancerians have a basic insecurity about money
and they take work very seriously. Don't play around or be silly, because
they won't tolerate that kind of inefficiency. It's a waste of time—which is
a waste of moneymaking potential. They are tenacious and expect you to
be the same way. Your boss is moody, so don't expect a happy face every
moment. In fact, the day could be like a roller coaster of emotions. If they
see that you are intent on doing a good job, you will be included in the
office family and will be there for a long time. Make sure your boss eats a
good lunch and has plenty of healthy snacks and he will be much happier.

CANCER IN THE BEDROOM

If you like cuddles, spoons, and soft kisses, you are with the right lover.
This is the most affectionate sign of the zodiac and will smother you with
kisses. This sign has a sensual, loving touch. Stroke your Cancerian lover's hair and caress her head in your lap. Rock her like a baby—Cancers
love that! They have a high need for affection, almost more than their
need for sex. With this sign, sex starts in the kitchen. Hold their hand,
bring them hot chocolate, and you will win their affection in bed. The

only thing that can affect the sexiness of this sign is their ⟨...⟩
swings. If they are extra tired because of taking care of the ⟨...⟩
you might only get a cuddle. But, hey, it will be the best cud ⟨...⟩
signs of the zodiac.

CANCER MALE PARTNER

Jeff is a real estate agent, who sells residential homes to his ⟨...⟩
been a professional for twenty years and loves his chosen care ⟨...⟩
he so good at what he does? His clients love him because he re ⟨...⟩
about them. They invite him to dinner with their family and have ⟨...⟩
to know him well over the years. He goes overboard to make su ⟨...⟩
homes are beautiful and ready for sale. He has sold thirteen hou ⟨...⟩
one family. Whenever the siblings move, they always call Jeff. Th ⟨...⟩
has a knack for seeing beauty in homes. No wonder Jeff is so su ⟨...⟩

Even though Cancer men might be a bit tough on the outside, ⟨...⟩
them have the heart and soul of a woman. That doesn't mean that ⟨...⟩
are feminine. Not at all. But it does mean that they can cook an am ⟨...⟩
ing meal, have a sharp style of dress, and know how to create a be ⟨...⟩
home. This sign is the perfect metrosexual male. I think they are ou ⟨...⟩
wardly tough to protect their inner, vulnerable nature. The manly pa ⟨...⟩
them doesn't want to show their softness and won't for quite a while ⟨...⟩
will need to feel very comfortable with you before he divulges anythi ⟨...⟩
about his personal life. But you could trick him by asking about his fa ⟨...⟩
That will always bring up deep feelings in him. Ask him about his rela ⟨...⟩
ship with his mother. That should do it. The sign of Cancer is related t ⟨...⟩
moon and the moon is related to mother. Oh, yes—if you want children ⟨...⟩
this is absolutely the very best father of all the signs of the zodiac.

Another wonderful part of the Cancer male—he is a fabulous provider. But he might take his sweet time to realize you are the one. Cancerian men are very particular about the women they date. They are
easily hurt and usually have had their hearts broken at least once. So
they are shy about committing their heart too quickly and maybe getting hurt again. This sign has a terrible time getting over previous loves.

ey can get depressed and melancholy even thinking about a former
ationship. If he is getting over a divorce, it will take years. So you
ve to be patient with this sensitive soul. Once he is finally in love, you
ll be flooded with flowers, candy, nice presents, text messages, and
mantic evenings galore. He won't easily take no for an answer.

So is there anything to watch out for with this wonderful man? You bet
ere is. His emotions could get the best of him, and maybe get the best
f you, too. If you want a man who is emotionally stable, he is not the one
or you. Since the moon is his planet, the lunatic side *will* show up occa-
ionally. He can go from a frown to a laugh in just a moment. But then the
rown could come back just as quickly. His feelings get easily hurt and,
like a little boy, he will act out. He will never admit it, but he loves being
babied. Even though you might not want to give him a hug when he's being
a brat, that is the best thing you could do to calm him down. Somehow,
he doesn't feel secure or wouldn't have acted out in the first place. This
sign has an insecure side that erupts regularly. They absolutely need to
feel emotionally as well as financially secure. If his bank account isn't
as big as he wants, he might be hard on himself as well as on everyone
else. He's just disappointed in himself, because he is the provider and has
missed his mark. That's when the moody Cancerian shows up. Ouch . . .

Will it be easy to love this sensitive man despite his moods? Yes,
because he really is a sweetheart underneath his hard, protective
exterior. Once his heart is open and he invites you to meet his mother,
you're in. But here is a big warning: Never get between a Cancer man
and his mother! You will lose. I'm very sure there are plenty of mama's
boys who are Cancerians. She is the primary woman in his life and he
will compare you to her often. At some point in his life, he will eventually
want his own family. You are lucky indeed if you have a Cancer man fall
in love with you. He will love you, cook for you, buy you the perfect dress
by himself, take care of the children, and provide security for his family. Your only job is to flow with his multitude of moods and not let any
of them get to you. You know you have a prince of a man, and if you can
handle his emotions, you will have a wonderful life together.

CANCER FEMALE PARTNER

Angela, a double Cancer, is a kindergarten teacher. In her classroom, she has twenty students who are all five years old. One of them is always holding her hand while the others huddle around trying to get their turn to hug her. She sees them all as her own and one day wants to have several children herself. Angela gets such a thrill seeing her kindergartners happily playing in the schoolyard. Lunchtime is always fun for everyone. But her favorite time of the day is naptime. Sometimes she just walks around and watches them sleep like little cherubs under her wing. She does feel like an angel of protection for her little ones.

Angela loves what she does for a living. The watery female Cancerian is perfect for helping children. This sign is the most domestic and nurturing of all. They are the best when they can touch and be close to people, as with Angela and her little students. Cancerians are loyal, patient, and very attentive to the needs of others. Loving food, Angela helps her students plant a vegetable garden each spring. After they all harvest the organic produce, she gives them a cooking class to show them how to prepare their bounty. Since this sign loves tradition, she has made a custom of ending the school year with a feast. The children, with the help of some parents and teachers, prepare an amazing dinner for the other classes. Everyone looks forward to it, dresses up, and has a fabulous time. It has ended up becoming the end-of-the-year graduation party. This is a female Cancer at her best.

If this sounds like your love interest, you are in for a wonderful ride. Sometimes rocky, yes, but it will be a worthwhile ride indeed. This is the sign that your mother will love. Take her home to meet your family and watch all the cooing and gushing start to happen—hugs, kisses, and casseroles everywhere. You might even feel that she and your mother and sisters are ganging up on you. How did that happen so fast? They just love her! They know that she is the best thing that ever happened to you and that you would be nuts not to keep this one. She will love you totally. No cheating on you with others or having a duplicitous life. She wants to be joined at the hip with you and your family. You will have great food in your stomach and a beautiful, cozy home. So why are you feeling a little nervous?

Is it the joined-at-the-hip part? Cancerians need that. So if you don't like intense intimacy, being checked on regularly, and her absolutely needing you to tell her how much you love her all the time, walk out the door right now. This is not the sign for you. If you don't like people too close, you will feel smothered by a female Cancer. You must have a part of you that wants someone in your life who will always, always be there for you. If you see that as meddling or possessiveness, it will never work. Admit it to yourself. You know exactly what I mean. Next to the intensely possessive Scorpio woman, Cancerians come in a close second. She likes nice things and you are one of her prized possessions. Did I tell you she is moody? Oops . . . should have said that in the first sentence. You have a very emotional, extremely sensitive, and easily hurt angel on your hands. Criticize or raise your voice to her and she will cry immediately and escape into her hard crab shell for protection. She might be in her bedroom for the weekend. Let her be with herself for a while—she's healing her emotional wounds.

Even though your angel can turn into a loony tune at times, yes, you miss her and her feminine ways. The moon is her planet and as it ebbs and flows, so does she. Get used to her rhythms. The full moon would not be as appealing if it was up all the time. Don't we look forward to the moon's cycle? Learn how to look forward to the emotional cycles of your sweet Cancer partner. Since she is a water sign, take her to the beach for a relaxing vacation. You will see her natural serenity and beauty emerge when all the stress is off her. So if you want a feminine angel who is totally dedicated to you, she might be the one. Loony or not . . . you love her.

CANCER FATHER FIGURE

Charles is a chef, who owns his own restaurant. It is a wholesome family restaurant that serves comfort food. He's owned it for twenty-two years and knows most of his patrons by name. He'll often sit down and join them for a meal. Each night, after all the customers leave, Charles puts out a spread of food for all the employees. It's a great time to have everyone socialize. Since Charles believes in families working together, all his employees are relatives. Plus, it's important to him for all his workers to learn how to support themselves. He even incorporates family time into the business. It doesn't get more Cancerian than sharing food with your loved ones!

Charles loves his family and it shows. He's always available when they need him. He gives the little ones big bear hugs as he picks them up to spin them around. The Cancer father is without a doubt, the best father of all the twelve signs. You are very lucky if your father is a Cancer. His purpose in life is to provide, nurture, and care for his family. He'll make you do your chores without question. Your father is relentless, but never aggressive. Oh, he has his moments, I'm sure, but it's all worth it when you see the tears in his eyes when he holds his new grandchild for the first time.

Often Cancerian fathers feel responsible for the members of their family as well as for their extended family. They will build a mother-in-law's guest cottage behind the house. You never know when his mother or your mother will need a place to live. He does not do this out of duty, but out of an overwhelming sense of nurturing that is inherent to his sign. He does it because it's the loving thing to do. Family is everything to him. Many Cancer fathers feel this responsibility within their neighborhood and are community leaders. They are not the leader with the big ego who serves for selfish reasons. Tooting their own horn isn't natural for Cancer. They help out of the goodness of their heart. This attitude extends to the idea of Cancerians being very patriotic. On a larger level, global unity and international cooperation are high on their priority list. Isn't that their real extended family?

Is your father calm and steady? I'm afraid not. He is connected with the changeable moon and it shows in his emotional patterns. Cancer is the moodiest of all the signs. Luckily, most of the time, he is caring and loving. But every now and then, watch out. He'll get moody, withdrawn, and vulnerable. Even though he's strong on the outside, he is very, very easily hurt. So don't take his emotions for granted. Care for him as much as he cares for you. He's a pretty good worrier and could let his family's problems get to him. But since he doesn't want to appear weak, he holds his emotions tightly inside. Remember the crab? OK, now I've said it. Yes, your dad is a crab sometimes! What does the crab do when he feels insecure? He pulls into himself to regroup. But don't worry— he'll reemerge when he feels safe again.

How do you make your dad feel comfortable? He's very sentimental, so honor his possessions. That old ratty baseball cap might seem like garbage to you, but to him it's precious and reminds him of his favorite team's championship game. Never, never clean out his room to surprise him! He'll hate it. I know it's a huge temptation, because he is the ultimate pack rat. The garage is full of old magazines, broken antique furniture, and boxes filled with mementos from his childhood. It's his stuff, so stay away from it! A better surprise would be to get the children together and make a nice meal for him and the family. Have a family workday and tackle cleaning up the alley or painting the fence together. He will love you sprucing up your home. That will make him happy, and as you know, you want your Cancer father happy, and not crabby. When he's smiling, then the entire family will be happy.

CANCER MOTHER FIGURE

Mary came from a family of eight siblings and always wanted a large family herself. She got her wish and has five beautiful little ones. She has four daughters and, after many prayers, finally had a son. He is the joy of her life. Now that two of the older girls are off to college and one is already married, she can focus on her little boy. Mary doesn't want him to grow up as fast as the others did. She thrives on being a mother; in fact, that it is all she cares about in her life. Every thought is about her family. She feels so lucky to have all her children and future grandchildren. What would she possibly do without them?

In the astrology world, the sign of Cancer is the archetype of the mother, plain and simple. The Cancer mother is the most domestic, devoted, nurturing, and protective mother of all the twelve signs. If you have a Cancer mother, you will experience pure motherly love. She really is like the mother hen who herds her chicks to safety. She makes sure they have enough food, comfortable shelter, and a safe family environment. The watery sign of Cancer is associated with the nurturing moon. Fertility and the female presence are strong here, and we see a lot of "earth mamas" in this sign. She has that comfortable, roundish body, and gives better hugs than anyone. There is always a pot of soup on the stove, as food is one of her expressions of love. Your mother is the type who will invite your friend over for Thanksgiving dinner because his family is away. She wants to take care of the children of the world.

This sign identifies so closely with her family that she may have a hard time cutting the apron strings. Oh, no—the dreaded empty nest fear. Since the parts of the body associated with this sign are the stomach and the breasts, many Cancerian mothers love to nurse their newborns. I've seen situations in which, even though the child is ready for real food, the mother still wants him to nurse. These mothers actually need to wean themselves and not the child. When the children grow up, the attachment is still there. This sign has a tendency to worry and be overly concerned for her children. You need to call home regularly and keep her informed. She is extremely sentimental and will save any memento you get her. Better yet, make something by hand and she will cherish it forever. She needs to receive as much love as she gives—remember that. Never take a Cancer mother for granted or else everyone will suffer.

What happens when the loving Cancer mother gets cross? The entire house can feel the vibe. You experience a heavy, down feeling when she's not happy. Remember that the moon, her planet, is notorious for mood swings and changes of emotions. It is proven that the full moon synchronizes with monthly heightened craziness in the world. The moon is luna, so the ones affected most by the emotional cycles of the moon are called *lunatics*. Therefore, officially, your mother is a loving lunatic at times. If you are reading this because your mother is a Cancer, you know just what I mean. The strangest little things can be set her off. Even though your mother seems strong on the outside, she is easily hurt on the inside. With the slightest criticism, you can see tears well up in her eyes. Oh, no—guilt. Just know that you have a sensitive mother and she needs to be treated gently.

If your mother is showered with unconditional love, you're safe. The typical Cancerian is very sentimental and loves family antiques and old photo albums. A great project would be genealogy or the study of your family tree. Many are avid collectors and have a very hard time getting rid of things. They are all precious keepsakes to her and she would hold onto them forever if she could. This sign has a love for little boxes kept together in a hidden drawer. Respect her secret drawer because one of the boxes probably contains that little necklace made out of shells that you gave to her when you were five years old. Prepare her dinner occasionally to show her how much you appreciate all the wonderful meals she has lovingly made for you.

Most important thing of all: Make a *huge deal* out of Mother's Day!

CANCER CHILD

Allison is the youngest child, so she has lots of attention from her parents and her brother and sisters. She is the baby of the family and loves it. Her older sisters dress her up in pretty clothes and pamper her. Her older brother takes her along to attract girls. She is the center of attention in her family. A bit spoiled? Well, yes. You see, Allison is a watery little Cancerian girl and is very sensitive. She doesn't like loud noises or scary images on TV. She's picky about her food. So everyone protects her. Are they protecting her too much? She doesn't think so.

Your little Cancerian angel came to you for pure love. This sign needs affection, lots of attention, warm hugs, and unconditional love. This child needs not only emotional security but also financial security, so open a savings account today. Your little one will feel much more secure with some money in the bank. Cancerian children are the most sensitive of all the signs and need your word that you will treat them gently. Children of this sign are easily hurt by a sharp, unthinking remark. They will remember it forever.

The infant of this sign is a dream—that is, if you have lots of time to hold your little one. They will need to be held and rocked a lot. Physical touch is usually the most important thing for this sign. This baby will love to nurse, since their parts of the body are the breasts and stomach. Buy one of those cloth baby slings so the baby can feel your warm body.

Right away you will notice the moods of your little Cancerian. One minute he is happy and the next he is crying. Boys born under this sign cry and cry and cry. They will, of course, cry for food, but they will also cry for affection. They need to be touched and held or they feel insecure. Buy the perfect teddy bear for a Cancerian baby. Many of them sleep with the same teddy bear for many years, until it is falling apart. The eyes are long gone, it's been stitched up everywhere, but it's Teddy!

Most Cancerians are big collectors/pack rats, so buy shelves and storage units for them. I know it's a feeble effort to make her room neat and orderly, but give it a try anyway. They will fill their shelves with precious objects of love. It doesn't matter whether they are rocks or dollies—to them they are treasures. Eventually, you might need to figure out how to clean out the toy chest. Negotiations will be necessary here. Don't just go in and throw things away or your little one will be trauma-tized for life. Not to put any pressure on you as the parent, but it's true. Try saying to her, "If you want a new toy, you need to give one away." Let her choose, or you will hear about it later, again and again. You are striking a balance between protecting her enough so that she will feel secure, but not so much that you spoil her.

Your little Cancerian might be a bit shy at school until she finds her best friend. Cancerians are not the most ambitious of students, but will do a good job because they don't want to disappoint you. Plus, they do like money and want to be successful so they can buy nice things. As soon as they are old enough, encourage them to get a summer job. Boys would be good at yard work or helping around the house. Girls are won-derful babysitters. Have them help you in the kitchen. Once they start making some money of their own, watch them blossom. Make sure they spend plenty of time with their grandparents. Plus, pets are great for the Cancerian child. Scruffy teaches them how to care for something, but also offers the unconditional love that only an animal can give.

CANCER PET

My sister works at a dog adoption center and told me the most family-oriented dog is a Cocker Spaniel. So I'm using that breed as an example. If you have kids who want to hold and play with an animal, get one born under the sign of Cancer. The animal will love all the affection and attention showered upon it. As a puppy, this is an easier sign to live with than others. As long as the food scene is good, they will be happy. But just like a human Cancerian, they are easily hurt and don't like to be scolded. If you see your little Cancer doggie under the furniture, something loud or scary just happened. This is probably not the best sign for a guard dog: They are just too gentle. Your Cancerian animal will probably feel best close to the house. As long as there is a backyard for some exercise, this sign doesn't have a need to run away. They know just what they want—a loving family.

ANIMALS FOR CANCER
Armadillo
Clam
Cow
Crab
Hen
Hog
Lobster
Opossum
Shrimp
Snail
Turtle

CANCER CELEBRITIES AND THEIR BIRTH DATES

Prince William	June 21
Cyndi Lauper	June 22
Kris Kristofferson	June 22
Meryl Streep	June 22
Randy Jackson	June 23
June Lockhart	June 25
George Orwell	June 25
Chris Isaak	June 26
Chris O'Donnell	June 26
Tobey Maguire	June 27
John Cusack	June 28
Kathy Bates	June 28
David Arkenstone	July 1
Liv Tyler	July 1
Princess Diana	July 1
Tom Cruise	July 3
The 14th Dalai Lama	July 6
Michelle Kwan	July 7
Ringo Starr	July 7
Kevin Bacon	July 8
Fred Savage	July 9
Tom Hanks	July 9
Jessica Simpson	July 10
Bill Cosby	July 12
Harrison Ford	July 13
Tommy Daniel Mottola Jr.	July 14
Nelson Mandela	July 18
Sandra Oh	July 20
Ernest Hemingway	July 21
Robin Williams	July 21

PERFECT GIFTS FOR CANCER

Cancerians love warm fuzzies. Comfort food and family sharing are high on their list. Their main sources of happiness are sentiment, home, family, and food. These sweet presents will make your Cancerian feel very special.

Sentiment

- Photo albums
- Silver picture frame
- Engraved silver goblet
- Soft pillows
- Anything handmade

Home

- New dining room table
- Soft sofa
- Sewing machine
- Barbecue grill or new kitchen, depending on your budget
- Subscription to a home improvement magazine

Family
- Family vacation
- Big-screen TV
- New dog
- Large, framed family portrait
- Genealogy chart or family tree

Food
- Gift certificate to a gourmet kitchen store
- Set of classic cookbooks
- Cook dinner for her

LEO

July 24–August 23

KEYWORDS

POSITIVE KEYWORDS

Confident

Charismatic

Royal

Playful

Proud

Sunny

CAUTION KEYWORDS

Arrogant

Demanding

Flashy

INFORMATION

FIFTH SIGN OF THE ZODIAC

Glyph: ♌

Planet: Sun

Symbol: Lion

Element: Fire

Mode: Fixed

Colors: Gold, Orange-Brown

Gemstones: Topaz, Amber

Metals: Gold, Brass

Body Parts: Heart, Spine

LEO: THE ENTERTAINER

Gene is a mega-Leo with several planets in the sign of the king. He is an entertainment lawyer and basically runs the world of show business. Gene is an icon in the entertainment world. You can also correctly call him a media mogul. The kings and queens of rock 'n' roll and pop music consult him before they make a career move or even think about signing that multimillion-dollar contract. Oh, yes: Gene does roar like a lion at times, but when it comes to entertainment he's the king of the jungle, so everyone always listens.

Just like Gene, Leos are the natural leaders of the zodiac. They were born with the uncanny ability of knowing what to do in most situations, without even thinking about it. Leo is the second fire sign, after Aries. I describe the Aries fire as the strike of a wooden match bursting into a bright, quick flame. By contrast, Leo is a roaring fire in a large, stone fireplace. This fire sign radiates warmth to its adoring fans, who huddle around the Leo for comfort from the cold. Leos love an audience—no, they need an audience. They are astrology's entertainers. Not that all Leos are onstage to sing or dance—although many of them are—but they are all very entertaining. Many have decided to use their creative talents as producers and directors. But all Leos, whether they are CEOs or sales-people, are engaging. They have a wonderful sense of humor and are always the center of attention—always. Their planet is the sun, which gives them a huge presence. Leos are cheerful, generous, and good-natured. So all goes well with Leos, as long as you know they are in charge. Otherwise, you will hear the loud roar of the lion.

One of the distinguishing features of Leos is their impressive stance. It is no surprise that this is the sign of royalty and the aristocratic life-style. Many jet-setters fall into this proud sign of the zodiac. Leos own glamour in a big way. They drive the fanciest Cadillac and own the big-gest home. The female lioness likes big, gold jewelry and, if she can afford it (and she usually can), designer clothing. Leos are also very attached to their long hair, which often resembles the lion's mane. They need to stand out in a crowd, and they do so with no effort. Leos don't walk—they strut. So if you see a confident, proud individual strutting in your direction and then she stops to pose, you can pretty much bet you are looking at a magnificent Leo.

IF YOU'RE A LEO, READ THIS!

I've never known any Leos who weren't proud of their sign. They are all thrilled to be the kings or queens of the zodiac. All the other signs look up to you, even if they won't tell you that. Are people jealous of you? They just wish they had your charisma, that's all. Why wouldn't everyone want to be the king or queen? But you are the benevolent royal who is very generous with your adoring subjects. If people need your ideas, you are always there for them. You have an amazing love of life and enough vitality to enjoy it fully. Leos are social powerhouses and are very popular. You are creative, ambitious, and have the golden touch. Leos are honest, kind, and fair to all. Do you know that your planet is the sun and your body part is the heart? No wonder Leos are so important—they are the center of the solar system as well as the center of the body. Now you know why you are so magnificent!

WHAT MAKES YOU HAPPY?

Being the Boss

Your life must give you the authority you deserve. You don't take direction well at all, so if you are under someone's thumb, you will be miserable. Oh, it might last for a while, but not for long. Eventually, hopefully sooner than later, you will take charge. You must be in charge of yourself and are usually responsible for others, too. Other signs might want to be taken care of, but not you. As a Leo, you need a clear and open path ahead with no one in the way. Leo is the perfect entrepreneur, so you might want to own your own business. You are very likely to succeed in the sales industry and can sell anything to anyone. Gifted with enthusiasm, you excite people with all the possibilities for your product.

Your sign of Leo is one of the most creative signs of the zodiac. Other signs are artistic, but none is better than you at turning their art or ingenious idea into money. Leo is also the sign of gambling, making you willing to try new projects. You have the golden touch and instinctively know how to be successful. Your positivity, combined with unbridled confidence, is a winning combo. I'll bet you have a great idea that you know could be the next pet rock. If any sign could pull it off, it's the incredible Leo.

The Ideal Leo Lifestyle

You own your own business, with no partners, and you are very successful. Not only does making money come very easily to you, but you also have figured out how to balance it with pleasure. You take many vacations with your family and don't ever scrimp on quality. Remember that Caribbean cruise when you took your family as well as inviting the best friends of your children? It was so much fun that everyone will be talking about it for a long time. You have enough money that you can be generous with your family and you even have extra money to give to your favorite charity. You are appreciated in your community. Laugh often and hug your loved ones every day.

Your Ultimate Dream

To be happy because you have achieved success. That means financial success as well as a rich personal life. You have the home of your dreams, filled with loving children and grandchildren who adore you. Leo is the sign of affection, and you are one of the best huggers of all the astrology signs. You feel secure because you are respected, cherished, and loved.

LEO STRENGTH

Leo is the proud sign of the natural leader. Not only do Leos feel comfortable as the center of attention, but others want them to lead. Being masters at delegation, they get projects accomplished easily. With the sun as their planet, they radiate a bright light to everyone they meet.

Leos walk with a sense of entitlement. They know that they are the ones in charge and everyone else does, too. Fortunately, they are good-natured, cheerful, and, almost always, incredibly positive. Leos are ambitious and think big. Blessed with the gift of enthusiasm as well as a golden touch, they just assume everything will work out the way they want it to. And it usually does. Leos are fun-loving and have a great sense of humor, with a roaring laugh. Since they are so playful, children love Leos. If you are lucky enough to have a Leo as a friend, you will have him for a long, long time. Leos are loyal and build long-term relationships.

LEO CHALLENGE

Arrogance is the biggest challenge for Leo. Although they will see it as confidence, others could see it as a show of superiority. Their big ego serves them well, but could rub people the wrong way at times. They are opinionated, dogmatic, and bossy. Leos have a huge need to be loved and adored. They are very proud and don't take personal criticism well at all. Leos don't like it when you won't let them lead. Conceit and vanity go with the sign of Leo. Often having a need to show off, moderation can easily balloon into extravagance. Many Leos have a loud, booming voice and are oblivious to its volume. Even though it's easy to brag about all their accomplishments, that can add to the problem. To sum it up per-fectly, one Leo I know has a plaque in his bathroom that says, "It's hard to be humble when you are as great as I am!"

MENTAL CHARACTERISTICS

Leos are very confident mentally. They have a natural talent for look-ing at the big picture and knowing how to achieve their goals almost effortlessly. Being a fire sign, they are blessed with a very quick and decisive mind. That powerful mind is why they are almost always suc-cessful. Leos are at their best when they can be creative and have an open avenue to reaching their goals. They get frustrated or even angry if they don't get their way. So stay out of the way of a charging lion. Using their gift of humor, Leos entertain as well as educate their subjects. Yes, they usually have a dedicated audience listening to their every word. Leo is the benevolent dictator who wants to dominate all. They have to watch out for the tendency to "know it all." A bit on the dogmatic side, they need to learn how to be open to the opinions of others. Leos like to be right—and they usually are right, to the dismay of many.

EMOTIONAL MAKEUP

If you need someone to hold your hand, you can ask a Leo. They usually are so emotionally secure that they can be there for you. Not prone to emotional weakness, they will help you feel better easily. One of the obvious occupations for a Leo is as a counselor, so you can count on them to comfort you. They are affectionate and goodhearted and truly want to help.

Leo is more emotional than they will admit. Pride is so important to this sign that they never want to seem vulnerable. But Leos are quite sensitive and easily hurt, even though they won't show it often. They are sentimental with family and friends. Just start a conversation about a family reunion and be ready to hear some sweet stories.

PHYSICAL CHARACTERISTICS
Appearance
Leo is an easy sign to recognize because of Leos' undeniably regal presence. The women walk with the aristocratic gait of a queen. The men have the authority and dignity of a king. They exude a confidence unmatched by any other sign of the zodiac. Their presence is commanding and they most definitely stand out in a crowd. Leos have piercing eyes, but the most striking feature is the lion's mane. It is well known that Leos have a strong attachment to their hair. I can see why, since most Leo women have a full head of long, amazing hair.

Fashion Sense
Leos are grand, and their fashion sense is nothing short of dramatic. Female Leos like big hair, striking makeup, and high fashion. They can wear spectacular ensembles that other signs could only dream of. Male

Leos are dignified and stylish. Leos pull it off with the flair and grace of royalty. The women like chunky, gold jewelry—the bigger the better. You will never see a female Leo sneak down to the store in sweats with dirty hair and no makeup. Won't happen. They like to be seen and have way too much pride to ever be caught looking less than magnificent.

Health Type

Leo is associated with both the heart and the spine. Since Leo is a fire sign, maybe the most important thing for them to remember is not to work so hard, because they get burned out and therefore exhausted. Striking a balance is important to the grand Leo, who lives life to the fullest. Leo is already stimulated, so they don't need much coffee. One of the worst things ever is an overcaffeinated Leo.

Exercise Approach

The competitive Leo likes sports, but Leos also like to win. So they will probably not participate unless they are experts at the sport. Looking foolish doesn't appeal to Leo at all. Aerobic exercise is good to keep the heart healthy and strong. Try circuit training, which combines weights and aerobics. If the Leo is in great shape, he likes to buy cool workout clothes and join a high-end gym so he can be noticed. If Leos need to get in shape, they do it in the privacy of their own home until they get buff, then go out and strut their stuff.

PROFESSIONAL LIFE

Leo is the entertainer, and entertain they must. Many actually are actors, singers, or musicians. Others have gone into producing or directing. Even if Leos don't pursue careers in the theater, they have a theatrical heart. The sales industry is perfect for the persuasive Leo. It is hard to say no to their sense of humor and commanding personality. Their natural leadership makes them quintessential business owners. Another area Leo owns is the luxury and glamour business. Leo is the stock trader, goldsmith, jeweler, as well as a professional gambler. What a sign!

Leo Employer

The Leo boss is one of the very best, due to the profound leadership skill of this sign. They are born to tell people what to do and they do it well. Since they love quality, you will have all the goodies you need to do your job. Leos are generous, so you will be well paid. They are the types who will take the entire office on a ski trip to Colorado. Of course, they always, always pick up the tab. But all these perks do not come without any effort on your part. They are very demanding, and if they are paying you well, they expect the best in return. You have to be totally dedicated when they need you. If you remember that they are always in charge without question, you will do just fine.

LEO IN THE BEDROOM

Leos are some of the best lovers of the zodiac. They must be in control and it is no different in bed. Leos, whether male or female, need to play the lead. They have a dramatic style that translates into passion in the bedroom. Even though they are grand on the outside, they are romantic, affectionate, sensitive, and even sentimental on the inside. Here is the trick: Flattery goes a long way with Leos. Tell him that he is the best, the sexiest, and the most amazing lover in the world. You will have a proud lion purring in your arms. Leos need your devotion—might I say, even adoration. If they are not *the* most important thing in your life, their feelings will be hurt deeply. So, go ahead and adore your incredible Leo. It's OK.

LEO MALE PARTNER

Joseph is a jeweler and travels the world in search of the rarest of gems. It's hard to know what shines more brightly—his jewelry or the light of his personality. He's charming, handsome, and rich. Linda met him at a gem and mineral show and was captivated by his charisma. They have been dating for one year and she's even more taken by him now than when they first met. He is truly a romantic, who wines and dines her and showers her with flowers and presents. Of course, many of his gifts are of fine jewelry, so she is one lucky girl. Yet, she has noticed that he makes all the reservations and most of the decisions. He's a real man and she loves how he takes control . . . most of the time.

Linda found out later that Joseph is not just a Leo, he's a double Leo. So she has a real lion on her hands. Leo is one of the most creative of all the signs, and it really shows with Joseph. He's always thinking of a new and fabulous piece of jewelry. Each design seems to be bigger and more dazzling than the last one. Of course, the price keeps going up, too. But his style is so recognizable that he sells as many pieces as he can make. Linda realizes that he's obsessed with his work and his lifestyle. His cell phone rings constantly and he always answers it, even when they are at dinner. At first she thought that was rude, but now knows he can't help it. Leo is a fire sign and he is always on the go. He talks fast, walks fast, and is always thinking about his next project. Now Linda sees why he is so successful: He works it.

Luckily, when they go on vacation, he really plays. She was afraid she fell in love with a workaholic, but not quite. Capricorn is the real workaholic. Leos balance hard work with strenuous play. And do they play! Only the very best will do for Joseph. Last summer they traveled to Greece and rented a gorgeous villa overlooking the Mediterranean for two months. They ate at the finest restaurants and shopped in the nicest little boutiques. He was chivalrous and protected her like a real man. He definitely spoiled her, and she loved it. He was extravagant not only with her but with their new friends. He attracted people to him like a magnet. Their villa was brimming with people most of the time. He loved to entertain, and they partied in grand style. Linda has her sun in Cancer and doesn't need to be the center of attention. Good thing, because Joseph played that role and did it with style and panache.

Linda realized after spending a summer with Joseph that his Leo was stronger than she thought. He always seemed to need to be in the limelight with their friends. Everything revolved around him. Even though he was funny, he talked loudly, which started to bother her. If Linda was going to be with Joseph, she knew that she would have to fit into his world. It was so grand that there wasn't room for another lifestyle.

Hey, she wasn't complaining, because it looks great from the outside. But she was starting to feel overwhelmed by his powerful personality. He made all the decisions for them. He talked over her when she had something to say, almost as if he wasn't really listening to her in the first place. His mind was set on most things and he was strongly opinionated. She figured out that two things could happen. Either she could get stronger, which isn't easy for anyone with a sun in Cancer, or she could be totally dominated by him.

After thinking about it, she decided that he was worth it after all. Maybe he's rubbing off on her, but she seems to have become stronger by being around him. She has learned to say what she wants, and, of course, he is generous with her no matter what. One thing about Leo men: They only take charge in a situation if there needs to be a leader. If everything is proceeding well, they are happy as clams. Joy bubbles to the surface with Leo. Happiness is their natural state of mind. They don't mean to intimidate people at all. Their energy is just so powerful that it radiates to all who come close. Remember the roaring fire in the stone fireplace? They teach us to be strong within ourselves, because we have to be strong around them or just give in. He wants a strong woman who can keep up with him and stand by his side. If you are with a Leo man, be prepared for quite an adventure. You have to be strong enough to handle him, yet relenting enough for him to feel like the king. If you can do that, you will be his queen.

LEO FEMALE PARTNER

Christina, a triple Leo, is an Academy Award–winning actress who was born into a famous acting family. Her mother is an actress and her father is a film producer. It was obvious, even as a child, that Christina inherited the amazing talent of her parents, only she had it times two. Everyone knew that she would be the most talented and successful of the family. Christina is tall, beautiful, and takes command naturally. When there are ten people on the stage, you just can't take your eyes off her. Being the center of attention is her destiny—she's a Leo!

Christina was born creative. Any chance she could get, she would sing and dance, and, with her family, she had plenty of opportunities. As a child, she started doing little parts in plays. Soon she flourished and wrote the scripts, designed the costumes, and was the star. Leos are great leaders and you can see their leadership traits emerging strongly, even as children. Christina is the perfect example of a Leo woman who has found her power. This commanding fire sign sparkles beautifully through her and she knew how to focus it on something she loved. It's particularly important for a Leo woman to find her niche in life. She needs to shine brilliantly and be seen and admired. Leo women are so grand that they outshine others without trying. She is stately and majestic, with a head of hair that would make Rapunzel jealous. Women envy Christina because of her extraordinary beauty and talent. She truly is a triple threat: She can sing, dance, and act. But her best talent is her unshaken confidence. She thinks big, wants to start directing in a few years, and eventually, she'll be the producer. It's written in the stars for this triple Leo.

Notice that I haven't mentioned anyone else? If you are interested in a Leo woman, you have your hands full. Is she worth it? Of course, but it's not without some effort on your part. You need to be strong enough to be able to stand next to a charismatic, magnetic star without feeling insecure. You could easily be relegated to her shadow. If your ego is stable enough to handle her getting all the attention, you will have a very exciting relationship. Leos are fun-loving, generous, romantic, and very affectionate. She's social and loves black-tie gala events, but she can work out with you at the gym, too. She's competitive and might even be in better shape than you. The main thing with a Leo woman is that you have to adjust to the fact that she is the star. Sorry, only one star to a family . . . and it's her. A perfect relationship for her would be a partner who is a combination of a fan, promoter, bodyguard, and lover.

Your Leo woman is a fire cat. Is that a wildcat? Sometimes. Leos need to be in charge, so don't even think about telling her what to do. Does she have a temper? Oh, yes! A perfect word to describe an indignant Leo woman is *diva*. Vanity and conceit are Leo's hallmarks. She needs you to adore her or you are in trouble. A bit on the narcissistic side, Leo women are in love with being in love and need an adoring partner. She can be spoiled and domineering if she feels threatened. Even though she is outwardly strong, she is inwardly quite sensitive. She can't take any criticism, so be careful how you make suggestions. If you are also a triple Leo and want to be in control, just walk out right now. It won't work and you know it.

Is your Leo beauty worth the drama? *Absolutely!* Remember how she makes you laugh when you are with her? You love her pure energy and vitality. It's as if she's plugged into the universal energy outlet and shines so brilliantly that she makes you want to be a better person. You can't be weak around her or she won't respect you. Are you strong enough for this wildcat? You have to be strong enough to stand by her side, but never block her light. If you can handle all her energy, you are blessed indeed to have your very own lioness. Grrrr . . .

LEO FATHER FIGURE

Cliff is a very successful owner of several businesses and well respected in the community. He's married and has two wonderful children. They live in a Leo-style home—big with all the trimmings. He even built a separate garage just for his toys—a Jeep, all-terrain vehicles, and a huge RV for trips. He is a devoted husband and father and is living his ideal life. Like most Leos, he works hard and takes pride in his work. Cliff is a contractor, developer, plays the stock market, and is even an inventor. Leo is one of the signs whose creativity and know-how turn their ideas into money. One of his inventions could easily catch on and bring in even more abundance. Leo has a golden touch—no wonder he's the king.

The Leo father is one of the very best dads of the zodiac. Since they are very driven, many grew up so quickly that they didn't have much of a childhood. So when they are adults, they connect with children almost on their level. They get down on the ground and wrestle with the boys. They take the girls out to movies or shopping. That's why they like their toys—so they can play, too. Cliff bought all-terrain vehicles for everyone so they could play together as a family. Leos think big and are very generous, especially with their children. They are fun-loving, positive, supportive, and funny, so everyone laughs around them. Leos are affectionate and are known for the best bear hugs ever. They are great providers and see it as a pleasure and not a burden. Leos are extremely proud fathers and will show pictures and brag about their children to anyone who will listen.

Many people are jealous of successful Leos because they have so much. But don't think that all wealthy Leos were born with silver spoons in their mouths—not so. Leo is the sign of self-made men. They are incredibly ambitious and hardworking. They can do anything they put their minds to because of their confidence. Leo is the most self-assured of all the astrology signs. They see obstacles as exciting challenges to overcome. Nothing much bothers a mature Leo male. Usually the Leo father is so powerful that he doesn't have to discipline his children too strongly. The children just want to please him out of respect. The children of most Leo fathers are successful, too. Everyone knows their Leo dad is the king and the leader of the family. No one ever questions his authority. It's just understood. You never want to hear the lion roar.

If your father is a Leo, you know what I mean about his unquestioned authority. Even though there is a lot of love in the house, there is also an underlying expectation of success. The Leo father is a wonderful role model and expects his children to perform to the best of their ability. No slouches allowed in the Leo household. He can be demanding, dogmatic, and set in his ways. But he's only looking out for your best interests, even though it doesn't seem like it now. Yes, he can be bossy and opinionated—he's a Leo. Being a fire sign, he is in high gear all the time. Can you keep up with him? He'll expect you to work as hard as he does. Leo is a tireless worker and not many can match his pace. Sometimes he runs himself ragged by trying to do too much and gets exhausted.

Even if you are not happy with him now, in a few years you will be very happy you have a Leo dad. When other kids are struggling with their parents or their schooling, you will have it quite easy in comparison. If you are doing your best and he can tell, he will provide you with everything you need to succeed. The trick is for you to do your very best—he'll know if you're slacking. A Leo can just sniff out laziness. You most definitely want your Leo father on your side! He is successful and wants the same for you. Respect him and honor him as the leader and provider and everything will go smoothly. Give him hugs and tell him you love him regularly. Have family gatherings with him seated at the head of the table. Leo is the king of the jungle and your Leo father is the king of your home.

LEO MOTHER FIGURE

Marilyn is a high-level international executive. She buys and sells businesses all over the world. Yes, she has twin daughters at home and manages to be a good mother, too. Marilyn's husband is a Pisces, an artist who actually prefers staying at home. They live in a mansion on a lovely estate with horses and lots of land. He has his art studio behind the house so he can create his sculptures and watch over the girls at the same time. Even though this might be an unusual setup for some families, it is perfect for Marilyn. Of course, she takes her daughters traveling all over the world with her. They've been to Paris, Hong Kong, London, and Sydney, and they are only fifteen years old. Marilyn sees to it that they have the best of everything, including education. She's in charge and that's perfect for them. Everybody is happy in this Leo household.

If there is one sign that can pull off being a super-mom, it's Leo. Marilyn is just as much in charge of her very successful business as she is in control of her home. Even from a distance she knows what's going on with everyone. Years ago she hired staff to help with the estate, so that makes it easier for everyone. Leos love opulence and Marilyn is a great example of this: She has created an amazing life-style. She stays in five-star hotels when she travels and demands the best wherever she goes. If the Leo father is the king, the Leo mother is the queen. Leo is the sign of royalty and Marilyn carries herself with the dignity and distinction of a queen. Her confident presence outshines everyone in her circle. She's tall, stately, aristocratic, and beautiful. Her best asset is her long, thick head of blond hair, which cascades down her back. But don't think that her beauty is her power—her intelligence reigns. No one messes with the queen . . . or a Leo mother.

Even though Marilyn works hard when she's away, she settles into family life when she is home. One of her preferred things to do with her daughters is to take them to spas for luxury treatments. She's very generous with them and they all have a great time when they are together. Even though her daughters are only fifteen years old, they have been pampered their entire lives. They know their signature nail color for pedicures. They know what facials they prefer and are not afraid to ask for what they want. They each have their favorite clothing designers. They luckily have inherited their mother's beauty as well as her gorgeous mane of hair. Personal appearance is very important to Leo mothers. She wants her home and family to be outstanding and will do everything she can to achieve that look.

If you have a Leo mother, you know what you can get away with . . . which isn't much. Somehow she always knows what you are up to. Is she intense at times? Yes, she's a fire lioness. She can roar with the best of them when she's not happy with situations. She's a bit on the dramatic side, so you want to make her happy. Like Marilyn, your mother will wear the pants in the family and everyone knows it. The husband of a Leo woman knows that, too. She can be opinionated and bossy if things are a bit messy and not to her liking. Even though she seems tough on the outside, she can get easily hurt if she's not respected. Honor her wishes and she will be happy. Compliment her when she looks particularly beautiful. Your mother is very sentimental, so sweet cards and presents will delight her.

A Leo mother is one of the proudest mothers of the entire zodiac. But you need to be upstanding so she can be proud of you. Make sure you take care of your appearance, and to make her real happy, have your room presentable at all times. She is honest, kind, and fair to all. But she will demand honesty from everyone in her family. She is very affectionate, fun-loving, and good-natured. Her natural state is one of happiness and joy. Leos are also very creative, so try starting a family project together. Surprise her with a family video photo album, or have everyone make her a collage of her favorite images. Your mother wants to be the center of attention, so be sure to remember her birthday with a party. If she feels loved and cherished, she will give all that love back to her family unconditionally. Not everyone is lucky enough to have a lioness for a mother.

LEO CHILD

Ashley is a radiant little five-year-old Leo girl. She seems much older than her young years because of her self-assurance. She is an only child and loves it that way. Her parents were older when they had her and want to give her everything they didn't have when they were children. She likes to wear her ballerina costume around the house. Her parents know when she wants to perform because she puts on her tiara. Even at the tender age of five, Ashley knows she's special. She's treated in a special way at home and expects that same attention out in the world. Knowing Leos, she'll get it!

Your little Leo is a star. If the Leo male is the king and the Leo female is the queen, then the Leo child is the prince or princess. This child came to you to be respected and honored as a leader, which is the destiny of a Leo. If you have several children, this Leo will be the one the rest look up to for advice. It doesn't matter if he is the middle child or the baby—he will still be the head of the pack. This child will be larger than life and you will be able to tell right away. The light shines brightly through this powerful astrological sign. Leo is a fire sign and will have all the energy of a lion cub. Who is in charge? Not you, that's for sure.

The Leo baby is affectionate and good-natured. You have a cheerful, outgoing, and confident little one, who will be very interactive with you and the rest of the family. Leo likes to be in the center of the action, so shower all the attention you possibly can on your little lion or lioness and you will have a happy baby.

Leo toddlers and children will be full of themselves in a good way. They will walk and talk early and with a pronounced sense of authority. How can a three-year-old exert authority? A Leo was born to be in charge and you had better get used to it early on. For example, select several toys that you approve of and then let your little Leo choose the right toy. Pretend that they are in charge of their lives . . . because, they really are in charge. It's important for little Leos to be with their peers so they can learn how to cooperate. They might want to tell their playmates what to do, which doesn't go over that well with the other children.

School is a good place for Leos. Since they are the born leaders, they need to have others to lead. As children, Leos are still learning leadership skills and might bump heads with other strong students. Enroll them in a leadership training class as soon as they are old enough. Leo is a very creative sign and they might enjoy dancing, art, or classes in acting or theater. They are dramatic and might throw a temper tantrum if they don't get what they want.

Leo teenagers are usually very popular and will often go to parties and overnight stays with friends. This is the perfect sign to run for class president, and they usually win! Their friends want to be like them, so you will have lots of activity at your house with their admirers. Give your Leo some responsibility—maybe a summer job. Leos like to have their own money to buy the goodies they love. And Leos love their goodies. They will want the latest gadgets, cool clothes, and expensive jewelry. They will want a nice car, even if it is their first one at sixteen years old. Only the best will do for a Leo.

The challenge for a Leo child is humility. It's hard for a Leo to be humble because of the extreme self-confidence inherent in that sign. As an adult, confidence is their best trait. As a child, it could be seen as bragging or conceit. Make sure not to diminish the large Leo personality. A Leo is supposed to be grand, regal, proud, and dramatic. So if you channel your Leo child in the right direction, you will have a bright, shining star.

LEO PET

If you want a majestic, confident family pet, choose one born under the sign of Leo. I'm using the grand German Shepherd as an example of a Leo dog. Like human Leos, this dog will need a lot of attention, so please do not get a Leo pet if you are at work all day long. As a puppy, this sign will be more mature than other zodiac signs. The Leo has a built-in maturity, which can be seen even in a puppy. Leos like activity, so make sure you have a yard for them to run in, and take them out in the country as much as you can. Leos are proud, and that holds true for the Leo dog as well. Get your dog groomed often, so he can feel secure about his appearance. If any dog wants a castle for a doghouse, it's a Leo. So spoil your Leo dog as you would spoil your Leo child. Only the best food and lodging for this dog. Go to the butcher for real bones! This is a good sign for a watchdog because they are likely to be protective and will take care of the children as a guardian. You can depend on your Leo dog to help the family. After all, he is the king of dogs!

ANIMALS FOR LEO
Lion
Lizard
Otter
Peacock
Pheasant
Seal
Tiger

LEO CELEBRITIES AND THEIR BIRTH DATES

Daniel Radcliffe	July 23
Jennifer Lopez	July 24
Amelia Earhart	July 24
Matt LeBlanc	July 25
Mick Jagger	July 26
Sandra Bullock	July 26
Carl Jung	July 26
Jacqueline Kennedy	July 28
Lisa Kudrow	July 30
J.K. Rowling	July 31
Yves Saint Laurent	August 1
Martha Stewart	August 3
Barack Obama	August 4
Charlize Theron	August 7
David Duchovny	August 7
Dustin Hoffman	August 8
Whitney Houston	August 9
Gillian Anderson	August 9
Antonio Banderas	August 10
Halle Berry	August 14
Debra Messing	August 15
Ben Affleck	August 15
Madonna	August 16
Robert De Niro	August 17
Christian Slater	August 18
Robert Redford	August 18
John Stamos	August 19
Bill Clinton	August 19
Matthew Perry	August 19
Kathleen Sullivan	August 20

PERFECT GIFTS FOR LEO

Leos are fun to buy presents for because they love goodies. The main interests are fine jewelry or art, creativity, theater, and gambling. Here are some suggestions for your Leo. Hint: They like things big. Leos like quality, so be prepared to spend a lot on this sign!

Fine Jewelry or Art
- Large, gold jewelry
- Tiara for women
- Crown for men
- Fine art
- Large, gold centerpiece
- Two lion sculptures to guard the entryway

Creativity
- Music collection
- Art supplies
- Classes in design

Theater
- Season tickets to the theater
- Concert tickets for their favorite musician
- Gift card to very nice restaurant
- Huge, flat-screen TV with surround sound

Gambling
- Lottery tickets
- Trip to Las Vegas
- Bottle of good Scotch
- Deluxe poker/blackjack table

VIRGO

August 24–September 23

KEYWORDS

POSITIVE KEYWORDS

Efficient

Detailed

Precise

Helpful

Factual

Modest

CAUTION KEYWORDS

Nagging

Worrier

Petty

INFORMATION

SIXTH SIGN OF THE ZODIAC

Glyph: ♍

Planet: Mercury

Symbol: Virgin

Element: Earth

Mode: Mutable

Colors: Brown, Camouflage

Gemstones: Jade, Jet

Metals: Bronze, Chrome

Body Part: Small Intestine

VIRGO: THE PERFECTIONIST

Michael is an accountant and loves what he does. Other people might think his job is boring, but since he's a Virgo, he finds it interesting, even exciting. Adding up numbers is exciting? It is for a Virgo. Michael enjoys seeing all the columns line up perfectly. It's a thrill for him when both sides of the ledger sheet agree. He finds joy in organizing things. This includes numbers, his files, and just about everything in his life. Virgo is the problem solver and will always find another problem to solve, happily.

Virgo is the perfectionist of the zodiac. Like Michael, Most Virgos are usually involved with some form of methodical planning and are excellent at follow-through. Their planet is Mercury, which offers them all the intelligence they need. Virgo's purpose in life is to analyze data and then find a solution. I always advise Aries that when they start something and get bored, give it to a Virgo to finish. One of my CEO clients only hires Virgo secretaries. I told him that was astrological discrimination, but he didn't care. He loves their efficiency and attention to detail. Virgo is the geek of the zodiac. Geek is a good thing—I would love to be a geek myself. What a pleasure it would be to feel totally comfortable with my computer when it's acting up. Balancing the checkbook is another wonderful Virgo talent. Taurus was the first earth sign and now Virgo is the second. Virgos' earthy style shines through with their great sense of discipline and effective work ethic. Virgos can easily handle jobs that would be too tedious for other signs. They see beauty in repetition and accuracy.

The symbol for Virgo is the virgin. But guess what? Not all Virgos are virgins. Surprise! So where does that virgin thing come from? The virgin, or the maiden, is holding a shaft of wheat in her hand. The dates of Virgo are from August 24 through September 23 each year. That historically is the time when the crops are harvested, therefore explaining the symbol of the sheaf of wheat. The maiden is self-contained and personifies purity in the zodiac. It is the sign of service to humanity. Many Virgos volunteer for charities or hospitals because of their huge hearts and deep sense of compassion for the world and those who are less fortunate. They take service very seriously and help in practical ways. Do you need someone to drive you to your car after it is repaired? What about a friend to help you move? Ask a caring Virgo and he will show up ready, and of course, always on time!

IF YOU'RE A VIRGO, READ THIS!

Even though your sign excels in organization, it's a myth that your entire life is neat. I call it the Virgo piles. You have a pile of papers that others would think is just a random stack, but not so. You have your own special system of organization. Many times it is organized chronologically and you can put your finger on the exact paper you want out of your Virgo pile. I tell others: Don't mess around with a Virgo's stuff. You have things in your exact order, even if others can't figure out your system. You have a Virgo system unique to your needs. Remember that you are an earth sign, so make sure you take time to experience nature to balance all your detailed activities. Maybe plant an herb garden or get involved with a community organization in your neighborhood. Be sure to have fun and laugh often. Focusing on projects comes easily to you, but you might have to make a concerted effort when it comes to playing.

WHAT MAKES YOU HAPPY?
Intellectual Stimulation

Mercury is your planet, which you share with Gemini. Where Gemini uses Mercury to communicate and chatter, you use your intelligence to analyze a situation and find a practical outcome. You have the best analytical mind in the zodiac when it comes to deciphering complex systems. Many Virgos make excellent systems analysts. Always challenge your mind by reading and studying difficult concepts. You feel happy when you learn something new. You like to have a plan and to chart your progress, so put your process on a spreadsheet so you can visualize the flow. You are the sign that accumulates scholarly degrees. Often, due to your innate lack of self-assurance, you feel as if you need more education to be prepared. Know that you can retain more details in your mind than almost anyone else. You are an expert at trivia and can wow the best of them with your wealth of information.

Surround yourself with people who stimulate your mind. Not prone to going to big, wild parties, you might enjoy hanging out at a coffee shop that caters to the intellectual crowd. You love to communicate if you are with very bright people. What a waste of time it is to be with people who just don't get it—you have to always explain yourself. You would rather be by yourself than to be with slow thinkers or dullards. Please . . . no dullards in a Virgo's life!

The Ideal Virgo Lifestyle

You work for a business that is stable and trauma-free. The people you work with appreciate your mind and consider you the logistics expert. Each day has a predictable, comfortable routine that makes you feel safe and secure in your surroundings. There is a beautiful patio filled with plants and a fountain and you take regular breaks to enjoy the fresh air. You take educational classes just to exercise your curious mind. Through these classes, you have met a group of intellectual friends who share your interest in learning. Being frugal, you have saved money and have even calculated the exact month and year when you can retire. Of course, it's all on a spreadsheet!

Your Ultimate Dream

To have a steady, reliable job for many years and feel appreciated and secure. You don't need to be the big boss, like Leo, but prefer doing your routine job perfectly. That will leave you time to read, take classes, and participate in all the personal development that excites you. You also want to have the time to volunteer for your favorite charity. Helping people is what truly nourishes your Virgo soul.

VIRGO STRENGTH

Virgos excel at solving problems that require a systematic approach, so I call them the fixers. They instinctively know how to fine-tune something so that it's more efficient. You love tools, whether it's a screwdriver or a computer. You are very, very smart. The Virgo mind is like a trapdoor, remembering every little detail. If any sign has a photographic memory, it's Virgo. Librarians use all the wonderful Virgo organizational skills nicely. The reference desk in a library is a perfect place for a Virgo. Remember the Dewey Decimal System? How much more Virgo can you get?

Virgo is the sign of service. With a strong interest in health and hygiene, many healers fall under this sign of the zodiac. You will see Virgos volunteering in hospitals or in the wellness arena. Virgos love animals and since you are here to serve, being a pet advocate comes easily to you. Many veterinarians and animal care workers are Virgos. As an earth sign, you have an amazingly green thumb and can grow plants effortlessly, so create a lovely home for the plants and animals in your care. This could carry into the green movement to help the global environment. You help not for personal recognition, but because it's the right thing to do.

VIRGO CHALLENGE

Worry is the biggest challenge for Virgos. They are the worrywarts of the zodiac and tend to fret about small things. Being the fixers of the zodiac, they need to acquire the wisdom to know what they can fix and the insight not to worry about what they can't fix. Also, not everyone wants to be fixed, so try not to solve the problems of others unless you are asked to help. There is a fine line between being analytical and critical. Virgos are critical of others, which doesn't always go over too well. They are also very self-critical and are always working toward their goals, but have a hard time accomplishing their ultimate mission. Often, earning all their different degrees is only a form of overcompensation. Everyone else is in awe of their intelligence except them. Cleanliness and germs are a big deal for this sign and Virgo leans toward hypochondria and depression. With a tendency to be timid and insecure and not being comfortable with casual hugs or intimacy, Virgos are often loners. If they do go to a party, they will stay on the outskirts, quietly talking with one or two people. Save the dancing on the tables for Sagittarians. A Virgo will be there to catch them when they fall.

MENTAL CHARACTERISTICS

Virgo has one of the finest minds in the zodiac. They are the analysts, technical writers, and mathematical geniuses. Being studious and detailed, they tackle statistics like it is a game to win. And they do win with their methodical and precise mind. The earth in this sign makes them relentless when they want to solve a problem. They eat up Sudoku puzzles and equations for breakfast. Typically they are modest, gentle, and have no need to be the center of attention. One tendency that could hold them back is their innate sense of inferiority and self-criticism. Often they don't feel good enough, which, of course, is not true. Everyone can tell them how smart they are, but they need to realize it themselves to truly succeed. Virgos are disciplined, meticulous, fastidious, and very efficient. They won't do something silly if they think it's a waste of their precious time. Hey, they could be solving an equation somewhere.

EMOTIONAL MAKEUP

Emotions don't come easily to the logical Virgo. You won't see them crying or outwardly expressing their emotions very often at all. They are most at home in that amazing Virgo mind, which totally dominates their life. They usually have nervous energy themselves and aren't the best at comforting others. But that doesn't mean that they don't care for humanity, because they definitely do care. They might be better at volunteering at the community health rally than holding your hand and commiserating with you. Intimate interaction is a little more difficult for Virgo, but they will work tirelessly for a worthy cause. Ask them to help out with practical, specific requests and they will be there for you every time. Can they do research to locate a good doctor for you on the Internet? Will they pick up some vitamins for you at the health food store? Will they take care of your cat when you go on a trip? How about helping you clean your house when you're moving? Now that's their forte.

PHYSICAL CHARACTERISTICS
Appearance
The Virgo body tends to have a wiry, lanky look. They have the lean muscles designed for endurance and can handle long, steady, hard work. The forehead is broad, which provides room for all those brains. They move in a nervous, twitchy way and are not known for the gentle grace of a Libra. Virgos have an intelligent expression with a business-like demeanor, as if they are always on an important deadline. I was at a restaurant once and saw a man next to me who just had to be a Virgo. He was folding his napkin with great intensity, over and over again absolutely perfectly. Fastidious, repetitive behavior spells Virgo!

Fashion Sense
There are two definite styles of Virgo fashion. One is the perfectly groomed, meticulous look of having every single hair in place all the time. Always pressed and perfectly clean, Virgo is an example of a precise, conservative dresser. Modest, with a tendency to be prudish, you won't see female Virgos in revealing clothing—ever. The other manner of Virgo style is disheveled and not at all interested in fashion, seeing it as a waste of both time and money. Think of the computer geek who slept in his clothes because he stayed up all night working on a project.

Health Type
The abdomen and small intestines are associated with the sign of Virgo. The biggest problem Virgos have is their propensity to worry and fret. Often that anxiety puts a strain on the digestive system and could cause irritable bowel syndrome if they aren't careful. Virgos are very interested in healthy practices like consuming organic food, herbs, and supplements. The trick is for them to be consistent and not give in to overwork. Relax! Your Virgo to-do list will still be there tomorrow!

Exercise Approach
Virgos have an inclination to be sedentary, due to all their detailed focus.

Many work on the computer for hours without a break. Virgos can be a bit on the stiff side and need to make sure they maintain their flexibility. Yoga and stretching are always good for this sign. Since Virgo is an earth sign, they enjoy walking and taking hikes in nature. Gardening is also a good exercise for Virgos since they have such a love for plants. Not very competitive, Virgos would rather work out by themselves. I tell them to just put exercise in their schedule and then they will have to do it. It's a Virgo thing.

PROFESSIONAL LIFE

Without a huge ego, Virgos are very happy to be a worker and not the boss. A Virgo will excel at a career that demands precision, like being an auditor, an accountant, a statistical analyst, a librarian, a data entry worker, an editor, a computer guru, a mathematician, or a chemist. Since they love the idea of good health, they also enjoy being doctors, dietitians, veterinarians, zookeepers, pharmacists, and massage therapists. The exactitude of a scientist belongs to Virgo. Other common Virgo careers are artisans, carpenters, graphic artists, and tailors. To summarize a Virgo, they are specialists at anything they put their minds to.

Virgo Employer

Expect to work hard for a Virgo boss. The atmosphere will be busy, efficient, and disciplined. It doesn't sound like a lot of fun, but you will get so much done that you will gain a tremendous sense of accomplishment. Make sure you are always on time, because your Virgo boss will be there early and you had better be there working by the time he arrives. Earn extra points by keeping the workplace clean and organized, because that will always please a Virgo. You will most likely be micromanaged by a Virgo. They want to do everything themselves because they think that they can do it better and more efficiently than anyone else. Do your job well or else you will end up with a stressed, anxious Virgo—not a pretty sight.

VIRGO IN THE BEDROOM

Due to the innate self-criticism of Virgo, often they take their time with relationships. Not comfortable with casual physical touch, they tend to be a bit stiff and aloof. If they are overweight or not happy with their bodies, they might decide not to take lovers at all. But when they do finally open up, they are incredible lovers. Virgo is the sign of technique and they will read and study anatomy and physiology until they can understand orgasms at a subatomic level. Also, their element of earth gives them a rare sensuality of touch. It's well known that Virgo is the sign of the sexual deviant, although only a Virgo can explain that dubious title.

VIRGO MALE PARTNER

Richard is the perfect example of a Virgo. He's a chemist and is working on new formulas that will help restore the natural balance after oil spills. The sign of Virgo is one of the best guardians of the environment of any sign. Richard is working tirelessly on a microorganism that will eat oil spills. Just sprinkle this powder and the oil disappears—and it's not toxic to the earth. Brilliant. Deborah, a dietitian, met Richard at a conference on new technologies concerning ecosystems. They share the same passion to help the world and are willing to take practical actions to make it happen. Luckily, she is also a Virgo, so she understands his studious, questioning mind. Richard is so bright and devoted to his cause that he must have a partner who shares his mission. Two Virgos working together—Nerds Unite to Help the World!

Richard takes what he does so seriously that he is obsessed with his project. He got his degree in environmental studies and combined that with his previous degree in chemistry. Together they gave him the education he needed to contribute to the world. Virgo is the sign of service, and must act in realistic ways to feel accomplished. Richard is scientific, methodical, analytical, and very dedicated to his work. His main focus in life is to figure out ways to eradicate toxic poisons from the environment. Virgos are studious, mathematical, and very detail-oriented; they are often experts down to the molecular level. The scientific method is a technique used by scientists to prove a theory by repeating the same test over and over again and finding the same outcome. Virgos love repetition and precise results. The scientific method was probably invented by a Virgo. Even though Richard might win the Nobel Prize for his discovery, he's not doing it to get credit. Cleanliness is very important to Virgo, so Richard is doing it to clean up the world around him.

Deborah realized right away that Richard has a destiny with a laser beam focused on his work. Since she shares his passion for serving the world, it might work for them as a couple. But if you want to be the recipient of his laser beam, this is not the sign for you. Virgos need a purpose in life and that purpose usually has to do with health, cleanliness, and service to humanity. This is the best sign for a worker in the green environmental movement. They need a cause and will work diligently until it's addressed. Virgo is an earth sign and Virgos need to be connected with the physical world, whether it's cleaning their house or cleaning the earth. Deborah and Richard have planted a vegetable and herb garden together, which serves their need to connect with clean soil. They are also vegetarians, like many Virgos, and grow only organic veggies, of course.

Does all this work sound exciting to you? Your Virgo man will have each day planned down to the minute and will have your schedule entered into his electronic calendar as well. He's programmed little alarms to sound throughout the day just to make sure he's on track. He has to be efficient because there are just so many important things on his Virgo to-do list. Yes, Virgos always, always have a detailed to-do list. They actually check off each completed task when it is done, but there is usually another task to take its place immediately. When is the last time you scrubbed your floor until you could see your face in the reflection? Do you organize the clothes in your closet by style and color? Are your vitamins lined up in alphabetical order? Well, if you like to sleep until noon, throw your clothes on the floor, hang out in your PJs, and watch mindless TV, that probably doesn't excite you at all. To be with a Virgo man, you need to have the dedication of a saint or it just won't work. Do you want him to organize your closet? Eeek, no thanks!

Typically insecure and timid, many Virgos are loners because they don't feel they deserve love. Why would she like me? I have nothing to offer her! Which, of course, is not true, but try to convince a Virgo of his worthiness sometime. Not an easy task. He won't accept compliments well, so go easy on all your gushy tries to talk him into a positive outlook. He's a skeptic and tends to be a realistic pessimist at heart. Because he's fussy over food, please don't surprise him with a spicy, exotic dinner. He'll pick it apart and complain, so it's not worth it. Save surprises for Aquarians—surprises make Virgos nervous.

If all this cleanliness and detail hasn't scared you off, you are in for a stable, loyal relationship with your dedicated Virgo. It takes a long time for your Virgo to commit himself, but when he does, he's in it for keeps. No playing around on you with this earth sign. He has a very strong conscience and couldn't do something wrong if he tried. Virgo has a huge amount of integrity and expects it in a relationship as well. Join in his cause to help the world and you will have a fulfilling Virgo lifestyle together.

VIRGO FEMALE PARTNER

Pamela, a research librarian, is also a Virgo. What a wonderful combination that is! She's very bright and curious, and has a definite talent for finding obscure information for people. She loves the written word and knows how to locate the perfect quote for any situation. She was a serious bookworm as a child and almost feels more comfortable around books than she does around people. That's why she loves being in the back rooms of the library, doing research. She's modest, gentle, and soft-spoken. But don't mistake her quietness for a lack of energy or focus, because she's a little powerhouse of intellect.

Pamela is living her perfect career choice with all the unlimited wealth of information that surrounds her in the library. Mercury, which is associated with intelligence, is her planet and shines brightly through her mind. She amazes people with the depth of detailed facts that she rattles off as if she has memorized them. With a talent for trivia, Virgo has one of the most studious, introspective, and disciplined minds of the entire zodiac. She feels comfortable with graphs, numbers, and even the infamous Dewey Decimal System. Did you ever figure that one out? I didn't. But her organized brain thinks that way. In a Virgo's mind everything has a perfect place. It would be so terribly inefficient to put something back that is out of order. What a waste of time and resources it would be to look for something that was stored in the wrong place. How does she know where to locate all this information? She's a Virgo!

She is very particular and even finicky about the placement of her books. Please don't ever put the Ms before the Ns or else she will tell you right away that it is incorrect. Virgos like—no, they *must have*— order. I know one Virgo who has to line up the vase of flowers exactly under the light fixture hanging over the dining room table. She will move the vase one-quarter of an inch (6 mm) over and over again until it's just perfect. I mean so precisely perfect that you could measure it and know the flowers are centered to the millimeter. Virgos don't do anything in a sloppy manner; they are not wired for inaccuracy. They just can't do it. Virgos get pleasure from repetition and don't mind tedious work that would bore an Aries silly. They actually enjoy the safety of doing menial work and knowing that they can do it perfectly. Virgo is the sign of the perfectionist and Virgos will repeat something continually until they get it right. But are they ever totally satisfied? Rarely.

If you are interested in a Virgo woman, there is one main question to ask yourself: Are you smart enough for her? She needs someone of equal intellect or she will be bored. If you can stimulate her mind, she might give you a chance. You must appreciate organization and have the willingness to make an effort to organize your life around her wishes. You will need to be patient with this one, because the earth in her doesn't move very fast in a relationship. Virgos tend to be insecure and quite self-critical. Being slightly prudish, she's not comfortable with much affection until she's in a committed relationship, so go slowly on the physical side at first. Let her open up to you and then you can be more demonstrative. Virgos can be inhibited and will need plenty of time to feel comfortable with a partner. She has to trust you, so become her best friend first; the hugs will come second. Is she worth all this work? You bet she is!

Pamela is the kind of a woman your mother and sisters will love. They will tell you that she is the best thing that ever happened to you and that you are nuts if you don't keep her in your life. But to keep her, you will have to be the best person you can possibly be for her to accept you. She will make you a better person if you choose her. Take her to a coffee shop with your laptops and go online and surf with her. Volunteer with her for that literacy program for underprivileged children on Saturday mornings. She will love quiet evenings at home reading together, leading to rich, long, intimate conversations. If you really want her, show her that you can offer her a stable, practical life with not many upsets or surprises. Hey, if you help clean her house, you will find a special place in her heart, forever.

VIRGO FATHER FIGURE

George, a successful tax attorney, works with numbers and graphs all day long. Since he's a double Virgo, he likes all the details and tax laws and is excellent at explaining them easily to his clients. His mind is very logical and linear, which is perfect for understanding the tax world. He thinks in linear time lines, and of course being punctual is a necessity in his business. George has been faithfully married for twenty years and has two sons. His time revolves around his work and his family. Not much else matters to him. To other signs, his life would be routine and maybe boring, but it is perfect for him. Virgos need security and a calm atmosphere or else they get nervous. George has a quiet yet busy office and then he goes home to a peaceful, stable family life. Now that is the repeatable rhythm that a Virgo loves.

George is one of the good guys several women passed up, thinking he was too nice. He didn't get married until later than all his siblings, but luckily, he found a woman who was perfect for him. His wife, a Leo, is quite strong. She is basically in charge of the home, which works just fine for George. Virgos are not keen on being in control and will often be submissive to others. So if your father is a quiet, more inward-looking type, that is what he is supposed to be. But don't think he's a wimp—he's not. Virgos exude a solid, intelligent, and gentle power. He can't do the bravado of a Leo or the cockiness of an Aries. He's not suave and debonair like a Libra. But your father is stable and will always be there for you. A Virgo father works relentlessly to make sure that his family's lifestyle is up to his high standards. Oh, yes, he will have tough standards to live up to and you will have to do your chores. That is an established Virgo fact. If you chose a father who is a Virgo, you must have wanted to learn about accuracy this lifetime. Oh, boy, accuracy! That sounds like fun . . . Not!

Actually, *fun* isn't a word that is associated with Virgo very much, unless you can find fun in cleaning, organizing, and generally wanting to improve the world. Depending on your attitude, that can be fun, right? Your father likes systems and spends lots of time systemizing your household. You will have definite routines that he sets for you. Cleanliness is very important to Virgos. If you are a slob, then your father will hound you mercilessly. He notices every tiny thing that is out of place or dirty. You will never be able to get away from his focused scrutiny, so you might as well keep things clean. Virgo is the sign of the perfectionist. He wants you to meet his high standards. Virgo's planet, Mercury, is associated with intelligence, so he takes education very seriously, and you had better, too. Believe me, you want your father to be the calm Virgo and not the upset Virgo.

When your Virgo father isn't happy, the critical father emerges. This sign is both self-critical and critical of others as well. You think he's petty and only sees what you're doing wrong instead of all the good things you are doing. Remember, he's the fixer. You only fix what is broken and not what's working. So he wants to help you fix what is broken by painstakingly pointing out your faults.

Virgos are prone to overly elaborate monologues. You ask a simple question about a lamp and five minutes later he's telling you how it's wired into the electricity of the house and now he's working toward the nation's energy grid. You just wanted to know how to plug it in! Better be taking notes, because his almost photographic memory will expect you to retain what he's just told you. He walks that line between being a realist and being a pessimist. So don't expect that he will support an impulsive whim—not without a spreadsheet, that is.

Okay, so maybe your Virgo father isn't one of the easiest and most lenient fathers of the zodiac. But you will be a better person because of him. Your father has a very high level of integrity and will raise his children to do the right thing, even when it's not the most popular thing to do. He has a strong need to help people in practical ways. He might have you clean the yard of your neighbor who just broke his leg. Or he will make you set up your aunt's first computer for her, even though you wanted to go out with your girlfriend. He will demand that you get excellent grades in school. No wild parties for friends at your home—sorry. I know these might sound like terrible things right now, but it is setting a foundation for your life that will always serve you. It might seem like you are growing up sooner than your friends are because of all the chores delegated to you by your Virgo father, but it's worth it. He's grooming you to be one of the good guys, too. You will soon find out that women like the good guys—really!

VIRGO MOTHER FIGURE

Leslie has two delightful and accomplished children and takes her motherhood seriously. She is the Virgo "earth mama" type of mother. She has an amazingly green thumb and lives in an organic home outside of the city in the foothills. She's created a paradise of exotic plants, herbs, and vegetable gardens. Leslie raised her children with all the wholesome values of a dedicated Virgo. Her children are lucky enough to eat homemade pies and yummy food with fresh flowers at the table. She did financial consulting part-time until her children were mostly grown. As she is ever the scholar, she returned to school and got an Executive MBA and is now doing estate planning for her private clients. Of course, she still has her garden, like a good little Virgo.

Leslie sounds pretty laid back for a Virgo, you say? Although many are, not all Virgos are uptight and focused on every little detail. There is a more gentle and earthy type of Virgo. Remember the maiden with the sheaf of wheat? Leslie is more of the maiden type, but also possesses the analytical, MBA side. Family was her first priority before she pursued a full-time professional career. Now she can take the dedication she has as a mother out to the world and help others. Leslie is the perfect combination of love, like the mother in her, and intellect. Mercury, the planet of intelligence, belongs to Virgo as well as Gemini. Virgos go much deeper than Gemini in their pursuit of learning. Gemini know just enough to talk about the subject, but Virgos research it and become experts. So Virgo is the expert specialist of all the signs, even if she is an earth mama.

If your mother is a Virgo, you must have wanted to learn about how you can succeed in life. She wants only the best for you and is here to help guide you toward your goals. That's one reason she is so focused on your education—because she knows that is the key for you to get what you want in life. If you are more highly educated, you earn more money and can take better care of yourself. But that will come with some criteria she sets for you as a child. This is the sign of discipline and a serious work ethic, so look forward to high expectations. Virgos are gentle and very powerful at the same time. She won't have temper tantrums like Aries moms or push you like Capricorns, but she will be relentless until you give in. Little by little, she will talk you into what is right for you. Sometimes you might want to just do it to shut her up, but, hey, whatever works for you. Just know she will eventually get her way, so resistance is futile.

Worry belongs to this sign and the Virgo mother is the master worrier. Just like Leslie, who put her life on hold until her children were almost adults, your Virgo mother might sacrifice herself for you instead of pursuing her own dreams. That can put pressure on both of you if her expectations are unrealistic or if you have a different plan for your life. Your Virgo mother is quite self-critical and might blame herself for your seeming disappointment in life. Remember, Virgo is the fixer and your mother wants to fix your problems. She might focus on the problems more than the successes, but that is the way Virgo fixes things. She has lots of inner nervous energy and tends to get anxious over small things. Not the social butterfly, she stays home rather than having a busy social schedule. That only gives her more time to pay attention to you and might add to her concern for her children. Know that you are the center of her world. Oh, maybe just a little pressure there.

The Virgo mother is one of the most dedicated mothers in the zodiac. If you ever need something, she is right there for you. You will never have to want for much of anything with her. What can you do to make her more relaxed? Always do your homework before you are asked. Study hard in school and be the very best student you can be. Keep a clean room and cheerfully do your chores as well as you can. Organize a workday to surprise her with a sparkling clean house. Help her plant a spring garden. You know how much she hates germs, so wash your hands so often that they shine. Clean children and a clean home will make your mother happy . . . and you do want your Virgo mother happy.

VIRGO CHILD

David is ten years old and already showing signs of being a genius. He is so advanced at math that he challenges his teachers. He's a mega-Virgo with several planets in that sign. So he's an extreme combination of the very best and the absolute worst of Virgo. Even though he's doing work at college level and beyond in math and physics, he struggles in school. David is so smart that the other kids have a hard time relating to him and he's a bit of a loner. Most of the time, he's fine with that. Besides, he's working on an equation that's more important than any old game, anyway.

Your Virgo child wants one thing from you: praise. They need for you to tell them how amazing and wonderful they are when they succeed. You see, Virgo is a very delicate combination of incredible intellect and fragile sense of self. Virgos are born self-critical, shy, and not very social. So, as parents, you need to counterbalance their self-doubt with positivity. Always build up their self-esteem and never criticize them. Now you know that you are raising a delicate genius.

As a baby, your Virgo will be easily entertained and won't need others around to be happy. Virgos have a great power of attention and will play with their toys of choice with full interest. Don't expect a real cuddle bug; they are too interested in what they are learning at the moment. Start a savings account right now for college! Read to your little Virgo every day and, please, no baby talk!

The Virgo child needs a routine, so make dinner and bedtime the same time each day. Often Virgo children are very fussy eaters and are notorious for picking at their food and complaining. In their defense, they are sensitive and probably know what their body needs. But it is a challenge for parents. Buy educational toys for Virgos . . . save the toy guns for Aries.

School is mostly comfortable for Virgo, or at least the educational part. No prodding to do homework; it's done before you even ask. The social scene is another story. Virgos usually feel uncomfortable in large groups and prefer a few close friends instead. They are usually found on the side of the schoolyard talking with a couple of good friends. A Virgo will gravitate to the brightest kids in class because they are the only ones who can understand his brilliant mind.

Teenage Virgos need to be focused on their education, because that is where they shine. Usually they are not athletic or socially adept, so the mental arena works best for them. Many Virgos are literal geniuses on computers and are working at full speed by the time they are teenagers. Virgo is the type who will start an Internet business out of his bedroom at fifteen years old and be a millionaire by the time he hits his eighteenth birthday.

The most challenging part of raising Virgos is to help them minimize their self-doubt. Often they will study, study, study and not quite feel ready to write that paper. Overpreparation due to lack of confidence is a Virgo trademark. Even though Virgos have the material down cold, often tests are tough because they freeze out of fear. Don't let them say they don't feel well on test day and need to stay home. Virgos are sensitive and can easily talk themselves into anxiety attacks. Anything you can do as a parent to bolster your Virgo's self-assurance is crucial. Your Virgo is studious, introspective, gentle, and so very intelligent. If Virgos only realized how incredible they are, they would be unstoppable.

VIRGO PET

An animal born under the sign of Virgo will be a loyal, dedicated pet to your family. But they have special needs and require a certain kind of a family. I'm using a Chihuahua as an example of a Virgo dog. Just like Chihuahuas, Virgos can get nervous with too much stress or wild activity in the house. If you have lots of kids running around making tons of noise or have a teenage rock star whose band practices every day in the basement, pass on getting a Virgo dog. An Aries Doberman would love being in the thick of things, but a Virgo Chihuahua would sit in the corner, shaking, and say, "Get me out of here!" Diminutive Virgo pets would be great for small, quiet, and calm families who live in an apartment without much of a yard. Make sure you don't feed a Virgo animal weird people food, because it will upset his sensitive digestive system. Stick to real healthy dog food and not many goodies. Maybe get a Virgo pet for your grandmother who wants a loyal lap dog and watches a lot of TV. Yes, that's a good match.

ANIMALS FOR VIRGO
Bird
Cat
Chicken
Deer
Dog
Duck
Hamster
Lynx
Owl
Sheep
Squirrel
Turkey

PERFECT GIFTS FOR VIRGO

Virgo is an easy sign to buy presents for and here are some suggestions. These are their main interests: tools, health, clothes, and plants. Here are some presents that any Virgo would love!

Tools
- The newest and fastest computer
- Bread maker
- Toolbox full of precise tools
- Draftsman drawing set

Health
- Insurance that covers alternative modalities
- Gift card from a health food store
- Massage and bodywork
- Fancy soap, shampoo, and body lotions

Clothes
- Gift card to a nice clothing store
- A nice watch
- A custom-built closet with lots of compartments

Plants
- Shopping spree at a plant nursery
- Large pots for planting
- A new tree for the backyard

VIRGO CELEBRITIES AND THEIR BIRTH DATES

Sean Connery	August 25
Tim Burton	August 25
Claudia Schiffer	August 25
Elvis Costello	August 25
Macaulay Culkin	August 26
Mother Teresa	August 26
Jack Black	August 28
LeAnn Rimes	August 28
Michael Jackson	August 29
Cameron Diaz	August 30
Richard Gere	August 31
Lily Tomlin	September 1
Keanu Reeves	September 2
Salma Hayek	September 2
Charlie Sheen	September 3
Beyoncé	September 4
Michael Keaton	September 5
Buddy Holly	September 7
Pink	September 8
Adam Sandler	September 9
Hugh Grant	September 9
Harry Connick Jr.	September 11
Prince Harry	September 15
Alexis Bledel	September 16
Lance Armstrong	September 18
Jada Pinkett Smith	September 18
Jimmy Fallon	September 19
Sophia Loren	September 20
Luke Wilson	September 21
Faith Hill	September 21

LIBRA

September 24–October 23

KEYWORDS

POSITIVE KEYWORDS

Balanced

Refined

Artistic

Charming

Easygoing

Romantic

CAUTION KEYWORDS

Indecisive

Lazy

Codependent

INFORMATION

SEVENTH SIGN OF THE ZODIAC

Glyph: ♎

Planet: Venus

Symbol: The Scales

Element: Air

Mode: Cardinal

Colors: Green, White

Gemstones: Aquamarine, Emerald

Metal: Copper

Body Parts: Kidneys, Urinary Tract

LIBRA: THE ROMANTIC

Jacqueline is thirty-two years old and she's a successful wedding planner. Her sun is in Libra, the sign of love and romance. She adores creating weddings that are truly magical. Her artistic eye and sense of beauty are perfect for making romantic wonderlands of love. Only one problem—she's not married and very much wants to be. Sometimes the beautiful weddings she creates are torturous for her when she knows that the big highlight of her night will be going home to feed her cats. It's just not fair . . .

Librans come into this world for one reason: to find true love. They are the eternal romantics who live for being in love. None of this "being satisfied with loving humanity" stuff for a Libra—they want the real thing, one-on-one, passionate, can't live without you kind of love. Their life partner is out there and they will search and search until they find their soul mate. Libra is the sign of rose-colored glasses, who always sees the very best in a potential partner. When Jacqueline attends weddings, you know she has her radar on and is scanning the audience for any potential mates. She wants a true partner and doesn't want to date just to be dating. Besides, Jacqueline can hear her biological clock ticking fast right now. That clock will turn into Big Ben in a couple of years, and it will gong so loudly that she'll hardly be able to hear what her new boyfriend is saying. She scared off the last one, she knows that for sure. Her tactic is to be sweet now and let him know her real needs later. That should work.

The symbol for Libra is the Scales, which represent the duality of the Libra and the partner. It also shows the need for balance and fairness, which is crucial for this sign. Librans strive for a balanced life, and for them that must include a partner. No loners in this sign. Gemini was the first air sign of communication and Libra is the second. Gemini love to talk to groups—actually, to anyone who will listen. Librans save their communication for their partner. They like cooing, private jokes, and pillow talk. That's the Libra style of communication, which is much more of an intimate version of air than Gemini's. What's the planet for Libra, who is so obsessed with love? It's Venus, of course, the planet of love. Librans have all the exquisite Venusian traits of refinement, harmony, sophistication, and kindness with the gift of social graces. I call them the Lovely Librans.

IF YOU'RE A LIBRA, READ THIS!

So how is your love life? I might as well get right to the point, because that's what's important to you. Don't worry one little bit if you are not with your soul mate right now. Eventually, it will happen. Sometimes as a Libra, you need to discover yourself first and then you can bring that person into the relationship. Have you had the life experiences you want yet? Make yourself happy just with you and then your partner will appear. Happiness attracts a partner much more easily than loneliness or desperation. Get involved with something that feeds your keen sense of beauty. Art or dance classes might be a possibility. What is your hobby? Join a club with other people who share the same interest. Know that your sign of Libra will continually attract possible mates, all the time. The flow of potential partners will never end. It's your destiny—you're a Libra!

WHAT MAKES YOU HAPPY?
A Committed Relationship

You must have love in your life to make you happy. Other signs might enjoy the single life, but not you. Companionship is without a doubt the most important thing to you. Real love is having someone who holds your hand and will help you when you need him. The Libra in you knows how to give unconditional love and wants that love returned. Happiness for you is love.

Since Venus is your planet, you also gain pleasure through beauty. Libra is the sign of the artist or at least the art appreciator. To make you happy, surround yourself with lovely works of art, beautiful fabrics, and enticing fragrances. Libra has the keenest sense of smell in the zodiac, so always have your favorite essential oils handy. Loving leisure, be sure to do plenty of lounging around in silk pajamas doing not much of anything but looking beautiful.

Love and beauty—now that's a wonderful combination for Libra. You would enjoy going to art gallery openings with your mate. Both of you are classy, even chic in your style. Librans are blessed with good looks, thanks to that wonderful Venus of yours. So you both are the envy of your social admirers, who watch you being embraced by your handsome lover. Yes, real Libra love and romance is yours.

Your Ultimate Dream
To have your dream partner in a romantic, fairy-tale marriage. He's handsome, rich, in charge of everything and treats you like a princess. You have two beautiful, well-mannered children and belong to the country club. You dabble at painting or maybe photography. With your talent as a fabulous hostess, you often entertain socially in your lovely home. Your life is perfectly designed for love and luxury. You lucky Libra!

LIBRA STRENGTH
Libra is best at cooperating with others. It is the sign of the diplomat and negotiator because they can see both sides of a situation easily. They use gentle reasoned argument instead of force. Libra avoids confrontation at all costs, even if that means giving in to make peace and harmony. Librans are the peacemakers; they love to bring people together from different sides of the fence to find common ground. Many models are Librans, due to their classic beauty and interest in the arts. They have a great sense of color and line and make distinguished artists. Refined, graceful, kind, and popular, Librans are at home in most social settings. Experts at etiquette, they could set a tea for royalty and enjoy it. Plus, you can bet that they wear the perfect dress for Her Majesty. Not an easy task, but Librans dream about dressing up at tea parties.

LIBRA CHALLENGE
Indecision is the hardest challenge for Libra. The Libran diplomat sees

both sides of an issue, but has a hard time aligning with one side or the other. Librans would rather sit on the fence until the situation just goes away, rather than taking action. That tendency to waffle or be fickle comes from a deeper feeling of insecurity in this sign. That insecurity, in turn, needs a Prince Charming who will take care of them and solve their problems. Whether a man or a woman, Libra defines the concept of codependency. In the need for keeping the peace, Libra will compromise and be controlled, or, worse, allow themselves to be abused, just so they won't be alone. Many would rather have a bad relationship than have no relationship at all. Another result of indecision is procrastination and a seeming laziness. Librans will say that they aren't really lazy: They just take time to appreciate the finer things in life.

MENTAL CHARACTERISTICS

Librans are good communicators, especially with their partner and family. Their voices are soft and they have the ability to look directly at their partners and actually listen to them. No darting eyes like Gemini. Focusing on the other is the forte of Librans. Don't confuse their gentle demeanor with a lack of intelligence, however, because they are very bright. Needing peace and harmony, they will often find themselves in the middle as a mediator to calm the situation. Librans have an incredible power of persuasion over people. They are charmers and can charm their way in and out of any situation. Librans find anything crude, ugly, coarse, or vulgar to be totally repugnant to them. They always avoid confrontation, sometimes to their detriment. They are people pleasers. But never underestimate a gentle Libra because they get what they want in very subtle ways. They are so slick that you don't even know you're being pushed in the direction where they want you to go.

EMOTIONAL MAKEUP

Libra is the most sensitive of the air signs, which include Gemini and Aquarius. Because of their interest in people, they can emotionally be present for their friends and personal relationships. They don't dwell on the past, like Cancers, or dream of the future, like Aquarians. They really live in the moment. Librans are born kind and can be insightful, especially if the problem involves your love life. They have a talent for calming people and have the gift of persuasion in convincing you that you can succeed. This sign has empathy for others because personally they relate. Due to their typically fickle nature, often they deal with emotions of the heart. They can get very involved with the personal interactions of others when it comes to their relationships. "He said this and then she said that" is a common conversation with their friends. You don't need to watch TV soap operas if you have a Libra in your life!

PHYSICAL CHARACTERISTICS
Appearance
The Libra body is long, well-proportioned, and has a refined, delicate facial structure. The distinguishing feature of this sign is the inherent poise and sophistication they show to the world. Never crude or rude, they convey the very best of social skills and etiquette. Associated with Venus, the planet of beauty, they are usually very good-looking, with smooth, creamy skin and fine, silky hair. Mild-mannered with an alluringly sweet voice, Librans are the most charming of all the astrology signs. Always beautifully coiffed, they slowly glide across the floor as if they were walking on an invisible cloud.

Fashion Sense
The stylish Libra always looks effortlessly polished. Librans prefer the classic, sophisticated style of quality clothing to the trendy, hip style of Gemini. Fond of pastels, Librans look pulled together even in their pajamas. They love the smooth touch of silk and natural fabrics against their delicate skin. Librans need quality and dislike anything loud or garish. Loving clothes fit for lounging, you could easily find a Libra in the best silk pajamas, leisurely stretched out on a velvet chaise lounge reading the current fashion magazine. Of course, next to her is either tea in a china teacup or a glass of wine in a crystal wineglass.

Health Type

The part of the body associated with Libra is the urinary tract, including the kidneys and bladder. Drinking lots of fresh, pure water is essential for those born under this dry air sign. Their skin is more on the dry side than oily and needs plenty of moisturizer. Librans love to eat creamy, rich, and sweet foods and enjoy eating out at fine restaurants. Often this love of the good life can cause them to develop weight issues. Librans have a delicate look, tend toward anemia, and do need a lot of rest. Aaah—a good use for those new silk pajamas!

Exercise Approach

Libra isn't very fond of most types of exercise. Getting sweaty and dirty doesn't appeal to the delicate sensibilities of a Libra. Forget running the marathon race like a Sagittarius, because it's just not going to happen. Those born under this sign will be lucky to put down their cup of tea to do a stretch every now and then. Oh, their intentions are good, but their social commitments and love of leisure always get in the way of strenuous exercise. Grace is one of the best Libra talents, so stretching and yoga classes are a wise choice. But ballroom dancing might be the best for this sign of beauty because they can get dressed up, be in the arms of a loving partner, and work out at the same time.

PROFESSIONAL LIFE

Naturally gifted in love and beauty, ideal Libra occupations make the world more beautiful. They enjoy being artists, jewelry appraisers, aestheticians, models, hairdressers and experts with cosmetics. Their creative side enables them to succeed as architects, interior designers, and art dealers. Libra is the sign of the diplomat, with talents in negotiating to facilitate collaboration between parties. World embassies are rich in Librans, I'm sure. In sports they would be the referees or umpires, imparting their sense of fairness to the game. But maybe the very best career for a Libra would be as a matchmaker, since her true forte is love.

Libra Employer

Of all the bosses, Libra is one of the most popular and well-liked. Librans will be fair with everyone in their gentle, almost shy manner. Your boss needs harmonious behavior between the employees and will not tolerate any swearing or crude statements. Bullies, go to work for an Aries who can handle you. *Nice and polite* is the phrase of the day in Libra land. The work surroundings need to be classy and artistic with music in the background for ambience. The biggest problem with your Libra boss is his lack of quick decision making. He will poll all members of the staff for their opinion and then ultimately decide by consensus. So expect your Libra boss to ask you for your ideas frequently, and then don't be surprised when he incorporates them into his decision. You must have patience with your Libra boss, but it's worth it because he is just so darn nice.

LIBRA IN THE BEDROOM

Libra is one of the best lovers of all the astrology signs. They love a gentle touch, slow kisses, and sexy words whispered softly. Start with flowers and chocolate to set the romantic mood. To top things off, buy an "I love you" card and prop it in front of a beautiful vase of flowers. Easily seduced, Libra lovers are passionate and almost insatiable in their appetite for love. Remember the importance of a fragrance, lots of candles, and smooth music to create an irresistible atmosphere. Just go ahead and put the DO NOT DISTURB sign on the door for the evening, because it's going to be good.

LIBRA MALE PARTNER

Kevin is a very well-known model whose face has graced the covers of many a fashion magazine. He's a Libra and has the beauty to prove it. They call him the pretty boy because of the exciting androgyny that characterizes his look. His tall, blond, Grecian style really sells magazines because the men like him as well as the women. But he's not only beautiful on the outside, he's also a genuinely nice person on the inside. He's as kind to the makeup artist on each photo shoot as he is to the director of the shoot. Of course, his personality and kindness account for his success, because looks only go so far. He's getting paid for his refined charm; no wonder he always has a smile on his handsome face.

Kevin is completely in his element in the world of fashion, with his planet Venus at his side. He truly lives the life of a jet-setter, dashing all over the world for the next photo shoot while getting paid and treated like a rock star. Many supermodels like Kevin are impossible to work with because of their huge, fragile egos. Not so with Kevin: He's known for being easy to work with on shoots. He's very accommodating and gracious, which only adds to his appeal. With impeccably good taste, Kevin attracts luxury like a magnet. Of course, he's wined and dined at only the best restaurants and clubs by his wealthy clients. Everyone wants to get their own photo op with Kevin because the picture will surely make the paper. The society page is the ideal forum for a Libra. They know they have really made it when they are the largest picture on the most read society page. Now that's success!

If you are interested in a Libra man, you need to be stylish as well. Can you keep up with his charismatic image and fast-paced lifestyle? Granted, not all Libra men are like Kevin, but they will have a suave and debonair demeanor. Kevin spends quite a long time getting ready in the bathroom in the morning. He probably takes more time than most women in front of the mirror. You have to be confident and not have too large an ego, because your Libra lover might attract more attention than you do. Not all women would feel comfortable sharing the mirror with their man. But shopping together sounds like fun. Libra men can shop with the best of them. With their impeccable taste, they often pick the perfect dress for you as a surprise. How does he know the ideal color, style, and size for you? He's a stylish Libra, remember?

If you want a macho guy who is going to take charge and be a man's man, you have the wrong partner. Libra men are gentle, fickle, and easily thrown off balance emotionally. Even if he's masculine, he has the heart of a woman. He's not the best at making decisions and might want you to make reservations at the restaurant of your choice. He hates confrontation and will instead be quiet and pout, or, worse yet, get whiny. Underneath it all is a deep fear of rejection, which is why he will so easily compromise and sacrifice to keep the peace. Librans tend to procrastinate, so you need to either do it yourself or have lots of patience with him. They have a slow and leisurely rhythm, so if you are an ambitious double Aries and like to run instead of walk, just turn and run the other way right now.

Once you realize that your lovely Libra man is worth it, you will start to see the true romantic in him emerge. Candlelight dinners for two at your favorite bistro? How about a huge bouquet of your most cherished flowers every birthday and anniversary, without fail? A foot rub on the sofa watching a romantic movie? Will he surprise you with breakfast in bed? You bet! All of these are in the daily routine of a sweet Libra man. This is the sign of a chivalrous man who is also a real gentleman. So if you want to live the good life with a handsome, tender, and charming partner, you might want to choose a gentleman Libra.

LIBRA FEMALE PARTNER

Laura is a professional ballroom dancer, who competes all over the world. She is a beautiful, tall, blond Libra with the beauty of Venus herself. The dance she specializes in is the elegant waltz, and she truly glides across the dance floor with grace and dignity in her flowing, feather-studded gowns. Even though Laura has a dance partner, many suitors have their eyes on her. Yes, she wants a relationship eventually, but now she needs to focus on her dancing and the many competitions next year. She has been invited all over the world to dance and loves the attention and the grand gala events she attends. She also visits her friends as she travels. Oh, yes, more suitors for this lovely Libran.

Laura loves to have her sun in Libra. To her, that represents grace and beauty. She was born to dance and feels her best on the dance floor when she's performing. The audience is mesmerized by her fluid movements and ease of covering the entire dance floor. She truly looks like she's gliding or dancing on air. Libra is an air sign and between the waltz and all the feathers, you could swear she's flying. The women wish they were like her and the men think she is the ultimate feminine creature. Some people show a little bit of jealousy toward Laura, but she doesn't let that bother her. She sees it as a compliment. Dancing is a very good thing for Laura because Librans can get caught in their minds thinking about their relationships with others. So it's a positive outlet for her to dance and feel her power through her glorious performances.

In addition to a graceful body, Laura is blessed with a very rich and busy social calendar. She loves getting dressed up, going to cocktail parties, and chatting with friends. Libra is the perfect social butterfly who can flit from one group seamlessly to another equally cool group of people. Laura is charming, kind, and always has a smile on her beautiful face. Some people get prettier and prettier the more you know them because of their inner beauty. That's the way it is with Librans—they grow on you. The more you know them, the more you like them. They will do anything for their good friends. If you miss your plane and you get in at 1:00 a.m., your Libra friend will still pick you up and do it with total love. Not much is an imposition on a good friend who is a Libra. You can count on Librans.

If you have met a sweet Libra woman and are falling in love, you need to ask yourself this question: Can you offer her the total commitment and love that she needs? No part-time romance for her. She needs a soul mate and will settle for nothing less. Also, like Laura, Librans are interested in the material world. She loves her feather gowns. They're part of her. So can you afford her? She likes very nice things, never gaudy or flashy, but expensive and classy. Your Venusian beauty needs pampering with mandatory spa days for manicures, pedicures, facials— the works. Emotionally unstable at times, she can have a fit of temper over something you did. You will apologize and tell her you love her more than anything and then you make up. She needs to be proud of your appearance, so no sloppy sweatsuits, please.

Once you've fallen in love with your lovely Libran, it's too late. You're hopelessly caught in her gentle, feminine power. So how do you keep your Libra love? You have to be romantic, very affectionate, and tell her you love her very often because Librans tend to be insecure in love.

Even if she knows you are her man, you must reassure her, and often. She is very peace-loving and even a hint of aggression is too much for her. Think tender kisses. Serenade her with music and poetry written just for her. Surprise her with little presents. A card and flowers will score you major points with her. What about giving her a massage with her favorite essential oil? Make sure you have decorated the room with candles and flowers to set a mood for romance. Is having a goddess in your arms worth a little romance? I think so.

LIBRA FATHER FIGURE

Andrew is an architect who designs high-end custom homes. His style is light, open, airy with great views. He's married and has three little girls he watches during the day. He designed their fabulous home with his perfect design studio right there. His wife is a lawyer and goes to an office each day, so he stays at home with the girls. The Libra father is one of the best stay-at-home dads. He and the girls get along so well and he's definitely not the authoritative type of father. Somehow they all have the same power. I call it the Libra happy home.

Andrew is an award-winning architect, and being an air sign, he really uses the air element as he incorporates space and air in all his designs. Their home is modern, almost all glass, with two stories and a great room with an open ceiling into the second story. When you stand in the living room with the glass walls, you feel as if you were outside. This stunning home is nestled in the foothills overlooking a lake. Of course, patios and decks surround the home to capture the 360-degree views. Andrew is also an artist, so his colorful pastels grace the walls, adding the needed beauty a Libra must have in his home. He and his wife entertain often and even have art openings in the great room. Everywhere you look, it says Libra.

Those born under this sign like the finer things in life, so Andrew and the girls have everything they want. They have a housekeeper and a cook so they don't have to do any dirty work and they can do what they please. Menial work never appealed to this sign of the artist. They are here with an aesthetic mission in life—to make things beautiful. Librans cannot tolerate unpleasant smells or messy surroundings. They are very sensitive and need a calm, serene atmosphere with no drama. Arguments and disagreements are very upsetting to their delicate system. Luckily, the girls get along very well and do lots of creative projects as a family. They all seem to have an artistic leaning, so Andrew has built them their own kids' art studio in which to play and create. Their home has a state-of-the-art sound system with gentle music in the background all the time. Librans love their music.

If your father is a Libra, you can count your lucky stars. You got one of the easiest dads ever. In fact, Libra fathers can be pushovers and spoil their kids rotten. The trusting Libra dad is in trouble if he has a quick-witted child who wants to take advantage of him. Who is in charge with a Libra dad? Sometimes it's the child who is the bully and sees him as an easy target. Librans fear confrontation, so the sensitive Libra dad often just gives in to keep peace and quiet in the house. Worse yet, they have been known to bribe the children into good behavior. Well, it doesn't take a sneaky kid very long to see that he might have some power over his dad. Because of the natural indecision of a Libra, you might hear, "We'll see what your mother says about this!" Indecision can give mixed messages to the children, who already think they are in charge.

The Libra father is very dedicated to the family and children. Venus is his planet and he exudes love, especially for his family. Your father is gentle, easygoing, and loves harmony in the house. No, he needs harmony in the house. There are very few things that upset your father, since he's easy to live with and quite kind. The number one upset for him is a disruptive household with people arguing or fighting. So please maintain a calm home to soothe his sensitive nature. The other thing is to be rushed. Librans have their own definite slow-paced rhythm and really hate to be rushed. The only time I ever got yelled at by a Libra—and it was intense and loud—was when I tried to rush him. Don't think he doesn't have a temper; it just takes a lot to trigger a Libra temper. But trust me: It's there if you push him hard enough. So be kind to your gentle Libra dad. He's a good one.

LIBRA MOTHER FIGURE

Elizabeth, a double Libra, is a stay-at-home mom by choice. Even as a child, all she wanted to do was to be a mother and take care of her family. She has four children, quite spread out in ages. She is ultrafeminine; adored being pregnant; and is now a very dedicated, loving mother. Luckily, her husband is a banker, so she doesn't have to worry about money, bills, or anything except her beautiful home and children. Good thing, because her forte is beauty and not bills.

Elizabeth is one of the best mothers I know, and somehow she seems to make it all look so easy. Her home is like one of those pictured on the front cover of a garden magazine. She always has the perfect centerpiece on the dining room table, with matching candles, fine art in gold leaf frames on the walls, with a housekeeper taking care of it all. Their dog is a flawlessly groomed poodle with pink bows and painted toenails—really! There is a fragrance of flowers in the air, and gentle music playing in the background. She never seems harried, even though she usually is busy. Her relaxed rhythm sets the tone for the household with the children being well-mannered and polite, even as toddlers. Her planet, Venus, is easy to see in her personality and in her lifestyle. The gentle, kind Libra style brings a sense of peace and harmony to her family, but it has to look good, too!

If your mother is a Libra, you understand what I mean by needing to look good. She can't tolerate messes or out-of-control behavior in any way. Librans do care what the neighbors think, so you can't leave your bike in the driveway or throw your clothes on the floor without her being on you. Librans need a sense of beauty and moderation and will never take life to extremes, so any wild and crazy ideas will be looked upon with disapproval. She doesn't need to yell at you to let you know that she is not pleased with your behavior. You know that expression. You won't be able to get away with much with your Libra mother, because she is one of the most dedicated mothers and will show a deep and abiding interest in your life. An Aquarian mother lets you do whatever you want; not so with a Libra mother. She's the type who wants to go with you when you are a freshman at college, pick out your dorm room décor, and then set up your room for you. You wanted to do that by yourself? Feel lucky that she cares so much and try not to be bothered that she's in your space. You will have plenty of time to be on your own—let her be the perfect mom for now.

As long as she has a fairly quiet and peaceful household, she will be happy. But if you argue, slam doors, or don't honor her special possessions, someone will be in trouble. Don't think that just because she's nice and kind she doesn't have a temper, because she does. Libra mothers aren't yellers and screamers like Aries, but they have a bad temper when they finally do get angry. She is very generous and will spoil her children with attention as well as with presents. Librans love the material world and want to share it with their loved ones. But don't take advantage of her generosity and kindness. She might seem so sweet that she doesn't know what is going on behind the scenes, but believe me, she does. Librans are very smart and instinctively know more than you think they do. That innocent façade hides the real person inside who gets what they want most of the time. They are so smooth that you don't even know you're being played. She can change from the goddess to the scary shrew in seconds if you don't watch out. So you'll probably want to be on her good side to get the beautiful goddess back.

LIBRA CHILD

Victoria, at five years old, is a pretty little blond Libra. Even at that young age, her parents can see her artistic bent. She danced to music as a baby, so they put her in tap and ballet. Now that she has her costumes and ballet slippers, that's all she wants to wear. She'll say, "Mommy, where is my tiara?" Victoria has three older brothers, and her parents really wanted a little girl. Well, they got the girliest little girl ever. Being the baby of the family works just fine for her, because they all spoil her with love and goodies. No hand-me-downs for Victoria—they buy her clothes at an upscale children's boutique. Only the best for this little princess.

The Libra child is a delicate angel and needs special attention because of her sensitive nature. Since Venus is Libra's planet, Librans are born with a gentle spirit. They came here to understand relationships and their primary relationship as a child is with a parent. Libra children are very social and need people close by to feel secure. Libra is an air sign of intelligence and needs to communicate all the time. Talk to your little angel and listen to what she has to say with all your heart. You have an angel talking to you.

As a baby, Libra is affectionate and will need a lot of attention to stay happy. This sign is very sensitive to bright lights and loud, sudden noises. So try to keep things gentle and calm and never raise your voice. Keep your Libra baby in your sight. You don't have to do much, just be there so he can see you. This is the most important statement about Libra I could ever make: *This sign does not like to be alone!* Neither Libra children nor Libra adults feel comfortable when they are by themselves. Have some music on and be sure to talk to your Libra baby often. Librans are so smart that they can understand you even as an infant.

The Libra toddler needs to be able to play with other kids. So if there are plenty of siblings, your Libra is in heaven. If she is an only child, you might want to consider preschool for the companionship of other kids. Just like Victoria, don't be surprised if your little Libra angel is very particular about her wardrobe. She has favorite dresses and insists on wearing them instead of that brown, checkered dress she never liked anyway. Think princess and you will do just fine.

School is a great place for Libra children, since they are both very smart and very social. They will meet their new best friend within days of the beginning of the school year. Librans need to feel comfortable in any social situation, so please teach them etiquette and good manners. A Libra wants to know how to set the table and where to put the water glass, really. Ballroom dance classes are good for Libra children, so they will know how to be gracious when they go to their first dance. All the culture you could introduce early on will definitely help them later.

The teenage Libra is Miss Popularity. Like Victoria, when she grows up a bit, she'll want to wear nice clothes and will always be invited to all the cool parties and dances. Be prepared for numerous slumber parties, with girls giggling through the night. She's popular because she really is a nice person and is kind to everyone. Libra makes the most exquisite debutante of all.

Librans are blessed indeed, but since they are so lucky, they tend to take things for granted. Their challenge is procrastination with maybe a touch of laziness. Librans are not known for being ambitious, so they need some extra help to keep on track. A little gentle discipline might be important to push them along a bit. Also, help them speak their mind. Insecure Librans need help building their confidence and the ability to think for themselves. Often Librans will defer to others instead of taking a stand on their own. Love your tender little Libra and you will get an angel's love in return.

LIBRA PET

Are you looking for an easygoing, loving pet? Then buy one born under the sign of Libra and you will be very happy. Libra is the sign of love and beauty and Libran pets need a calm, gentle environment. I've chosen a fancy poodle as an example of Libra. Just like human Librans, animals have the same sensitivity characteristic of that sign. They don't like loud, abrupt noises or even very much frantic activity. Save the crazy running around for an Aries puppy, because it would upset the Libra's delicate sensibilities. Your Libra dog wants a very comfy doggie bed in every room where people spend time. You need one in the den with the TV, one in the bedroom, and one in the kitchen to make your Libra doggie happy. The Libra dog is one of the most social dogs of the entire zodiac. They don't do well when left by themselves at all. Also, groom them often, because they love to feel clean and attractive. Look at this pretty poodle!

ANIMALS FOR LIBRA
Butterfly
Koala Bear
Lamb
Panda Bear
Raccoon
Swan

PERFECT GIFTS FOR LIBRA

The lovely Libran is easy to buy for because Librans just love beauty and luxury. These are their main interests: romance, art, and shopping. Plan to spend a lot on this sign—they like nice things. It's better to buy them one expensive present than several small ones. Remember that the special care and elegance of the packaging is almost as important as the contents. Here are some suggestions they will most definitely like!

Romance

- Charm bracelet with pictures
- Two engraved silver wineglasses
- Two tickets for a spa vacation
- Two silver candlesticks with dripless white candles
- Intimate dinner for two
- Concert tickets
- Essential oils for massage
- Silk pajamas

Art

- Family portrait
- Goddess sculpture
- Art or flower arranging classes
- A Picasso, a Rembrandt, or a Van Gogh
- An original, but pricey art print

Shopping

- A gift card to the most expensive clothing store you can find
- Fashion accessories like silk scarves or ties
- Fine jewelry
- Fly her and a girlfriend to Paris for a shopping spree
- Expensive perfume

LIBRA CELEBRITIES AND THEIR BIRTH DATES

Bruce Springsteen	September 23
F. Scott Fitzgerald	September 24
Will Smith Jr.	September 25
Catherine Zeta-Jones	September 25
Christopher Reeve	September 25
Michael Douglas	September 25
Barbara Walters	September 25
T.S. Eliot	September 26
Gwyneth Paltrow	September 27
Hilary Duff	September 28
Brigitte Bardot	September 28
Julie Andrews	October 1
Jimmy Carter Jr.	October 1
Ann Richards	October 1
Mahatma Gandhi	October 2
Sting	October 2
Susan Sarandon	October 4
Kate Winslet	October 5
Yo-Yo Ma	October 7
Simon Cowell	October 7
Desmond Tutu	October 7
Matt Damon	October 8
Sigourney Weaver	October 8
John Lennon	October 9
Sharon Osbourne	October 9
Paul Simon	October 13
Ralph Lauren	October 14
Usher	October 14
Eminem	October 17
Carrie Fisher	October 21

SCORPIO

October 24–November 22

KEYWORDS

POSITIVE KEYWORDS

Focused

Secretive

Intense

Sexual

Purposeful

CAUTION KEYWORDS

Calculating

Jealous

Manipulative

Dark

INFORMATION

EIGHTH SIGN OF THE ZODIAC

Glyph: ♏

Planet: Pluto

Symbols: Scorpion, Serpent, Eagle

Element: Water

Mode: Fixed

Colors: Crimson, Black

Gemstone: Alexandrite

Metal: Uranium

Body Parts: Pelvis, Sex Organs

SCORPIO: THE STRATEGIST

Vincent is a mega-Scorpio and he's a classic example of this intense sign. A real spy, he works for the CIA, but of course, no one knows that. "Vincent" is an alias; it's not even his real name. He's fearless and has a sense of stealth, the quality of remaining invisible. He has a sixth sense about people, just seems to know when something isn't right, and his poker face never gives any secrets away. Scorpios love intrigue and mystery, so spying is a perfect profession for Vincent, or whoever he is.

Scorpio is the most misunderstood of all the twelve astrology signs, and I can see why. Scorpios are truly secretive and won't let anyone into their private world. Scorpio is the second water sign after Cancer. The water of the sign of Cancer is like a bubbling brook in front of a cottage. By contrast, Scorpio is the dark, deep, murky water of twelve thousand leagues under the sea. Since water represents emotions, Scorpio's feelings are hard to reach and even harder to understand. The all-powerful Pluto is Scorpio's planet, so it's no wonder they're strong. Pluto brutally takes away, but then gives something precious back in return. Adding to their complexity, Scorpio is the only sign that has three different symbols: the scorpion, the serpent, and the eagle or phoenix bird. The lowest level of the Scorpio personality is the scorpion with his well-known deadly stinger. This side of Scorpio can be vengeful, sarcastic, jealous, and very controlling. Up one level is the serpent, who is the shrewd businessperson whose interactions are not quite illegal, but often ethically questionable. Luckily, the highest Scorpio is the eagle or the phoenix bird. The eagle is the spiritual healer that flies over the world, sending down powerful light to help transform the world. Finally, the phoenix bird rises out of the ashes of destruction and is reborn anew. The lower part of Scorpio is menacing, so everyone is always happy to see the eagle.

Vincent never got married, for obvious reasons. His life is all about secrets that he can't share with anyone, even a wife. But he does have girlfriends everywhere and has an exciting sex life. He loves his life of intrigue; even his love life has to be full of secrecy by extension. He gets a chance to travel all over the world investigating international financial criminals and enjoys seeing them put away. Scorpios are strong-willed, passionate, streetwise, and love exacting vengeance—perfect for a spy. Vincent is dark, swarthy, moody, and temperamental. But in a very strange way, the shadowy mystery is incredibly sexy . . . even if it is a little scary.

IF YOU'RE A SCORPIO, READ THIS!

Even though people misunderstand your sign, I hope you know that you are the most powerful sign of the entire zodiac! The Scorpio level of power makes you a conduit to unlimited universal energy. In fact, your power is so strong that you need to learn how to harness it. If not, it's so hot that it can burn you or others if it's not directed carefully. Scorpios instinctively know that true renewal also requires letting go of old habits. That's why your sign is involved with death and rebirth. Yours is the only sign that really understands the cycles and rhythms of life. Everyone knows that you are private and not the best communicator, but it's not because you just stubbornly hold in your words. It's because you are figuring it out in your mind before you speak your truth. When you do speak with your incredible depth of profound wisdom, the world listens.

WHAT MAKES YOU HAPPY?
Privacy

You must have some alone time regularly to achieve happiness. The Libra social calendar of cocktail parties would drive you nuts. Actually, happy isn't a very good Scorpio word anyway. You would feel more comfortable with words like intense, focus, fearlessness, strength, passion, and sex. All that light surface stuff bores you and seems so superficial that it's silly. You need something deep and puzzling that reaches your inner core or it's a waste of time: You'd rather be home by yourself watching an old mystery movie.

Money makes you happy. Taurus and Scorpio are the two signs of money in the zodiac. The Scorpio in you has a need for financial security, and you are willing to work hard to achieve that success. Many Scorpios are mega-millionaires because of their uncanny ability to focus themselves on a project until it's completed. You just know how to sniff out money wherever it is hidden.

Scorpios need emotional security as much as they need financial security. Since your emotions run so very deep, having a few very good friends or confidants is important. Try not to isolate yourself too much or you will get hermitlike and it will be harder to connect with people. Get some fresh air and experience something outside your comfort zone on occasion. Do something that scares you once a month.

The Ideal Scorpio Lifestyle

You are a consultant who advises your clients on investments and estate planning. Your office is in your home and you do most of your business over the phone or the Internet. Meeting with your clients just to chat never appealed to you. Since you are so good at investing, you also manage your own portfolio and assets. Many Scorpios are night owls and prefer working at night and sleeping during the day. So you have blinds up and like a darker atmosphere. Bright lights and loud music are not your style. Maybe play some blues in the background to set the mood.

Your Ultimate Dream

To have a double life, something full of mystery like the Scorpio spy story. You have several bank accounts in different banks, just for the thrill. You have several groups of friends who don't know each other, and you like it that way. It's James Bond and Sherlock Holmes rolled into one fascinating lifestyle.

SCORPIO STRENGTH

Scorpio is the strongest sign of the zodiac. Of course, Scorpios have the power of Pluto behind them. This sign enjoys doing the dirty work that other signs could never handle. Who else could see the beauty in the falling leaves that die? A Scorpio realizes that they turn into compost and then into the flowers of spring. Scorpios understand the natural cycles of life better than anyone else. They are also the most psychic of all the signs, except maybe Pisces. Scorpios need to trust their intuition as it comes through and then act on it. Being very strategic, they are great chess players or military generals because of their shrewdness when it comes to planning an attack. Their love of intrigue gives them a mind that can solve complex problems easily. They are compellingly attractive and sexy without even trying. The Scorpio charisma and penetrating stare makes you feel as if you are being hypnotized by their magical power—and you are!

SCORPIO CHALLENGE

Isolation is the biggest challenge for a Scorpio. They tend to keep to themselves and cannot communicate or share emotionally very easily at all. In fact, they are terrible at it. You can live with a Scorpio your entire life and not feel as if you really know her. When a Scorpio gets burned, she broods and then wants to retreat so as not to get hurt again; then she becomes the hermit type and does not venture out much. Naturally suspicious, if Scorpios feel insecure in love, they are by far the most jealous and vindictive of all twelve astrology signs. A scorned Scorpio will do anything to get back at the perpetrator. I feel sorry for the aggressor, because Scorpio is never a victim. They go for the jugular every time. This sign burns their bridges totally when they find out that someone has wronged them. You get only one chance with a Scorpio: No apology will ever be accepted once the line is drawn in the sand. It's over.

MENTAL CHARACTERISTICS

Scorpios are very smart; actually the most street smart of all the signs. It's almost impossible to fool a Scorpio, who has an instinct for discovering anything sneaky. The calculating Scorpio mind can solve the most difficult puzzles easily. Scorpios love a challenge and know they can meet it. The Scorpio mind is similar to the unnerving Scorpio stare, in that it feels like a laser beaming through you. A Scorpio's mind is a laser, too, and can focus on a task until it's completed. No quitters among Scorpios. Introverts by nature, they are the silent wise ones instead of the Gemini nervous, chatty type. In fact, talkative, bouncy types bother Scorpio. They prefer silence. That laser beam of thought often yields to obsessions and a need for instant gratification. Try not to push yourself too hard, because an exhausted Scorpio is distant, sarcastic, and controlling.

EMOTIONAL MAKEUP

Scorpio lives in the bottomless sea of emotions all the time. They are experts at feeling deeply and passionately. It's a waste of time for Scorpio to be involved with anything that is shallow. This sign goes deeper than all twelve signs combined. They can never pretend or fake anything—what's the purpose of doing that? Feel it and then move on to another emotion. That's why Scorpios spend so much time by themselves—to explore their innermost depths without the distraction of the outside world. That emotional introspection feeds the Scorpio soul.

If you have a problem and need consoling, you can always ask a Scorpio. It doesn't matter how troubling the situation is, they can handle it. Many Scorpios are volunteer hospice workers and they are really good at that. Now that's a job not everyone could handle, but this sign understands that life and death are one and are never to be feared. So you can feel safe emotionally with your Scorpio—just don't ask him anything personal about himself.

PHYSICAL CHARACTERISTICS

Appearance

Scorpios are one of the easiest signs to recognize. Their laser beam Scorpio stare is hard to miss. When they look at you, it feels as if you were naked and they can see right into your soul. Their deep-set eyes penetrate through you and stare without ever blinking. They are usually dark in coloring, often with dark hair and dark eyes, and exude a distinctly mysterious look. Oftentimes, you can't tell their heritage, since they could be from any of several parts of the world. Many have long hair and bangs to cover up their face. Some of the men even wear beards. If Scorpio could have a superpower, it would be to be invisible.

Fashion Sense

Scorpio style is sexy and exotic. Scorpios prefer dark colors, which actually look good with their dark complexion or hair color. Black, red, and maroon are their preferred colors. They tend toward the dramatic in style and color. No bright, geometric designs, please. Sleek and sexy—that's the look that works well for the sensuous Scorpio. A good look for women is a little black dress, long gold chains, black sling-back stilettos, and an ankle bracelet. Top it off with large dark shades and a hooded cape just in case they want go incognito. Smoky eyes and red lipstick, of course. Men can handle a black power suit, a nice black shirt, and a red tie.

Health Type

The Scorpio part of the body is the pelvis, which explains the sexual association with this sign. The reproductive and sexual organs belong to Scorpio. Maybe this is why this sign is so comfortable with sex. Scorpio tends to binge on food or alcohol when they feel low and need to strive for a moderate, healthy diet. The other part of the pelvis is the colon, or the organ of elimination. How perfect for the sexual and refuse departments to both be within the Scorpio domain. Scorpios see as clean and normal what others see as dirty.

Exercise Approach

Scorpio is a water sign, so swimming is a natural for Scorpios. Physically strong and blessed with endurance, many take it so seriously that they become competitive swimmers and will stay with it their entire life. This sign is passionate and needs intensity in their exercise. They get obsessed with a sport, tend to overwork themselves, and need to avoid straining their muscles or overdoing it. Moderation doesn't come easily to intense Scorpios, but they need to try to temper their exercise regimen. The martial arts appeal to this sign, especially the forms that incorporate esoteric practices like breathing and meditation. For a spectator sport, what about heading to a demolition derby for fun?

PROFESSIONAL LIFE

A career that involves solving puzzles or mysteries appeals to the sleuthlike Scorpio. They make great private investigators, archeologists, bounty hunters, creditors, researchers, detectives, deep-sea divers, and magicians. Another career path for Scorpio might involve life and death, such as an estate lawyer, an insurance agent, a cemetery or hospice worker, a mortician, or a pathologist. They are good at waste disposal, like plumbers, and experts on the effects of toxic chemicals in the environment. The sexy side of them would enjoy being a gynecologist, a sex therapist, a stripper, a hooker, or a mistress. Exciting choice of careers, Scorpio!

Scorpio Employer

The Scorpio boss is one of the calmest of all; that is, if he likes you. He has a sixth sense about people and will instantly take a liking to you or not. If not, you probably won't get the job. If you did, he has accepted you as part of the team and will expect you to perform. He's a great role model, because Scorpios are tireless workers until the project is done. The work atmosphere will be a controlled one, and he won't tolerate drama or emotional outbursts. Always guarded, you could never trick your Scorpio boss because he intuitively knows your inner motives. One warning with a Scorpio boss: Be sure to keep the finances clear and organized. Inherently suspicious, he watches everyone closely, all the time.

SCORPIO IN THE BEDROOM

If there is one master lover, it has to be Scorpio. Scorpios are intensely passionate and insatiable lovers. They can passionately kiss for one entire hour and then take four hours for foreplay. OK, pretty much anything goes for a Scorpio: costumes, masks, domination, cross-dressing. Gemini like to talk in bed. Scorpios need silence. They don't want any distractions so they can focus on what they're doing. Red satin sheets, mirrors, romantic music, incense, and candles will set a sultry Scorpio mood. Passion and total immersion are necessities with Scorpios. This sign feels comfortable in dark and forbidden places, so sex is perfect for them. Blindfolds and handcuffs, anyone?

SCORPIO MALE PARTNER

Simon is a Scorpio, and he's a financial wizard during the day. He wheels and deals with the biggest international monetary institutions and clients. At night he takes off his coat and tie and puts on his white gauze Indian tunic to teach kundalini yoga at his holistic center. He is a great example of a high-level Scorpio eagle who channels his intensity into healing humanity. Simon is an expert at playing gongs, which use sound and vibration to create a shift in consciousness. He's dark and handsome and has a kind, caring look about him. Yet you get the sense that there is so much more under the surface.

Simon is the perfect example of an evolved Scorpio who chose to use the positive personality traits of his sign. Each Scorpio has the choice of whether he wants to be the stinging scorpion or the soaring eagle. We have free will to become the very best of our sign or to stay stuck in the worst of our sign. It's our choice. Simon chose the high road to help the world with his Scorpio energy. One of the best Scorpio strengths is their innate understanding of money. Somehow they just know how to work the system and due to their dogged perseverance, they nearly always succeed. There are lots of Scorpios in the financial world strategizing about creative ways to make money. It's their forte to deal with shared resources and other people's money. But will it give them the depth of insight they crave?

That's why Simon balanced his financial days with his spiritual nights. He needed more. The other talent of a Scorpio is to investigate the complexities of a situation until he really understands it thoroughly. Scorpios' main object of investigation is nothing less than their eternal soul. What am I here to contribute this lifetime? What is God? Am I part of God? If I am part of God, what do I do now? These are the kinds of questions that eagle Scorpios think about in the middle of the night. Tough questions, but so worth the effort.

Simon teaches yoga and meditation to help him answer some of those questions. Here is a story about how Scorpio energy works. I was at Simon's holistic center once when he led a group of underprivileged, rowdy, out-of-control teenagers, sent there for a yoga class. Good luck, Simon. They were hitting each other, yelling, and being totally disrespectful and rebellious. What to do? He gave them each a pillow, had them lie down, and started to play the gong. The vibration was so powerful that the transformation was like magic. There was a calming, palpable energy that floated down and put these teenage rebels into a dream state for about half an hour. Considering the condition of their lives, that was probably the most relaxed they had ever been. When they got up, they were hugging each other and joyous. It brought tears to my eyes. I'm sure they will never be the same again. Not one word was said during the gong session. I watched a miracle happen that day . . . a Scorpio miracle.

Like most Scorpios, Simon had some challenges earlier in his life, but has transformed them into something positive. Scorpios need a rebirth to bring about their self-realization. Often they go through a personal vision quest to test their strength. Their planet Pluto tests their strength and power. As a result, all the wimps are weeded out. Only the strong Scorpios survive. Once Scorpio has accepted his internal power, anything is possible. The only challenge I can see left for Simon is the Scorpio tendency to push himself relentlessly. My homework for Simon is to take more vacations with his beautiful wife and son on an island somewhere. The work will always be there when he returns.

SCORPIO FEMALE PARTNER

Alexis is a plastic surgeon who loves transforming her clients into new people. She looks like the classic Scorpio, with long, dark hair; deep, penetrating eyes; and a mysterious aura. Of course she's amazingly beautiful and walks like a cat. Her steps are so quiet that she's always surprising people. Alexis started out as an artist—actually a sculptor—so she has an eye for beauty and what it takes to perform artistic alchemy. She told me that she didn't like the medium of clay and realized she preferred flesh. What a Scorpio statement!

The notorious Scorpio woman is universally feared by anyone who knows astrology. They are the most seductive as well as the most dangerous of all women. They possess an almost irresistible magnetic attraction and you can't keep your eyes off them. The Scorpio woman is similar to a spider who catches you in her web of intrigue and then has her way with you. If she likes you, you're in for the experience of your life. If she doesn't, run for cover and try to protect yourself. She will want to know everything about you while artfully dodging any answers about herself. Her perfect poker face will never give you a hint of her secrets, that's for sure. Can you imagine a female Pluto? If you can, that is the female Scorpio. This is the sign of controlling others and she is always in charge, always—even if you don't know it.

Alexis uses her Scorpio traits quite well in business. Scorpios love money and drive themselves to success with pleasure. She has an elegant, two-story office that includes a high-end skin care salon as well as an operating room for plastic surgery. She offers facials, makeovers, liposuction, implants, face-lifts, as well as many other body-part lifts. People fly in from all over the world for her combination of technical skill and artistic style. She charges a lot, but has no shortage of patients, so they must find it worthwhile. Alexis runs her operation like a tight ship and probably works the hardest of anyone there. She's demanding and expects quality from her employees, but is willing to pay them for it. All her staff members have their health insurance, 401k, and retirement covered, so she has very little turnover. Her staff has been with her for years. Oh, yes: They each get one free procedure a year, which is a great beauty incentive for all the hard work.

Even though this next story isn't about Alexis, it's just too good a female Scorpio story not to tell. Another one of my clients is a more jealous type of Scorpio and her boyfriend had just broken up with her. The scorned female Scorpio is the scariest creature on earth. She suspected that he had another girlfriend and hid in the bushes in front of his house all night waiting for him to return. Just as she thought, around 2:00 in the morning he brought a woman home, and as they were standing and kissing by the front door, she jumped out of the bushes and started screaming at him. The poor new girlfriend ran off in total fright as the Scorpio stayed there grilling the guilty guy. So if you are interested in a female Scorpio, beware. Never try to get away with anything behind her back. You will get caught, guaranteed. And no matter how pleasurable the secret, it will never be worth it when she catches and punishes you. Oh, one other thing: Scorpio women never forget.

I don't want to scare you away from your new girlfriend, so how can you keep your sex kitten without getting burned? First of all, be honest, because she always knows what's happening underneath the surface anyway. She's the most intuitive of all women; her sixth sense is amazing. Realize that she's in control. She's eminently good at it, so why challenge her? Let her be alone when she needs space. Believe me, you don't want to be around her when she's in a private mood. If you can stay on her good side, you have the most passionate and exotic woman ever. You know you can't leave her, because the memory of her would haunt you forever. The question is this: Can you handle her power?

SCORPIO FATHER FIGURE

Jack, a mega-Scorpio, is a professional poker player. He's married and has one son, Jacob, who is also a Scorpio. His wife, a Libra, is a stay-at-home mom. Jack travels all over the world playing poker competitions and wins quite often. He wears his trademark beard, black cowboy hat, dark sunglasses, and his Scorpio poker face. When he does win, he wins millions at a time. Of course, he loses millions other times, too. It's a gamble, but this Scorpio definitely comes out on top. He's one of the most well-known and feared poker players on the circuit.

Jack is a star on the poker channel and is on TV all the time. I smile when I see him because he's such a great Scorpio. Not everyone looks like their sign, but you could so guess Jack as a Scorpio. His long black hair and black beard add to the look of intensity that he uses to intimidate his opponents. Something else that makes him such a great player is the Scorpio talent for complex problem solving. Plus Scorpios always have a battle plan. The Scorpio mind is calculating and very strategic, which is perfect for poker. They are also psychic and that has to help, too. Jack is well-known for being the master of the sneak attack.

His audience probably thinks this is his game face, but ironically he wears that same face at home. Even though he travels a lot by himself, he needs his private time when he gets home, too. His office is dark and cavelike, with papers and boxes everywhere. It would make a Gemini or Aquarius claustrophobic, but he sees it as safe and secure. Luckily, his son Jacob is also a Scorpio and is actually much like his dad. He spends most of his time in his bedroom playing on his computer, while his dad is alone in his office. If Jack's wife or son want to talk to him, they have to knock on his door and Jack will answer, "Come in." Scorpios are typically curt and right to the point, so no idle chatting happening in there. The two Scorpios are very content—it's just the Libra wife who feels left out. Luckily, she has her friends and Libra social life. Good thing, because there isn't much communication happening with her Scorpio men.

If your dad is a Scorpio, you understand this scenario. He might not be a poker player, but he could be. As you probably know already, this is not the easiest of fathers to have. Scorpio dads are usually demanding of their kids and not very generous. He's strict and fairly suspicious of foul play, even if you are innocent. You can never get away with hiding anything from him, so don't even try. Once he catches you hiding something from him, he won't trust you ever again. He's set in his ways and not at all flexible when it comes to change. There's no screaming like an Aries. Instead, he'll give you the Scorpio cold stare. It's an icy-cold stare that goes through you like the north wind. I'd take a yelling any day over the dreaded Scorpio stare.

Why is your Scorpio father so tough on you? He wants you to be strong on your own, and if he was there to help you with every little problem, you'd never figure it out by yourself. In his mind, by being hard on you, he's helping you grow up strong. The purpose of a Scorpio father is to make his children tough. So I'll bet your father is doing that, right? Do you feel more powerful because of him? Scorpio dads are harder to appreciate when you're young, but as you mature, you will realize he was the perfect dad for you.

SCORPIO MOTHER FIGURE

Joan is the mother of three children and runs a tight household. Before she got married, she was a very successful prosecuting attorney. It was her plan to then marry and have three children, which she did right on schedule. Her husband is also a lawyer and works at his office while she stays home with their children. Scorpios are not very domestic and Joan might lack the gushy emotions and affection of a Cancer or Libra mother, but her children know she loves them. She's very protective and will defend them against any foe with her poisonous stinger. Well, that's one Scorpionic way to give love.

Joan is a loyal and very dedicated mother, even if she isn't very demonstrative. She's not a hugger and a kisser, but her dedication is so strong that none of her children ever feel neglected. In fact, she's very involved in their lives. If you wanted a lenient mother, you would have chosen an Aquarius. The Scorpio mother is a strict and demanding parent because she wants her children to succeed in the world. She hates weakness in anyone and will raise her children to be strong so they can protect themselves in life. She's also not a screamer, but instead gives you the famous Scorpio stare. That's the scariest thing in the world. You want to be good so you don't have that experience very often.

The Scorpio mother keeps an organized and clean house. Nothing too out of control will do for her because she knows how to create systems. The dishes are cleaned in a specific way. Laundry is done on Saturday. She likes to be in control and will make sure that everyone knows that rule. Because she's a lawyer, Joan has no trouble implementing rules and regulations. No loosey-goosey household with your Scorpio mom. Everyone will know their chores and when they need to be finished. Dinner is on time and you'd better be there with your hands washed. Cleaning day is always fun for a Scorpio mom, who wants to know what's in every little corner in her house. Yes, she will notice if you hide your dirty laundry in your closet instead of taking care of it on washing day. Remember your mom is psychic, so nothing gets past her. You never want to break her trust because her naturally suspicious nature will be focused directly on you, and nobody wants that.

Scorpio is a born sleuth and is insanely curious about the secrets of other people. That's why they excel as investigators and detectives. But having a sleuth as a mother might be a challenge. If she even suspects for one minute that you're hiding something, never fear, she will go through your drawers while you're at school to find it. And who knows all the other things she will find looking for it. She will know where you surf on the Internet and how many text messages you have. So having a Scorpio mother ensures honesty in you or you will face the consequences. Going in her purse is how you could get in the very most trouble with her. Never, ever rummage through a Scorpio mother's purse or there will be hell to pay. She never forgets anything—she will know just how much money she had in there, down to the last penny.

Your Scorpio mother has a need for privacy and when she's in her leave-me-alone mode, do just that. Leave her alone until she is ready to take up her domestic duties once again. The water of a Scorpio runs so deeply that she will have to visit her inner world to stay connected to herself. So when you see that DO NOT DISTURB sign on her door, please respect it. Pluto is her planet and he doesn't like to be bothered or you will see a female version of him. Not a pretty sight.

SCORPIO CHILD

Jacob is the Scorpio son of Jack, the poker player. Both he and his father are double Scorpios, so I have to use him for my Scorpio child.

Jacob takes after his father in many ways. Even though Jack is very smart, Jacob is a little genius and might even have a sharper mathematical mind than his father. Jacob is so focused on computer science and math that he is pursuing college-level studies even though he is only eleven years old. What does he want to be when he grows up? A poker player.

Your Scorpio child is very special, even if you don't totally understand him. They are mysteries and are still figuring themselves out as children, so they will need to spend a lot of time alone. Don't worry if your little Scorpio stays in his room for hours by himself. Just like Jacob, he's learning intensely, even in quiet. Scorpios enjoy solitude. To them it offers time to focus on their pet project without distractions. This sign often sees the outside world as a big distraction from what's important inside.

The baby Scorpio has a very intense expression on his face, as if he's trying to figure out something very, very important. So what if he's only one month old? He still has a mission to investigate his inner feelings. The eyes—it's always the Scorpio eyes. This baby will lock gazes with you as if he were looking in to your soul. He is.

Scorpios like to be in control and a Scorpio toddler is no different. Your little one will challenge you as a mother. Who is in charge? Sweet Libra or Pisces mothers will have to be as strong as they can possibly be to exert any semblance of authority over the Scorpio child. You will need to learn how to outstare your little Scorpio, who is a master at the stare. Yelling won't work because your little one will pull into a deep shell and become quiet and inhibited. Outstaring him is the only way to be on his level. Practice in the mirror. It's not easy.

The scholastic part of school is comfortable for the competitive, intelligent Scorpio. Scorpios particularly excel in math, science, and technology. Invest in a microscope or a chemistry set for your little Scorpio. They will enjoy hours of study. But the social side of school might not be as easy for them. Also, Scorpio children might prefer a reptile cage with an iguana or unusual lizards instead of a fluffy little white dog. Typically shy and reserved, they usually have a couple of good, loyal friends instead of being in the superficial, popular crowd. Encourage your Scorpio child to talk out his problems, as he tends to keep things bottled up inside.

Scorpios need to be involved intensely with hobbies or something that captivates their interest. They are competitive and have to burn off both emotional and physical energy, so try enrolling them in a swimming class. All Scorpios are private and like secrets—even the children. Get a sign to hang on his bedroom door that says, "JACOB'S ROOM. KEEP OUT!" Also, he'll love this: Buy him a sturdy, metal box with a key. There is only one key to the box and he's hidden it somewhere. Respect his need for privacy and you will have a contented Scorpio in your house. Here's a little hint: Scorpios are usually more comfortable as adults because they have more control of their lives. So let your little Scorpio be in charge of his life and he will be happy . . . well, as happy as a Scorpio can get.

SCORPIO PET

All Scorpios have an intense personality and an animal born under this sign is no different. Why did I choose a Dachshund as a Scorpio dog? This dog is actually a hound and can sneak into small spaces because of his long, compact body. Bred to scent, chase, and flush out badgers from their underground burrows, this is the only dog certified to hunt both above- and underground. If he sees something moving in a little hole, he's on it and instantly kills it. That can be a little shocking for small children. Scorpio dogs can be a little more temperamental than those born under other signs, so even though he's a little one, he'll want to be in charge of the other dogs in the family. He's the tough one who will need his own doggie bed, as they don't like to share much. So if you live on the land and have gophers, this is a great choice. Since Scorpios cherish their privacy, quiet apartment life might also work nicely for a Scorpio dog.

ANIMALS FOR SCORPIO

Buzzard

Eagle

Ferret

Hawk

Insects

Mouse

Reptiles

Rodents

Scorpion

Skunk

Snake

Spider

Vulture

Wolverine

SCORPIO CELEBRITIES AND THEIR BIRTH DATES

Johnny Carson	October 23
Dylan McDermott	October 26
Hillary Rodham Clinton	October 26
Keith Urban	October 26
Theodore Roosevelt	October 27
Joaquin Phoenix	October 28
Julia Roberts	October 28
Bill Gates	October 28
Richard Dreyfuss	October 29
Gavin Rossdale	October 30
Dan Rather	October 31
Betsy Palmer	November 1
Matthew McConaughey	November 4
Walter Cronkite	November 4
Art Garfunkel	November 5
Ethan Hawke	November 6
Sally Field	November 6
Calista Flockhart	November 11
Demi Moore	November 11
Leonardo DiCaprio	November 11
Anne Hathaway	November 12
Chris Noth	November 13
Prince Charles of Windsor	November 14
Martin Scorsese	November 17
Lorne Michaels	November 17
Owen Wilson	November 18
Meg Ryan	November 19
Jodie Foster	November 19
Goldie Hawn	November 21

PERFECT GIFTS FOR SCORPIO

Scorpios are quite particular about their gifts, so this list will help you when it comes to buying them presents. Scorpio interests include mystery, intellectual investigation, intensity, and sex. Never give a Scorpio an unwrapped present; double-wrap it to add to the intrigue.

Mystery
- DVD selection of noir or mystery films
- Oversized, black, hooded cashmere cape
- Dark sunglasses and large, floppy hat
- Small binoculars
- James Bond–type surveillance equipment

Intellectual Investigation
- Books about real-life mysteries, crime, and spy secrets
- Puzzles and brain teasers
- Games of strategy
- Personal diary or journal with a key

Intensity

- Extreme sports like bungee jumping
- Skydiving lessons
- Cave exploration
- A class in martial arts

Sex

- *The Kama Sutra*
- Black and red lingerie with a long black robe for women
- A black silk smoking jacket for men
- Massage oil
- Sexy literature like *Lady Chatterley's Lover*
- A tiny digital video camera

SAGITTARIUS

November 23–December 21

KEYWORDS

POSITIVE KEYWORDS

Adventurous

Idealistic

Outspoken

Open-minded

Footloose

Educated

CAUTION KEYWORDS

Tactless

Rambling

Exaggerating

INFORMATION

NINTH SIGN OF THE ZODIAC

Glyph: ♐

Planet: Jupiter

Symbol: Centaur

Element: Fire

Mode: Mutable

Colors: Scarlet, Khaki

Gemstones: Opal, Cat's Eye

Metal: Tin

Body Parts: Hips, Thighs

SAGITTARIUS: THE EXPLORER

William is a perfect Sagittarius. He was lucky enough to be born into a very wealthy family, so he can do what he wants with his life. He has chosen to spend his time learning. He's a perpetual student and is focusing now on metaphysics and the esoteric, which, of course, includes astrology. He lives on a lake with his wife in a nice house, but nothing outrageous. The largest room in the house is the library, which is filled from floor to ceiling with rare and fascinating books.

The highest purpose of Sagittarius is to expand the mind and discover new ways of thinking. International travel is one of many ways Sagittarians learn about broad concepts and foreign cultures. They must explore and it doesn't matter to them whether the journey is mental or physical. The symbol for this sign is the centaur or half-man/half-horse with his bow and arrow aiming at his next adventure. Sagittarius is the last fire sign, following Aries and Leo. Aries is the fire of a wooden match burning brightly, and Leo is the huge stone fireplace with people huddled around for warmth. By contrast, the Sagittarian fire consists of fireworks that shoot high in the sky for everyone to see. Sagittarius is even more expansive than the other fire signs, due to the power of Jupiter, Sagittarians' planet. Jupiter is the largest planet in our solar system and does everything in a big, even grandiose way. It is the planet of abundance, the philanthropist, and Santa Claus. No wonder Sags are so lucky.

One interesting note is that Sagittarius is the only sign that has a nickname. William calls himself a Sag. I'm not surprised, which is why I've named Sag the stand-up comedian: They have the best sense of humor of all the signs. They even have a Jupiter-like booming laugh. Sags have grand expectations of what the world has to offer them. They often walk innocently into fantastic situations of good fortune that others could only dream of finding. Take a look at lucky William, who reads spiritual books by the lake all day. Hmmm, nice life, Sag!

William travels all over the world, experiencing new adventures in pursuit of higher knowledge. I first met him in Tucson when he was on his way between exploring the pyramids in Egypt and Peru to hike Machu Picchu with a shaman. He travels like that all year round. Sagittarians have an intellectual restlessness that fuels them their entire lives. It's similar to having an insatiable appetite for learning because you were starved before. They just can't get enough.

IF YOU'RE A SAGITTARIUS, READ THIS!

I'll bet you are happy you're a Sagittarius! You do know that your sign is the most fortunate of all the twelve signs of the zodiac, right? If someone is going to win the lottery, guess what? It's you. Trust your good luck, because it's your destiny to have easy windfalls. Sags have a huge zest for life and want to enthusiastically squeeze everything they can into one lifetime. You will always push the envelope. Go way beyond the norm and maybe you'll be satisfied. Broaden your horizons, and, yes, search for the Holy Grail. If anyone could find that elusive treasure, it's a Sagittarian. Do you want to travel around the world? Do it! Do you want to write a book? Do that, too! You can do anything you can imagine, and I'm sure your dreams are boundless. No sign dreams larger than a Sagittarian.

WHAT MAKES YOU HAPPY?
The Ideal Sagittarian Lifestyle

You are fluent in several languages, travel internationally, and own an import/export business. With friends all over the world representing a variety of cultures, you have the life people read about in novels of international adventure. Your business is so successful that you can give a percentage of your profits to some of the indigenous peoples you meet on your nomadic journeys. You write a travel blog telling everyone about your experiences. One day you want to compile all your travel adventures into a book that's a journal of your fascinating life. The Sagittarius mission is to have no regrets.

Your Ultimate Dream

To be a philanthropist and be able to give money away freely to your family, friends, and pet causes. The library in your home is one of the most comprehensive you've ever seen. You are totally free to pursue any direction you want. You travel often on long journeys to wherever you want, whenever you want.

SAGITTARIUS STRENGTH

When it comes to thinking big, Sagittarians are the best. They were born with the gifts of enthusiasm, optimism, and discovery combined with an outgoing personality and a great sense of humor. People like Sags, and what's not to like? They're fun, generous, intelligent, and are always going on some outrageous trip. The ability to think expansively makes them open-minded, liberal, and adventurous enough to actually go to Rio de Janeiro for Carnival instead of just talking about it. Learning foreign languages is easy for this sign, since they are the true citizens of the world. Sagittarians have a talent for keeping up with international current events, so long talks in coffee shops about politics and social unrest appeal to them. They believe that goals are easy to reach without working terribly hard. However, I think their greatest strength is the typical Sagittarian attitude that they are surrounded by good fortune. And they are!

SAGITTARIAN CHALLENGE

Being opinionated is the biggest Sagittarian challenge. Yes, they are very bright and well-informed, but they can be intellectually smug and believe they know more than anyone else. Some astrologers call them the "know-it-alls" of the zodiac. The perfect example is the college professor who is an expert on a particular subject and lords it over everyone else. They are very impatient, quick-tempered, and self-absorbed. They have an extreme restlessness that borders on a "grass is greener" mentality. They are never quite satisfied. Many have a loud voice and some are practical jokers and prone to exaggeration. Lacking tact, Sagittarians are brutally candid and frank to a fault. The Sag husband will tell his wife that she doesn't look good in that dress as they walk out the door to go to a party. They hate being told what to do by a partner, their boss, or even the government. Sagittarius is the gypsy of the zodiac.

MENTAL CHARACTERISTICS

Sagittarius is very bright and loves the process of education and learning. Sagittarians are the eternal students of the zodiac. This sign is perfect for taking a trip to Italy to learn about Tuscan cooking and how to combine it with the perfect wine. Also, some Sags teach themselves new languages simply for the challenge of learning something new. Hey, you never know when one of those languages will come in handy on a vacation! Sagittarians are very strong in their beliefs and possess excellent debating skills. Although, the typical Sagittarian mind does tend to ramble, somehow magically it eventually comes back to the main point. Since they learn things so quickly, they don't have patience to interact with slow thinkers or talkers. A typical Sag will get up and abruptly leave a dry conversation with no apology. Mentally very restless, they always need to keep their minds involved in something interesting.

EMOTIONAL MAKEUP

Sagittarius is one of the least emotional signs in the zodiac. This fire sign is just too impatient and busy to be able to sit down very long and listen to someone's problems. Don't get me wrong: They are humanitarians and care very much about the plight of refugees or starvation in developing countries. Many actually travel and volunteer, helping to build homes after a hurricane, or call their congressman to voice their opinion about an important issue that is being voted on this week. However, don't ask them to get too personally involved, as they might begin to feel uncomfortable, and will probably be too busy to help.

Even on a personal level, Sagittarians would rather do something interesting than sit around emoting about anything for very long. Isn't there an activity that they can do to feel better? I'll just bet there is!

PHYSICAL CHARACTERISTICS
Appearance
The Sagittarian body is typically tall, even lanky. The Sagittarian head is long with a high forehead and prominent teeth. Sags have an athletic, sporty style about them. I've found that they are inclined to stoop and need to focus on their posture. Their walk is hurried with a look that says they have somewhere to go and are just walking out the door. Never slow and graceful like a Libran, the Sag is on a mission. You don't want to miss that plane!

Fashion Sense
The busy Sagittarian likes a more relaxed, sporty style. No frills or lace, like a Libra or Pisces. The casual Sag wants to be ready for any situation that arises, so her clothes must be stylish, but also functional and comfortable. A great look for a Sag is a modern version of the safari jacket. Khaki with lots of pockets would do the trick for this on-the-go fire sign. Practical but fashionable shoes are a must. Oh, Sagittarians can get dressed up, but they still need to be able to run to catch that last shuttle.

Health Type
The sign of Sagittarius is associated with the hips and thighs, and the mobility of the body. Sagittarius doesn't understand moderation and instead can be quite overindulgent. They truly believe that more is better. Sagittarians often binge on food or drink and like eating heartily. Therefore, many grapple with weight problems. Where do they carry their excess weight? In their hips and thighs, and that can contribute to a pear-shaped body. The Sag restlessness and impatience often create a reckless tendency, especially for young Sagittarians. Take it easy, Sag!

Exercise Approach
Sagittarius hates anything boring or repetitive, so they need to pick an exercise program that keeps them motivated and interested. Not known for their ambition, many need to be coaxed into working out. Sags enjoy

hiking in nature over the dreadmill—oops, I meant treadmill. Sags would see it as a dreadmill and prefer the outdoors anytime. This sign has a restless and nervous energy that nature helps to calm. Since their symbol is the centaur, half-man/half-horse, many enjoy archery as well as horseback riding.

PROFESSIONAL LIFE

Sagittarius is the natural academic, so being a college professor is one of the perfect careers for this sign. Using their vast intelligence, they are great advertisers, publishers, lawyers, or even judges. The restless part of them thrives on foreign affairs, as an adventurer, guide, interpreter, travel agent, or missionary. Since they love philosophy and religion, many pursue a calling as members of the clergy, religious scholars, missionaries, or evangelists. Loving both travel and being their own boss, the international import/export entrepreneur is more than likely a happy Sagittarian.

Sagittarius Employer

Do you like your new Sagittarian boss? Well, that answer probably depends on the day and his mood. You know he's smart and he sure is funny, but he's so erratic and unpredictable that you can't figure him out. You will discover that your Sagittarian boss is impatient. He's here today and gone tomorrow and you will have to make excuses or apologize for him missing appointments. However, his worst trait is the brutally honest way he points out your faults. He's totally tactless and even criticizes you in front of everyone. He's not trying to be mean or to demean you; he just thinks you want to hear the naked truth. On the other hand, you can depend on his sincerity when he does give you a compliment. He can only speak the truth, even if it hurts. Luckily, he is mostly the happy-go-lucky and humorous Sagittarian that everybody loves.

SAGITTARIUS IN THE BEDROOM

Sagittarians are good lovers if you let them be the initiators in the bedroom. They are not the most spontaneous lovers, since they're often involved with another activity that is totally captivating their energy. You need to learn to be very flexible with a Sagittarian, as they have a short attention span and their mood can change at a moment's notice. Timing is everything, so wait until he's in the mood and then you'll have an active participant. They like to be in unusual places, so be creative. Travel somewhere, even if it's just staying in a bed-and-breakfast a little ways out of town, or try the excitement of an airplane. I'll bet it was a Sagittarian who invented the Mile High Club.

SAGITTARIUS MALE PARTNER

James is a triple Sagittarius and feels so fortunate that he's named his business !LUCKY JAME$! Since Sag is the sign of abundance, what kind of a Jupiter business is that? A casino! The fire in Sagittarius likes to do things big, like a fireworks display. James may be the most confident Sag I know. He always radiates a sense of optimism and self-assurance. He attracts money like a magnet because of his expansive view of life. He's fearless and nothing is too big for him; in fact, he has no interest in small ventures whatsoever. What a waste of time when you could be opening another casino!

James is the best example of a male Sagittarian of anyone I know, so I had to use his story. A casino? You have to think big to decide to open a casino. Sags think bigger than all the other signs combined. How could James not think expansively with the huge planet Jupiter egging him on? Jupiter is the largest planet in the solar system and symbolizes good fortune, adventure, development, and ultimate success. The confidence of Jupiter with the element of fire is a dynamic combination when directed constructively, which he does in grand Sag style. James is so upbeat and confident that he could easily be an inspirational speaker regarding money and success. He has the Sag wisdom of knowing how to go beyond the everyday reality of life and transform it into a colossal victory. Also, James is blessed to have five planets in the sign of Capricorn, which makes him a wonderful businessman. The combination of Capricorn business acumen and fearless Sagittarius optimism makes him a definite winner. I guess that's good if you own a casino!

If you're interested in a Sagittarian man, you must be adventurous. He is so full of energy and thirst for the unknown, just for the sake of discovery, that you will have to learn how to keep up with him. If you have a Cancer sun and want a normal life in front of the TV each night watching the same shows, this is definitely not the sign for you. A Sagittarian is not known for his emotional coziness or need for domestic bliss. He detests routine, being held down or told what to do by you, by a boss or by the world. Sagittarians do better being their own bosses because they don't take direction very well at all. They have a fear of small spaces or a confined lifestyle. Your Sag will always be looking at distant vistas and needs a partner who shares that wanderlust. You never know: The grass might really be greener over there! He walks fast and is always headed somewhere. Can you keep up with him? Or do you want to? Sags are straightforward and will always tell you the truth, even if you don't want to hear it. He's incredibly outspoken, impatient, opinionated, and restless. Oh, yes: You will most likely have to fit into his life and not the other way around. Are you flexible enough to move to a remote part of the world? You had better be willing to jump on the back of that horse and ride; otherwise, he'll leave you in the dust.

Sagittarians have fabulous lives if you like discovering new worlds and learning unfamiliar customs in foreign lands. Oh, I didn't tell you that the !LUCKY JAME$! casino is in Eastern Europe. How much more Sag can you get than opening a casino in a totally foreign country! Knowing him, he'll have several casinos in no time at all. James is fulfilling his destiny as a Sagittarian to live as big as he thinks. Anything less would be totally unsatisfying. Can he do it? I'd bet on him!

SAGITTARIUS FEMALE PARTNER

Louise owns an award-winning travel agency. But like the Sagittarian she is, she only deals with high-end travel and clients. First class and five-star—that's her Sag style, and very worthy of abundant Jupiter. She's tall, slender, beautiful, and always on the go. With her insanely long legs and almost masculine fast stride, everyone is always running a little just to keep up with her. They had better keep up, because she's definitely not going to slow down for anyone. Is she in London now? No, she just left for Thailand to try out a new spa.

Like most Sagittarians, Louise has always had a passion for travel. As a child, she collected maps and loved studying other cultures. Luckily, her father was an ambassador, so she got a chance to travel and actually live in several foreign countries. She had her seventh birthday in Hong Kong and turned sixteen in Paris. Louise has friends and family all over and visits them regularly. Of course, she opened her agency so she could have a personal excuse to travel. Louise is fluent in four languages and is now learning Portuguese just for fun. Her intention is to teach herself seven languages and she's already well on her way to accomplishing that goal. Once she's mastered all those languages, she'll be able to go anywhere and interact easily with anyone.

Even though this Sagittarian has a nice town house, she sure isn't home very often. This sign is not known for domestic leanings. No soup on the stove or doggie waiting for her when she gets home. Sometimes she doesn't come home for a month at a time, so how could she have a dog? At times, Louise is almost manic in her need to travel. It seems as if she's searching for an elusive treasure that she just has to find in this lifetime, or else. There is no other option for the gypsy Sagittarius. Remember the centaur with his bow and arrow, aiming for distant lands? I think they release the arrow and then run over there to see where it landed. Then they pick up the arrow again, aim anew, and release again. This pattern is repeated throughout their entire lives.

Have you met an exciting Sagittarius? Well, there are a couple of warnings about her. She will always be honest with you, but you may not like her method of delivery. Tact is not—let me repeat, *not*—a Sagittarian virtue. She can be brutally truthful to the point of insult. Plus Sags are also known for their quick temper. So if you are a sensitive Pisces who gets your feelings hurt easily and has to talk it out with your therapist, please leave now before you get crushed. She has no mercy for wimps and was the captain of her debate team in college. So you don't have a chance if you aren't worldly, highly educated, and a mental giant. She only respects someone who can be her equal, and that requires big shoes. Luckily, her brutal honesty is also her redeeming quality. When she does compliment you, it is so genuine and sincere that you know she believes it from the bottom of her heart. You melt and almost forget that ten minutes ago she cut you to the core.

But if you can stand up to your Sagittarian beauty and keep her interested, you are in for the ride of your life. Keep a bag packed at all times, because she could call you at midnight to meet her in the morning for a trip to the Caribbean. Are you going to pass that up? No way! Just like Louise, your Sag is incredibly exciting, adventurous, open-minded and willing to try anything once. You need to know if you can keep up with her. She gets bored very easily, so you have to be even more exciting than she is. Can you do that?

SAGITTARIUS FATHER FIGURE

Matthew was a professor of archeology who specialized in theology and comparative religions in ancient cultures. When he got tenure, he started traveling to some of the regions he had only studied in books. When he made his journeys, it was like the world had changed from black and white into a prism of colors. He was hooked. So at a rare family meeting, he announced his new career: treasure hunter. His family thought he had gone off the deep end, but had to support him anyway. Well, he became an Indiana Jones–type character and searched the world for ancient, missing treasures. Leave it to a well-educated and lucky Sagittarian, because he actually found some . . . and still searches for more to this day.

Since Matthew's area of expertise is in theology and ancient wisdom, his treasures aren't gold and jewels. He considers his riches to be much more precious than any old box filled with gold. Matthew searches for ancient manuscripts and tablets that might encode the mystery of the origin of the world. Sagittarians are always intellectually curious and have wonderful minds for discovering new thoughts or, in Matthew's case, old thoughts.

The mission for Sagittarius is the pursuit of knowledge, and Matthew embarks on that mission literally with his treasure hunts. Publishing is also associated with this sign, so it was easy for Matthew to have his findings presented in peer-reviewed archeology journals. But someday he wants to write a book himself. He envisions a coffee-table book with amazing pictures and maps. He wants to share this ancient knowledge with the world, like a generous Sag.

Sagittarius, which is not a domestic sign, values movement, travel, and discovery more than a traditional, settled life. Sags would see too much stability as boring when there is so much to see and learn in the world. Even when he was in college, Matthew was quite busy. He always had so many projects in motion that he wasn't home much. When he was, his family always had fun with him. Matthew loves the outdoors and takes the family camping whenever he can. Since he was a teacher and had summers off, they went on long camping vacations in the wilds. One year they visited ghost towns in the Southwest. Of course, he made them all write an essay for school about their summer vacation. Their family also shares a love of sports and Matthew is always at their soccer and baseball games, loudly cheering them on to victory. Of course, now that he's a treasure hunter, they see even less of him.

If your father is a Sagittarian, there are a few things you need to know about his personality. When he's involved with a project, please don't bother him until he's done. A Sagittarian gets completely caught up in his activity. It doesn't matter whether he's watching a movie, reading the newspaper or answering his e-mail. He needs to finish it before he can refocus on what you want. Timing is everything with your Sag dad. If you disturb him before he's ready to be interrupted, he could be impatient and quick-tempered with you. Also, since Sagittarians are bright and informed, he could be the professor who knows it all. They have an intellectual smugness and think they are right. Darn thing is, most of the time they are right. He might be sharp with you, but it's only the fireworks going off every now and then. Remember: Sags tell the total truth with no sugarcoating, so be prepared to hear his straightforward, candid opinion.

Matthew's children are happy to have their Sagittarian dad, even if he is gone much of the time. The children each speak three languages and have traveled all over the world with him on fantastic treasure hunts. His family will never forget that trip to Egypt when they first saw the pyramids and then cruised down the Nile on a boat watching the sunset. Christmas vacation this year will be spent climbing Mt. Mauna Kea in Hawaii and studying the ancient Hawaiian Kahuna tradition. Next summer they're planning a trip to Nepal and will be hiking the Himalayas in search of a hidden monastery. No wonder Matthew's children love him—what a life they have with their Sag dad!

SAGITTARIUS MOTHER FIGURE

Kelly was a tomboy as a child and she always wanted boys when she became a mother. She got her wish: She has three sons and they live on a ranch. Her husband is a cattle rancher, so they have thousands of acres and raise animals. In addition to cattle, they have several horses, two dogs, three cats, four goats, and lots of chickens. Every day is different on the ranch. One day they're mending fences, the next day they have to drive into town for supplies, and next week is a cattle drive. Kelly wanted an active life and she sure got one. The worst thing for a Sag is to be bored. Well, that's not going to happen with this Sagittarian mother!

 Kelly loves her life on the ranch. A Sagittarian needs to keep busy to be happy and her Western lifestyle definitely gives her plenty to do. She's a real cowgirl. This fire sign has a huge zest for living and needs a life large enough to keep her interest. One of her favorite things to do with her family is to ride their horses up to this steep cliff that overlooks several valleys. Usually they pack a picnic lunch and sit down on a blanket to talk.

Since Sagittarians are prone to claustrophobia, the incredibly expansive view feeds her need for open spaces. In fact, that is her little sanctuary when she needs some space to think. Sometimes she escapes on her horse by herself and just rides and rides for miles. She loves the feeling of wind blowing through her hair as she gallops across her ranch. Kelly very much relates to her symbol, the centaur, because she almost feels more comfortable on a horse than on the ground.

Sagittarians are inherently restless and nervous, which is why they always need to keep busy. Kelly has a perfect lifestyle for her sign, since there is always something to do on the ranch. To be comfortable, Sags need to feel as if they are always expanding their horizons. The status quo just doesn't cut it for a Sag. Maybe a Virgo likes routine and repetition, not a Sagittarian. Kelly is always seeking new experiences. Yesterday they went to one part of the ranch; today let's try the south 40 instead. Very adventurous, she's always looking for exciting activities for her boys. What about us building a shed today? Her boys say, "But Mom, we don't know how to build a shed." No problem, she'll have them study shed building on the Internet and then they can start. Nothing is ever too difficult for the intelligent Sagittarius to learn.

If your mother is a Sagittarius, you are one of the lucky ones. She has an outgoing and vivacious personality and is almost always in a good mood. She makes you laugh a lot because her outrageous sense of humor keeps everyone laughing. Even though there is typically plenty of laughter in a home with a Sag mother, she does have her moments. This fire sign needs to have interests or hobbies outside the home to be totally happy. So support her when she goes out with her girlfriends on that getaway, even if it is to Paris. She must escape on occasion to feed her Sagittarian need to try new things. She'll come home with cool French presents and don't be surprised if one of them is Fast French lessons on CD. Your mom picks up languages easily and wants to speak French with you. Even though she is easygoing, don't think you can slide on your education. If you want to keep your mother on your side, get good grades in school!

Your Sag mother will have a lively household with lots of noise, activity, and kids running in and out of the house. She will encourage you to expand your life to the fullest. Education is very important to the Sag mother, so focus on your dream and she will help you make it a reality. Do you want to go to Europe after high school and before college? She'll agree with you instead of making you work a stupid summer job that you hate. She wants you to be happy. Sagittarians have a commonsense wisdom that expands as they mature. So your mother will usually know the right thing for you. Trust her.

SAGITTARIUS CHILD

Ten-year-old Connor is a Sagittarian. Even as a baby he was so full of energy that his parents had a hard time keeping up with him. Now he jumps on his bicycle and is gone as soon as he comes home from school. Fortunately, he is a wonderful student and loves to learn. His favorite subject is biology and he usually has a frog in his pocket to surprise his mother. He's almost always in a good mood, unless his mom forces him to do something he doesn't want to do. She realized early on that he has his own agenda.

Your Sagittarius child wants one main thing from you: the freedom to do what he wants. I know that it's a bit hard for a parent to give your little one total freedom. But you will find out right away that your child knows what is best for him. Just like Connor, who hops on his bike and zooms through the neighborhood, he knows where he wants to go. This sign does not take direction well at all and will debate you about most of your decisions. Why? You'll hear that word a lot! If you can logically convince your Sag that it's a good thing, he will comply easily. If you don't present a good enough case, you lose.

The baby Sagittarian is restless and not as cuddly as, say, a Pisces baby. They are too interested in everything going on around them to be passively held. Sag and Gemini babies are the most claustrophobic and won't handle time in a playpen well at all. Have lots of space for those two signs, in particular, or you will have screaming babies.

The Sagittarian toddler will walk and talk early. Those born under this sign will climb up the drapes if they are cooped inside too much. Sags love the outdoors, so ideally you'll have a backyard with lots of room and a tree or two to climb. Put in a swing set as well as a sandbox: Sags get bored easily and need lots of stimulus.

School is a natural place for the intelligent Sagittarius. They are very bright and excel academically, so build up an excellent library, read to them daily, and buy a fast computer for your little one. Sagittarians are born restless and often have loud, boisterous voices that might need to be toned down as children. You will find your Sag to be outspoken, often prone to exaggeration, so try to keep her straight on details. You will be amazed at how easily your Sag will learn a foreign language, so start her speaking another language very early.

Not only will the Sagittarian teenager do very well scholastically, but he is generally interested in sports, too. This sign is outgoing, confident, and usually has lots of friends. Take your Sag and several of his friends on a camping trip for fun. Nature always calms down a Sagittarian and it will be a great opportunity for him to learn survival skills. Since Sag is a fire sign, I've seen many born under this sign who love to build and maintain campfires. Give your Sag fire duty and watch him shine with responsibility.

The challenge for Sagittarians is defiance of authority. It's not only your authority that they will question, but also their teachers', their government's, and society's itself. In a Sag mind, no one can tell him what to do. Period. And they are so darn smart that they can start to convince you that you were wrong after all. Sagittarians are the masters of debate and no other sign can equal their clever logic. So your responsibility as a parent is to be an authority figure without your Sagittarian catching on. Good luck!

SAGITTARIUS PET

If you want a pet that is full of energy and loves to run, choose one born under the sign of Sagittarius. When I was selecting a dog for each sign, this was one of the easiest ones to choose. A Greyhound is born to run—look at his aerodynamic body! Whether your Sag dog is a Greyhound or not, all Sagittarian dogs need space to run. A Sag puppy will be all over the place and will take a while to mature. This restless sign needs space for almost constant activity. So if you have several very active kids all running around, this is a great choice for your family. Make sure you have a large enough backyard for lots of exercise for your Sagittarian pooch. But if you have a cramped little apartment, do not choose a Sagittarian! Hint: This is not the dog for your grandmother.

ANIMALS FOR SAGITTARIUS
Horse
Kangaroo
Leopard
Porcupine
Racehorse

PERFECT GIFTS FOR SAGITTARIUS

Sagittarians are fun to buy for because of all their interests. Here are their main areas of interest: travel, education, and the outdoors. These will give you some ideas for your Sagittarius.

Travel
- Rugged luggage
- Cool backpack
- GPS device
- Language interpreter gadget
- Airline passes to anywhere
- Leather passport cover

Education
- Geography class
- World atlas
- Gift card to a bookstore
- Foreign language classes
- A globe

Outdoors
- Hiking boots
- A safari jacket
- An archery set
- Camping equipment

SAGITTARIUS CELEBRITIES AND THEIR BIRTH DATES

Scarlett Johansson	November 22
George Eliot	November 22
Miley Cyrus	November 23
Katherine Heigl	November 24
Henri de Toulouse-Lautrec	November 24
Christina Applegate	November 25
Tina Turner	November 26
Michael Vartan	November 27
Jimi Hendrix	November 27
Jon Stewart	November 28
Dick Clark	November 30
Ben Stiller	November 30
Mark Twain	November 30
Bette Midler	December 1
Gianni Versace	December 2
Julianne Moore	December 3
Brendan Fraser	December 3
Marisa Tomei	December 4
Tyra Banks	December 4
Teri Hatcher	December 8
Judi Dench	December 9
Kenneth Branagh	December 10
Teri Garr	December 11
Jamie Foxx	December 13
Benjamin Bratt	December 16
Brad Pitt	December 18
Katie Holmes	December 18
Jake Gyllenhaal	December 19
Chris Evert	December 21
Kiefer Sutherland	December 21

CAPRICORN

December 22–January 20

KEYWORDS

POSITIVE KEYWORDS

Dependable

Serious

Accomplished

Competent

Presentable

Sophisticated

CAUTION KEYWORDS

Pessimistic

Cold

Rigid

INFORMATION

TENTH SIGN OF THE ZODIAC

Glyph: ♑

Planet: Saturn

Symbol: Goat

Element: Earth

Mode: Cardinal

Colors: Black, Slate Gray

Gemstones: Diamond, Obsidian

Metal: Lead

Body Parts: Knees, Skin, Teeth

CAPRICORN: THE EXECUTIVE

Clark is an attorney who specializes in real estate law, which is perfect for a Capricorn. He carries a sense of authority and a bit of superiority with him in business meetings. As an earthy Capricorn, he speaks with confidence and always has a detailed plan for his clients. Clark travels around the world looking at new properties for business as well as for second or third homes for his wealthy clients. He insists they always stay in five-star hotels, of course.

Capricorns are here to accomplish their goals and they always have a list of responsibilities on their agenda. This is the last earth sign following Taurus and Virgo. The earth of Taurus likes his creature comforts and Virgo's earth wants everything in place. The earth of Capricorn has mastered duty and achievement. This is the most driven and dedicated of all the zodiac signs. Capricorns' seriousness is not a surprise because the planet associated with Capricorn is the dreaded Saturn. Why is Saturn the least popular planet? He's the taskmaster. You have to actually work with Saturn, rather than doing all the fun stuff you can do with Jupiter. Saturn makes sure you get all your bills and taxes organized. Saturn is the one who will have you do a five-year projection of your business plan. Yes, that's lots of time devoted to reading reports and making up budgets. Fun? Maybe not for you, but for a Capricorn, it's a joy.

The symbol of Capricorn is the goat. Actually it's the mythological animal called the goat fish. This animal represents extremes in heights and depths. The sure-footed goat climbs craggy hills with confidence and stability and always gets where he wants to go. The fish can swim to the bottom of the ocean with diligence and perseverance in order to fulfill his mission. Capricorns are astrology's overachievers and will work until they reach their goals. They never quit until they're finished and see the goal reached, and done with quality in mind. Halfway just won't cut it for the ambitious Capricorn. Status, reputation, and recognition are of the utmost importance to this sign. They climb the ladder of success to reap the rewards of their hard work. Just like Clark, all Capricorns exude an air of authority. People automatically respect their maturity and ability to accomplish daunting feats of organization. They might not be fun and goofy like a Gemini, but if you want to get something done, ask a Capricorn.

IF YOU'RE A CAPRICORN, READ THIS!

You can feel proud that your sign is the most dedicated and accomplished sign of all. As a Capricorn, you do what you say you're going to do. You have to . . . because you gave your word. Integrity and conscientiousness are wonderful Capricorn traits and will always keep you on track. You know that if you apply yourself and work hard, you can succeed in doing anything. Your reputation for excellence is important to you, as are the rewards you receive for such valiant efforts. Because of your natural sense of clout, people bestow on you the recognition that you want and so richly deserve. Capricorn is the sign of ambition. How can you get to the next rung on the ladder? You know you're never going to be truly satisfied until you're at the top, so make a plan with a time line; it will make you feel better.

WHAT MAKES YOU HAPPY?
Recognition

Why work so hard if you're not getting acknowledged for everything that you do? As a Capricorn, you actually enjoy getting things accomplished. That sense of fulfillment you get when you complete a project is what you live for this lifetime. You are happiest when you are working at a career that is steady, constant, and secure. A nice routine feels safe and reliable. Remember, your earth element likes to know that your feet are firmly planted on the ground, standing on a solid foundation. You are both patient and ambitious, which is a fabulous combination. Capricorns are known for their perseverance and ability to focus on an objective until it comes to a successful completion.

But there is something even more important to your happiness than security and that is your reputation and public status. You need the people you work with to respect you. If they don't value your incredible contribution, then leave, because you aren't in the right situation. You should be admired for your dedication and attention to detail. You need to be recognized as an authority in your field: Yours is the voice of mature wisdom. Hey, an award every now and then might be nice, too. They would all be lost without you and they know it. That should make you happy!

The Ideal Capricorn Lifestyle

You're a CEO in a Fortune 500 company, and because of your hard work and dedication, you have earned all the perks. Everyone admires and respects you for your important contribution to the company. Part of your package is special parking, a huge corner office, and the much-sought-after key to the VIP washroom. You are happy with your achievements as well as your fat pension. All that hard work paid off!

CAPRICORN STRENGTH

Capricorns are fabulous organizers, managers, and achievers of any-thing they put their minds to. This sign was born mature and with the gift of being trustworthy. They are conscientious, persistent, goal-oriented, and have a sense of purpose. Many of my most successful and wealthy clients are Capricorns, and I'm not surprised. They walk with the air of an aristocrat and are always sophisticated and appropriate. Capricorns are dignified, and a male Capricorn falls into the father figure role easily, no matter what his age. Common sense, patience, and, as a result, the inevitable tolerance of others belongs to Capricorn. But maybe the best of their traits is their ability to achieve mastery of their work, which comes after years of applying their determination in the quest to reach a desired outcome. Capricorns have a plan, and their goal is to do it, whatever it is!

CAPRICORN CHALLENGE

Being overwhelmed is the biggest challenge for the hardworking Cap-ricorn. Oftentimes, Capricorns take on more than they can handle and therefore feel rushed and stressed over their volume of work. They either need to learn how to delegate, as Leo does, or learn how to say "No!" When Capricorns feel overburdened, they seem to be carrying a huge weight on their shoulders and even look down at the ground as they walk. If this sign is just too overwhelmed, he turns into the Capricorn hermit. The challenge side of Capricorn is stuck somewhere between reality and pessimism. Capricorns tend to have rigid attitudes about life and often walk with a stiff awkwardness. They are usually inhibited, cautious, and definitely won't be the ones drunk, dancing on a table at that wild party. In fact, Capricorns are usually the safe designated drivers who don't drink at all. They exemplify sobriety and are proud of it.

MENTAL CHARACTERISTICS

Capricorns are very methodical and detailed thinkers and have a solid grasp of complicated documents that Pisces would see as hieroglyphics. Think of your tax accountant, who looks at all those boxes on your tax return and just knows which ones to check, almost automatically. This sign is the best organizer and manager of them all. Capricorns like having a plan and are good at actually following it. But open-mindedness is not one of their virtues: Save that for Gemini and Aquarius. The Capricorn mind is linear and thinks in a defined dimension—no abstract stream of consciousness here. They prefer a script rather than winging it, like a Leo. Rather conservative and stoic, they respect self-discipline in themselves and others. Capricorn tends to be a bit of a snob, scorning poverty and those lacking ambition. In their eyes, everyone can be successful if they apply themselves, and they don't understand why everyone isn't. Because not everyone is a Capricorn!

EMOTIONAL MAKEUP

Capricorn is perhaps the least emotional sign of them all. They are innately inhibited and feel quite uncomfortable with the emotional world. Capricorns like to accomplish a mission to organize projects, so listening to your problems isn't easy for them. They have stable emotions and just can't relate. You will feel slighted and they will feel inadequate to help you. So don't even bother. Save your Capricorn friend to help you plan the logistics of your situation. Ask her to help you make a list of everything you have to get done to solve your problem. They want to help, but they need to help you "Capricorn style."

Personally, Capricorns are not going to share their most intimate feelings with you or with anyone. That would make them feel way too vulnerable, and why make themselves feel worse than they do already? This sign wants to do a practical job to get things moving. That's the Capricorn way.

PHYSICAL CHARACTERISTICS
Appearance
There are two distinctly different looks to a Capricorn. The positive side of this sign is very distinguished, sophisticated with an aura of reserved dignity. This style of Capricorn is classy in dress and in attitude. By constrast, the more solemn type of Capricorn is very easy to recognize. They walk slowly, with heavy footsteps, and tend to look down with an expression of worry or severity. This type of Capricorn has a dark cloud over his head. A Capricorn typically has an angular body, a long head and nose, thin lips, and a strong but narrow chin.

Fashion Sense
Capricorns have a conservative and classic style of dress. No wild colors or patterns for this earth sign. They lean toward dark, muted colors and don't want to stand out in a crowd like Leo. Capricorns favor slate gray, navy, or black with their business suits. They often adopt a classy monochromatic color scheme. The more earthy type of Capricorn, who might be a potter or landscape designer, prefers solid colors as opposed to prints—mostly browns and earth tones rather than the Scorpio black and red. Even if they do work outside, Capricorns all pay attention to their appearance and always want to look good. They are the sophisticated Capricorn, after all.

Health Types
The most important mineral with Capricorn is calcium, which affects the skin, the hair, the teeth, and the skeletal system. The precise skel-

etal body part that relates to this sign is the knees. The calcium of Capricorn actually holds up the body, so it's important. But, Capricorns need to counterbalance their natural stiffness or tendency to be rigid by striving for flexibility. Keep an eye on the calcium levels of a Capricorn. Capricorns with a very sedentary lifestyle and no stretching could develop arthritis. Good reason to take that yoga class!

Exercise Approach

Capricorns need to pay particular attention to maintaining their flexibility. Their Saturn-type bodies are naturally stiff and with their tendency to be sedentary, stretching and yoga are almost a necessity. Since Capricorn is an earth sign, they like hiking in the outdoors. At least encourage them take a break from their work and walk around the block regularly. Capricorns have an affinity for repetition and are blessed with patience, so weight training would be a great exercise for the plodding Capricorn. Get outside and breathe, Capricorn!

PROFESSIONAL LIFE

Capricorn is one of the most effective authority figures in the zodiac, and those born under this sign excel as chief executives, managers, organizers, economists, and administrators. Another career path for this highly structured sign is in construction or engineering, possibly becoming a foreman or contractor. Some Capricorns who focus on their creativity and combine it with a talent for using natural materials are excellent potters, sculptors, and leather workers. Also, those born under this physical earth sign make great physicists, geologists, mountain climbers, and diamond cutters.

Capricorn Employer

The Capricorn boss is tough. He's the disciplinarian and taskmaster of the zodiac, so don't even think you can sneak out early. He's always the first one at the office and the last one to leave and he expects you to be the same way. Capricorns are gruff and often grunt in response to your questions, unlike the Gemini boss who talks all day. The Capricorn boss is the quintessential quiet boss who sits behind his desk working like a stoic, driven commander-in-chief. He demands consistent, hard work from his employees. No purple nail polish or wild music—he prefers class and sophistication in the workplace. But he is actually much kinder on the inside than he appears on the outside. As long as he realizes that you are sincere, he will be fair and just, even if he is a little rough around the edges.

CAPRICORN IN THE BEDROOM

Capricorns are good lovers if you handle them correctly, since they are only comfortable with more conservative styles of lovemaking. Don't expect flowers, candy, or a gushy "I love you" very often, as the inhibited Capricorn just can't do it. That doesn't mean that they don't love you, but don't expect the kind of romance you'd get with the sugar-sweet Libra or you will be terribly disappointed. Also, they don't give or receive compliments well. Too fluffy for them; they'll get embarrassed instead. Save the revealing styles for Scorpio because anything too overtly sexy in public will turn Capricorns off. Let them be in charge, and once they lose their inhibitions, this amazing earthy sensuality emerges in them. Remember the attention to detail and perseverance of Capricorn? Now those are great traits in a lover!

CAPRICORN MALE PARTNER

Paul is a double Capricorn and a potter. Not everyone looks like their sign, but Paul is so ruggedly handsome that you could guess his sign easily. He lives on an old adobe ranch in the desert and has his pottery studio on his land. A week will go by when he won't see anyone except for his horses and his faithful dogs, and he likes it that way. The pottery calls him, and he could work in his studio from dawn to dusk and often does just that. Paul is so good that his works of art are in museums and galleries, and are cherished by private collectors all over the world. Leave it to a Capricorn to figure out how to make his living from the earth.

Paul is not only an earth sign—he's surrounded by earth. He loves the feel of clay in his hands and has declared it his favorite medium. His style is a bit rough, yet he still creates simple and elegant works of art. Even

though he's an official cowboy, he listens to classical music and loves opera, like a good high-class Capricorn. The view from his studio is of the majestic Rocky Mountains that change in color from purple to light pink and then to hot fuchsia right before sunset. You can hear the coyotes at night yipping their calls to each other as they search for their evening meal. He likes to ride his horse in the predawn and watch the sunrise with his dogs. After a hearty breakfast, Paul, with a red kerchief around his neck, heads out to his open-air studio to throw some more pots. He just got a large commission from a museum and is excited to implement a newly developed style. Not everyone uses their element as literally as this earthy Capricorn, but it sure works for him.

As you can see, not all Capricorns wear suits and ties and go to an office each day. Many, like Paul, prefer to work in nature. The need to feel connected to the earth is very powerful within this sign. However, Capricorns all have a strong work ethic, in that they take their life's work very seriously. Their strong sense of integrity and need for excellence are traits that shine through, even if they are riding a horse on their ranch. They are conscientious, dedicated, and very, very responsible. In fact, I've named the Capricorn planet, Saturn, Mr. Responsibility! There is no way a Capricorn can flake out—they just aren't wired for failure. They persevere with diligence until their project is fully completed, since they need to feel proud of what they accomplish. Remember, their reputation is on the line, so they have to do it right.

If you are involved with a Capricorn, there are a few things you must know. Capricorn is the sign of the workaholic, so that part of their life is a major priority to them. They can be a bit of a hermit while they work and don't appreciate being bothered until they are finished. Typically,

Capricorn is guarded in relationships and they don't do casual love affairs. They are restrained, rigid, and feel awkward in most casual social situations. So don't ever surprise your Capricorn by bringing over your wild friends to meet him. He'll be cold, sober, and will definitely be a killjoy when others are spontaneous and having fun. When Capricorns are out of their comfort zone, they are stiff, quiet, cautious, and won't contribute to your little surprise party.

Even though your Capricorn might not be a social giant, like Libra, he has amazingly positive traits that you will adore. If you want a stable, mature partner who will create a solid life with you, he's the one. He loves his family and will be there without question when his loved ones need him. Capricorn is the father figure of the zodiac, no matter what his age. He is mature even as a child and will be the naturally responsible one to take care of the family. Capricorns are late bloomers and might take their sweet time to commit to a long-term relationship. But when they do fall in love, it's forever. This sign doesn't like instability and change at all, so they mate for life. He prides himself on being a good provider. So be patient with your Capricorn man, because he's worth it. You can always count on a Capricorn!

CAPRICORN FEMALE PARTNER
Carol is a triple Capricorn, lives in New York City, and is a self-proclaimed socialite. She was fortunate enough to be born into a very wealthy family and will never have to work. So she spends much of her time working on her charitable foundation, organizing fund-raisers and large charity events. She prefers calling them charity galas. Carol is slender, tall, and brunette, and has the air of an aristocrat. She went to boarding schools in Europe and speaks three different languages. I call her a classic Capricorn sophisticated socialite.

Carol lives in an old brownstone on the Upper East Side of Manhattan, and loves her lifestyle. She has staff plus a personal assistant to help manage her complicated life. Even though she doesn't have an official career, you would never know it by her busy schedule. She has a meeting with her accountant at 10:00 a.m., then a luncheon with her women's charity group at noon, just before her weekly massage and pedicure at 3:00 p.m. She's converted one of her bedrooms to a massage and spa room and another one into a home gym. She's more comfortable exercising in her own brownstone than at a local gym, even if it the nicest one in town. Her hairdresser and makeup artist come over to prepare her for the evening. Tonight is a dinner with some new friends she met on her last trip to Paris, and she wants to look her best.

Female Capricorns have a profound sense of dignity about them. Even if they aren't as fortunate as Carol, they all have a classy and ambitious air of authority. In Carol's case, she was raised to be a New York socialite by her parents and always lived in a privileged world. Like many wealthy people, her parents instilled in her the knowledge that along with privilege comes social responsibility. She takes it very seriously and is on the board of directors for several charities; she is also the president of her own charitable foundation. You can tell that all her hard work has not gone unnoticed by all the plaques and framed newspaper articles she has mounted on the wall of her home office. She's very proud of her accomplishments and is always willing to talk about her achievements. Capricorns don't brag, actually—they just want some recognition for all their hard work.

If you are seeing a Capricorn woman, you must know this: Even if she isn't in the economic class of Carol, she wants to be. Their status and social standing in the community are of the utmost importance to them. Capricorns feel like they are aristocrats, no matter what their income level. *Prestige* is a wonderful Capricorn word, and you will need to be able to achieve some level of high social standing in your community or you won't have a chance. A female Capricorn must have a partner who has a life plan and can offer her the security that she needs to be happy. If there is a sign who could marry for money or status, it's a Capricorn woman. Let me rephrase that—she might not marry only for money, but she won't even consider a mate who doesn't have high status and a great stock portfolio. Yes, she's a material girl. So here is your question: Can you live up to your Capricorn's expectations?

You think you can be worthy of your Capricorn? Great! But consider this: You will have to share her lofty aspirations and be able to achieve amazing things to earn her respect. A Capricorn woman very much needs to respect her partner. She's very ambitious, and you had better be even more ambitious than she is. I know it might feel as if you are applying for a job and need a fabulous resume. You got it. But if you can gain her respect, you will have a dedicated and loyal life partner. Lucky you!

CAPRICORN FATHER FIGURE

John, an engineer, works for a company that creates systems for NASA. He has worked on most of the space missions as well as on the space shuttle and loves what he does. I always enjoy watching videos of astronauts in space, knowing that he had a big part in their success. John has two children, yet spends many late hours at his important job. In addition, he travels a lot, visiting other government facilities. Luckily, he takes his family on vacations during the summer. Everyone looks forward to spending time with him whenever they can. He loves his children, but needs to organize his time so he can spend even more time with them. Ah, the Capricorn life.

John is a classic Capricorn, who looks and acts like a textbook version of his sign. He has a serious look on his face all the time, as if there is something he's trying to figure out in his head. Oftentimes, Capricorns have furrowed brows as they intensely focus on their current thought. This is the sign of the detail-oriented thinker, which exemplifies a Capricorn engineer. This earth sign is excellent at physics and needs to know exactly how things work. John is also an astro-physicist and loves playing with objects that defy gravity and the known forces of nature. One of his specialties is discovering mathematical perfection in nature and as well as in the solar system. His office looks like it belongs to a mad scientist, with oddly shaped models everywhere. John will sit for hours staring out in space and then suddenly write down a long equation. Only a Capricorn has that level of attention and focus. With a mind like that, no wonder he can land on Mars.

Capricorn's life is built around accomplishing his goals. John's purpose in life is to understand physics as no one else has before. He

dreams in equations and lives in the land of physics. His focus is so profound that he's not even slightly interested in anything else. If I mention
a current movie or TV show, he looks at me as if I'm wasting his precious time even bringing it up. In the next sentence, he's talking about
a new discovery he's working on, as if I had never mentioned the show.
Unless you are interested in theoretical physics, there is no other conversation. Period. I fondly remember one long evening we spent talking
about the physical problems of the world. I'd keep throwing out an issue
and he'd think a bit and then come up with a solution. What about water
shortages? Global warming? Nuclear pollution? All solved with his
amazing mind. After that evening, I've always felt safer in this world.

If you have a Capricorn father, you must have wanted a sense of
structure. Even if he's not an engineer, like John, he will have a mind
that has a focus on objectives. He is very dedicated to his career and will
need to make special time for his family. Capricorns are not the most
domestic of the astrology signs, so he's probably not the most affectionate of fathers. Don't mistake his stiffness for a lack of love; he just can't
express his emotions well with anyone. So don't take it personally. He
will tend to warn you about all the bad things in life. It's his way of trying
to protect you. Remember the quiet donkey in Winnie the Pooh—Eeyore?
A Capricorn is like that character. He's incredibly lovable and intelligent,
yet keeps it all inside and is known to be gloomy. If your dad is quiet and
a bit on the gloomy side, he's being true to his sign. It has nothing to do
with you—he just has a lot on his mind.

Capricorn is the sign of self-mastery. Your father is not only focused
on mastering his own field, but also on promoting his children's success. What can you do to make your Capricorn father pleased with
you? He's not happy with impulsive, harebrained schemes or dubious
plans. Remember, he's an earth sign and needs to have things easily
explained to him so that his linear, engineer-type mind can understand
them. So put your dreams on a spreadsheet with a time line and he'll
be more supportive. As a Capricorn, one of his missions is for you to
succeed, too.

CAPRICORN MOTHER FIGURE

Virginia, a double Capricorn, has three children. She's a stay-at-home mother and loves keeping a close eye on her children. Even though she doesn't officially work at a career, you would never know it. She's the president of the Junior League as well as being on the advisory boards of both the art museum and the opera company. Her home is always immaculate, even though no one has ever seen her struggle to put things in order. She is just so organized that nothing much ever gets out of place. Virginia doesn't put up with any disruptions or drama in her home. Capricorns like a smooth and elegant household and will make sure it stays that way.

Even though Virginia is stricter than other mothers, she's not mean. But she does have a high standard of what is acceptable in her home. Earth signs are connected with the material world, and Capricorn mothers want their home to be beautiful and in good order. Like most female Capricorns, Virginia married very well. Her husband owns several banks, so money is almost no object. Of course, she has staff to help her run her large, traditional Tudor home, but she's in charge. I'd call it a mansion, but she calls it her home. You won't be able to get away with much if your mother is a Capricorn. She somehow knows when things are out of control and won't stand for it. Those born under this sign appreciate organization and discipline and will try to instill those traits in their children. Instead of being an affectionate hugger and kisser, she's more like a mentor to her children. She loves you, but Capricorns have a hard time expressing physical affection.

Of all the signs, Capricorns have one of the strongest work ethics. They are always busy doing something productive. You won't catch your mother spending hours on the sofa watching soap operas, that's for sure. She runs a tight schedule for both herself and her family. Tradition and historical reverence are important to Capricorns, so the family photo album, including old, musty albums of ancestors, are cherished. Even the family crest is usually displayed prominently in the den or foyer of her home. Genealogy, or the study of family history, is favored with the sun signs of Cancer and Capricorn. Your mother values hard work in her children because she knows it will lead to success in your career. She is a good role model for you—look how hard she works!

Even though the Capricorn mother is strict and requires her children to be accountable and honest, she does listen to you. She might not listen to you when you are going on about something she considers frivolous, but if you tell her what you learned today in science class, she's all ears. She might not get overly excited or animated, but you can tell that she's taking an interest by the subtle expression of approval on her face. Her expression of disapproval makes her look like she's smelling something bad; she does that nose-crinkle-and-one-raised-eyebrow look that you know oh so well. Rebellious teenage years are a challenge for the controlling Capricorn mother. Remember, she's a more traditional mom, so act with as much maturity as you can muster to make her happy. She won't raise her voice, but you know all too well her opinion of the situation. She will either quietly approve or quietly disapprove. But I'll bet you want to see that little smile and not the nose crinkle any day.

Don't think that you got a raw deal with a Capricorn mother. She is totally devoted to her children and her family and will do anything for them. Like Virginia, she is very eager for her children to be successful in life. Her mission is to prepare you for the adult world of work and responsibility. So she will give you chores and responsibilities early to make you strong as an adult. She would love you to be so successful that you are recognized in your field as an expert. Then she knows she did her job.

CAPRICORN CHILD

Dylan is a seven-year-old Capricorn, but he was born mature. He was always more serene and focused than all the other kids. It's almost as though he's their father figure, even at the tender age of seven. He has two older sisters, but he acts like the older brother to them. Everyone recognizes his sense of authority and respects him for it. He's so mature that he's already started a business selling holiday cards out of his bedroom. His mother was concerned and asked me about his little venture. I told her to open up a bank account for him so he has some capital. He is a Capricorn, after all.

Your Capricorn child was born an adult. I know that sounds strange, but it's true. The odd thing about this sign is that as children, they seem much older than their years. But as they age, they get younger. The most cheerful and youthful Capricorn is much older. It's almost a reverse-age illusion. They came here ready to get something done and you can tell by the serious expression on their face. As their parent, you have to teach them how to play and enjoy their childhood. They will be adults soon enough—if they are not adults already.

Capricorn babies are not as affectionate as those born under other signs, like Pisces or Cancer. They are really good babies because they are self-contained and easily entertain themselves. They like safety and routine, so they like a playpen, unlike the claustrophobic Gemini. But please don't talk baby talk to your little Capricorn; she will look at you disapprovingly, like you are being silly.

As a small child, your little one's movements are slower and more deliberate than most children's. A Capricorn won't be running around wildly like an Aries. This sign needs a set schedule at home. Capricorns want to eat at the same time and go to bed early. Also, they have a very long attention span and will be able to focus on an activity quite well. Because they are born under the sign of the builder, good toys for Capricorns might be clay, building blocks, or a truck. Capricorns are naturally quiet and timid, so if they ask for something, give it to them.

School is a comfortable place for the ambitious and scholarly Capricorn. Virgo and Capricorn are the only signs you probably won't have to ask to do their homework. It's already done before you ask. Those born under this sign usually know their purpose in life quite early, so support their hobbies. A great example: A little boy who collects rocks as a child might grow up to be a geologist. Cautious and serious, they need to be encouraged to laugh and have more fun.

Typically, the teenage Capricorn is studious in school and takes on a job as soon as he is old enough. Capricorns like to have their own money and are ambitious enough, like little Dylan, to start businesses early. Socially, they will usually have a few good friends but aren't drawn in by the superficial crowd or the rowdy troublemakers. Your Capricorn is too conservative to want to get mixed up with questionable types. So don't worry about the awful teenage years—you get it much easier with a mature Capricorn.

Your challenge for your little Capricorn is to teach her how to play. If you are a Gemini or a Leo parent, let your playfulness come out and you'll do just fine. But the question here is this: Who is the real adult—the playful parent or the serious child? I put my money on the Capricorn.

CAPRICORN PET

If you want a calm and mature pet, choose one born under the sign of Capricorn. As a puppy, this sign won't be as goofy as, say, Aries, Gemini, or Sagittarius puppies. Capricorns are known for their dignity and patience and would be good for small children. The wonderful example I'm using for Capricorn is the magnificent Saint Bernard. Remember, they are the large rescue dogs from the Swiss Alps who trudge through snowdrifts to save poor lost skiers. This breed is famous for their dedication, common sense, and loyalty. You don't have to get a Saint Bernard, of course, but consider a Capricorn if you want a calm, stable pet for your family. Hint: This *is* a good dog for your grandmother! Well, maybe not the Saint Bernard . . .

ANIMALS FOR CAPRICORN
Alligator
Amphibian
Crocodile
Frog
Giraffe
Goat
Salamander
Wolf

PERFECT GIFTS FOR CAPRICORN

Capricorns like gifts that are useful and practical. A love of elegance also characterizes this sophisticated sign. Here are Capricorns' main interests: business, luxury, clothing, and good-quality home furnishings. These suggestions will definitely make your Capricorn smile!

Business
- Leather monogrammed briefcase
- Expensive pen-and-pencil set
- Executive desk set
- Electronic organizer

Luxury
- Gift card to a classy restaurant
- Museum or art gallery tickets
- Tickets to the opera
- Rolex watch
- Leather-bound first editions of favorite books

Clothing
- Silk bathrobe
- Gift card to a classic, very nice clothing store
- Quality jacket or blazer

Home Furnishings
- Antiques
- Good-quality furniture
- Landscaping sculptures
- Overstuffed recliner

CAPRICORN CELEBRITIES AND THEIR BIRTH DATES

Helena Christensen	December 25
Jared Leto	December 26
Denzel Washington	December 28
Mackenzie Rosman	December 28
Sienna Miller	December 28
Jude Law	December 29
Mary Tyler Moore	December 29
Tiger Woods	December 30
Val Kilmer	December 31
Anthony Hopkins	December 31
Mel Gibson	January 3
Julia Ormond	January 4
Dyan Cannon	January 4
Diane Keaton	January 5
Joan of Arc	January 6
Nicolas Cage	January 7
David Bowie	January 8
Amanda Peet	January 11
Mary J. Blige	January 11
Julia Louis-Dreyfus	January 13
Orlando Bloom	January 13
Patrick Dempsey	January 13
Faye Dunaway	January 14
Martin Luther King Jr.	January 15
Jim Carrey	January 17
Kevin Costner	January 18
Cary Grant	January 18
Dolly Parton	January 19
Shelley Fabares	January 19
Edgar Allen Poe	January 19

AQUARIUS

January 21–February 19

KEYWORDS

POSITIVE KEYWORDS

Individualistic

Humanitarian

Unconventional

Modern

Bohemian

Friendly

CAUTION KEYWORDS

Scattered

Detached

Insensitive

INFORMATION

ELEVENTH SIGN OF THE ZODIAC

Glyph: ♒

Planet: Uranus

Symbol: Water Bearer

Element: Air

Mode: Fixed

Colors: Indigo, Electric Blue

Gemstones: Lapis, Turquoise

Metal: Aluminum

Body Parts: Ankle, Blood

AQUARIUS: THE REBEL

Zachary, seventeen years old, is a double Aquarius and lives on his computer, actually on the Internet. He's so smart that most of the kids in his school can't relate to him, so he's more comfortable online. As an Aquarian, he is very, very independent and definitely uses an alias. In fact, he's part of a huge subculture that is addicted to massive multiplayer online gaming. Zachary doesn't just have an alias—he has created an entire virtual character for himself. His online community or guild needs him to play their games. He's completely connected yet totally separate. Now that's a real Aquarian!

Aquarius is the free spirit or the rebel of the zodiac. Aquarians' purpose is to break the outdated paradigm and usher in the new. Aquarius is the last of the air signs after Gemini and Libra. All air signs are excellent communicators, yet they have different audiences. Gemini, the student teacher, will speak to anyone who wants to learn. Libra, the romantic, is best at talking with her loved ones and very good friends. Aquarius is the communicator for organizations, society, and to the entire world. The symbol for Aquarius is the water bearer, pouring from the urn onto humanity. I want to clarify some confusion about this sign. Although Aquarius sounds like water and even has a water bearer as its symbol, it is an air sign! The water bearer is actually pouring the air of wisdom over the world. The glyph for Aquarius looks like energy waves and is much more aligned with electricity. Water is way too soft for the radical Aquarian: They prefer lightning!

It's no wonder that Aquarians are rebels: Their planet is the notorious Uranus. I call Uranus the planet of surprises, but you could also call it the planet of disruption and upset. It brings sudden, unexpected, and shocking revolution. Uranus represents the theory of chaos, which shows that expansion is not random and is a necessary part of evolution. Aquarians are the harbingers of change and only look toward the future. Let Cancers and Capricorns reflect on the past—Aquarius invents the future. This is the sign of the genius and, just like Zachary,

Aquarius is a whiz on the computer. Zachary always has his earbuds in and listens to loud, edgy, electronic music while he's online and offline. They are a permanent feature around his neck. This sign is fabulous at multitasking, especially when it comes to electronics. Aquarius was born hardwired to the cyberworld.

IF YOU'RE AN AQUARIUS, READ THIS!

Aquarius is here to break the rules! You like to be different and I want to tell you that it's your job to break the mold and view life as a series of exciting stages. I'm giving you permission to always go against mass culture and the norm. You are a forward thinker and not many have your grand view of the future. In your interactions with the world, you tend to be somewhat private because very few people understand you. To me, Aquarius is someone who stands on a hill with an incredible vista and can see everyone in his valley working and living their lives. Aquarius has an overall perspective on life and incredible wisdom as a result. If there is another Aquarian close by, he has his own hill and his own valley. Freedom and independence are the most important goals for you to achieve in this lifetime. If you always dance to your own music, you will be true to your Aquarian principles. It's OK to be radical—at least it is for you!

WHAT MAKES YOU HAPPY?

Independence

You must have freedom in your life or you will be miserable. Virgos like repetition, so please save that for them. With independence, you will create an exciting life for yourself, full of surprises and excitement. Free will is an Aquarian concept, and you want to choose something new and cutting edge just because you can. Why travel to a familiar place every vacation when the entire world beckons you? It's like eating the same old meal over and over again. Boring! Your sign is here to seek change and wants something new each and every day.

Aquarius is the sign of the inventor, so trust your creativity. Allow yourself plenty of time and space to experiment with your brilliant new

ideas. In the astrology world, Aquarius is the genius. Did you realize that? That's why Aquarians are the futurists, scientists, and space
explorers. You are here to seek the truth and open the curtains to the
dark and repressed. It's perfect that Aquarius follows Capricorn, the
sign of limitations. The purpose of Aquarius is to break the barriers of
confinement and free both yourself and society. The ultimate Aquarian
contribution is your love of humanitarian causes. Your sign knows that if
many gather together with one purpose in mind, change will occur. Join
a club or organization and work with people who share your interest
in repairing the world. What makes an Aquarian happy? Shocking the
world into change!

The Ideal Aquarian Lifestyle

You live with a group of friends on some land you collectively bought
and are totally off the grid. There is a well for pure water, solar panels
for electricity, and Internet access from a satellite. Each of you has your
own home and is independent, but you share a separate community
center for gatherings, parties, or Sunday dinner. You are all financially
successful and work from your homes in cottage industries or with
Internet businesses. Each house is different, and they are all wired for
sound with the newest and coolest technologies available. The group
has learned how to work together without jealousy, emotional rifts, or
drama. Aquarius wants to create a true model for utopian living.

Your Ultimate Dream

To live your life always being true to yourself. You never have to compromise your ideals or take orders from anyone—not a partner, the
government, religion, or society. You feel totally free every day to choose
spontaneously what you want to do.

AQUARIUS STRENGTH

Aquarians are best at promoting change. They are always discontent
with old-fashioned, outmoded concepts and will be the ones who offer

innovative and brilliant suggestions for better ways of doing things. Typically, you might see this sign at coffee shops engrossed in intellectual discussions about politics and revolution late into the night. One of their best talents is networking and knowing how to work with groups, clubs, and organizations to promote social reform. They love to fight for a cause and will work tirelessly in a group to improve the world. Somehow they can help tragic causes without getting emotionally involved. Aquarians have the unique talent of being almost completely detached. They love humanity but are not as good with personal interactions. Oh, they are very friendly and want to help. But you won't see any tears or emotional outbursts over their cause or about anything else, for that matter. They would say, "Everything is perfect . . . it's all meant to be. Just let it go."

AQUARIUS CHALLENGE

Being scattered is the biggest challenge for Aquarius. They all have an internal restlessness that underlies their actions. That restlessness helps them to promote change, but it can also make them nervous and shaky. They need to finish one project before starting the next. Aquarius is known for being unpredictable and impulsive. I named Aquarius the rebel for a reason. Since independence is so important to them, if they feel held down personally, these defiant rebels fight for their rights. When they are liberated, then the free spirit takes over, which is, of course, their intention. Many Aquarians lean toward being nonchalant, indifferent, and aloof. They seem to occupy a position above all the strife and struggle in the world and people resent or envy their lack of emotional involvement. An eccentric Aquarian could become so detached that she turns into the eccentric old lady with all the cats at the end of the block who never has any visitors.

MENTAL CHARACTERISTICS

Aquarius is the most open-minded of all the signs. They love the avant-garde and outrageous and are never judgmental of any other lifestyle or opinion. Intellectually curious, Aquarius enjoys learning about almost everything, especially new philosophies and ideals. This sign is always up on the current trends and futuristic plans for humanity. Aquarians somehow discover stories before they hit the paper and pride themselves on being in the know. At a coffee shop, an Aquarian would serendipitously bump into the developer who is putting in that new solar plant outside of town. Aquarians are optimistic, unconventional, and progressive. In fact, they detest naysayers or killjoys. "Why not? Let's just do it!" That is the Aquarian mantra.

EMOTIONAL MAKEUP

I might as well just say it: Aquarians are terrible at emotions. They are so darned detached that they can't even understand why people cry. None of the air signs—Gemini, Libra, and Aquarius—are very emotional. But I think Aquarius is the worst. Oh, it's not that they don't care— they totally love humanity and want to help the world at large. It's just the one-on-one that makes them uncomfortable. An Aquarian friend wants to talk you into letting it go and not worrying about the situation. That technique might work when you are almost over the trauma, but it doesn't help much when you are in the midst of tears. The sign of Aquarius looks at all the upcoming prospects and wants to brainstorm with you about your future. They have an amazing level of wisdom, so when you are ready to look ahead, call on an Aquarian, but not before.

PHYSICAL CHARACTERISTICS
Appearance
The Aquarian body is tall and slender. They typically have deep-set eyes that are wide apart. Many have an almost androgynous or even alien look to them. But the distinguishing feature of an Aquarian is the noble and outstanding profile. There is a kindness toward everyone that you can feel in their personality. Aquarians are very friendly and have a stunning and genuine smile for the world. Nothing much bothers a detached Aquarian. They usually have a gentle voice and no loud laugh—they mostly smile.

Fashion Sense

The trendy and youthful Aquarius stands out with her striking fashion sense. The bohemian, artsy, gypsy-like, or unusual look appeals to the inventive Aquarius. They like colorful, sometimes wild, geometric patterns. Aquarians can combine outrageous costume jewelry and accessories and make them look good. Capricorns or Virgos would be cringing, but Aquarius loves pushing the creative envelope. They are particularly fond of electric blue and silver. This bold sign can actually pull off mixing stripes and polka dots without looking ridiculous.

Health Type

One of the parts of the body associated with Aquarius is the lower legs, including the calves and ankles. It's wise for this sign to wear comfortable shoes to avoid a sprained ankle. The other part connected with this sign is the circulating blood in the body. If Aquarians spend too much time sitting at the computer, that could result in swollen ankles. Often there is so much energy going through an Aquarian body that they can get shaky if they get exhausted. But overall, this is a healthy sign; Aquarians are just too disconnected from emotional turmoil and would never worry enough to let anything much affect their health.

Exercise Approach

Aquarius gets bored easily and prefers cross-training to one form of exercise exclusively. One day walk, the next take a yoga class, the next day swim, and the following day don't do anything physical at all. Make sure to do some weight training, especially to strengthen the calves and ankles. Getting outdoors will help dissipate the excess energy of Aquarius. Nature always has a calming effect on this air sign. I've noticed that Aquarians like grand vistas, so find the tallest hill or mountain and explore heights while you hike: The view will make you more willing to break out into a sweat.

PROFESSIONAL LIFE

Aquarians are very independent and don't take direction well at all, so they are better at being entrepreneurs or consultants, if at all possible. Many are high-tech guru types and work as computer experts, software programmers, electricians, machinists, mechanics, or lighting specialists. Since they look ahead, many are futurists, inventors, scientists, or unofficial trendsetters. Of course, humanitarian ventures like nonprofit corporations, social advocacy groups, and sociology very much appeal to Aquarians. Interestingly enough, this is the sign of the astrologer. But if they could get paid for it, the perfect Aquarian career would be as a dissident or an anarchist. What do you do for a living? Oh, I'm an Aquarian anarchist!

Aquarian Employer

The Aquarian boss is a rarity, because this sign hates a regular 9-to-5 job. They are more likely to be the mad scientist inventor in a laboratory late at night. But if you do have an Aquarian as a boss, be prepared for an unpredictable workplace. He'll give you new assignments often, just assuming you can handle anything he throws at you. Every day is a bit different and tends to be scattered, so just get used to it. Aquarians are never judgmental and will not be bothered by any unusual lifestyle or idiosyncrasies among their employees. What will upset your Aquarian boss is any form or dishonesty, laziness, or cheating. You will be dismissed or fired in an instant with no expression of emotion or guilt. You are gone in a flash and he moves on without a thought of your past performance.

AQUARIUS IN THE BEDROOM

Aquarius is one of the most adventurous of lovers and will surprise you with exciting, new, and unconventional techniques. Gee, you never tried that position before? Well, why not? Maybe due to their planet, Uranus, pretty much anything goes with an Aquarius. I know that Scorpios are known for being intense lovers, but I think Aquarians even outdo the Scorpio lover. Scorpios are comfortable with the body, but Aquarians love trying new experiences in bed. This sign enjoys shocking people, so you're in for a treat with an Aquarian lover—that is, if you're adventurous as well. Shy or inexperienced lovers or prudes, beware. This is not the sign for the faint of heart in the bedroom. Officially, Aquarius is the sign of sexual perversion. Hey, why not?

AQUARIUS MALE PARTNER

Brandon is a twenty-five-year-old software developer who is a double Aquarian. He created social networking software that enables people to get together via the Internet. Because of his efforts, now people can connect with each other easily through their computers. The Aquarian goal is to unify the world, and Brandon certainly has done that through his brilliant software. He happily sits in front of a bank of computers every day and comes up with new and improved versions of his programs. He created an entirely new way for people to communicate. Brandon is a computer genius who knew what people needed: each other.

Brandon has a quirky Aquarian lifestyle. He's independent and is definitely his own boss, and that's something he knew he needed very early in life. He wrote his software in high school as a class project and it was so good that everyone wanted to use it. So he turned it into a business right away and never went to college. Aquarians are very unconventional in their styles of education. Did he need college? Apparently not. He never quite fit into traditional settings anyway. Even his daily routine is not the norm. Mostly a night owl, Brandon stays up working on his software until around 4:00 or 5:00 in the morning and sleeps until 1:00 or 2:00 in the afternoon. He eats cold food right out of a can with a plastic fork and his office looks like some kind of weird science experiment. Pretty scary. There was nowhere for me to sit down, so I had to sit on a box. Even though he's worth millions, his house looks like a warehouse. I'd say he's an eccentric and he's only twenty-five years old!

Of course, not all Aquarians are as odd as Brandon, but most are. It's the sign of the nonconformist or the radical renegade—the bad boy of the zodiac. He's not bad as in getting into trouble; he just doesn't fit in well and is always an outsider. If you want a socially acceptable, suave, romantic partner, find a nice Libra. Aquarians are not the easiest sign in a relationship. They don't know how to open themselves up emotionally and need so much independence that they often come off as aloof and indifferent. No coziness with this intellectual air sign. Brandon doesn't have a girlfriend and isn't even interested in a romantic relationship. He says he'll never get married because he doesn't like anyone around all the time. I think he's a bit agoraphobic myself, but who knows. Aquarians usually have quirky and weird habits unique to them.

If you are interested in an Aquarian, here are some tips to keep him. Aquarians will not tolerate even a hint of jealousy! Independence is their most valued possession and they guard it fiercely. Even casually asking about his day might be too intrusive for him. Definitely any checking up on him will make an Aquarian run away as fast as his legs can carry him. Please, never ask Aquarians how they feel emotionally or you will just get a cold shoulder and the quickest change of subject you've ever seen. Oftentimes, Aquarians get married much later in life, if at all. I know two Aquarians married to each other who have come up with an interesting solution to their need for independence. They each bought a separate house right next to each other. One night they sleep in her house and the next night they sleep in his house. Probably the third night they sleep apart. Hey, it works for them beautifully!

Don't feel sorry for Brandon, thinking that he has no social life. He has an amazingly rich virtual social life. Remember, he develops social networking software. Like a true Aquarian, he has very good friends all over the world whom he has never met in person. It really doesn't matter to an Aquarius whether you are in the room or on the monitor. I think they actually prefer the virtual version of a relationship to the real, more awkward, emotional version based in reality. Is your Aquarian virtual or real?

AQUARIUS FEMALE PARTNER

V. is a huge rock star. She's an Aquarian and I'm calling her V. Her real name is a household word since she's a genuine pop icon who performs to sellout crowds all over the world. She's a musical genius, an amazing dancer, and a charismatic, dynamic entertainer. Her audience adores her and she truly loves what she does. Personally she's quite spiritual and incorporates higher consciousness into her music. Once V. gets back from a tour, she's on to her next CD and new world tour. Definitely life in the fast lane. Even though it's incredibly exciting, she feels quite isolated from a real relationship by being on the road all the time.

An Aquarian needs an unusual life and V. sure has made an interesting one for herself. Every day is different in her world. She works out daily with a trainer to keep her athletic physique. But she spends most of her time in her home music studio working on her next CD. I had the incredible pleasure of watching her create a song in her studio. She was in another reality entirely when she came up with the lyrics. I truly experienced someone who was in the zone. It was one take and perfect. Wow. I can see why rock stars make the outrageous sums of money they do. She really has a natural gift and is using it to the max. Aquarius is the creative genius, the inventor, and the entrepreneur. They innately know what the collective wants. It's like having their thumbs on the pulse of humanity. V. combines all those fabulous talents and has turned them into an empire for herself. She stays up all night and sleeps all day. By the way, you don't want to bother an Aquarian when she is in her private mode or you will be sorry.

I have never met an Aquarian who wasn't very protective of his independence and freedom. This is the sign of the free spirit and you need to honor that to be able to spend any time at all with your Aquarian. They will not tolerate any amount of control or jealousy from anyone, let alone a partner. Yet, Aquarians have a probing interest in the lives of others. He will likely know everything about you and has not yet told you one little morsel about his life. You probably don't feel comfortable even broaching the subject of his private life without feeling like you are invading his personal space. You know he doesn't like that. I've noticed that many Aquarians have a larger personal space around them than other signs. Where Scorpios might stand too close, Aquarians need a larger space of safety around them. I know one Aquarian woman who stands about eight feet away when she talks with you. It was odd at first; now I'm used to the Aquarian space thing.

Even though Aquarians need independence, it also causes them some problems. The flip side of freedom is loneliness. This sign keeps people at a safe distance by collecting many impersonal relationships. Once the emotions get too deep, they bolt. Then you will see the friendly, yet frustratingly detached Aquarian. Another Aquarian defense mechanism is being so busy that it could lead to their being scattered. Look at the Aquarian image, with all the arrows going in every direction. That is what a nervous Aquarian looks like.

I know it sounds like this is a tricky sign in a partner, but the positive side of Aquarius is so worth their quirky challenges. A good way to gain the respect and love of an Aquarius is to start out as her friend. Aquarians need to forge a common bond with personal interests or community involvements. Find out her favorite hobby and try to take a real interest in it; she will like that. Give her all the space she needs and without even a vibe of control. Otherwise, she will sniff out your intentions and call you on them. But once an Aquarian woman does fall in love, she is a loyal partner. She is easy to be with because of her huge level of tolerance. As long as you don't control her, she doesn't care what you do. No micromanaging with her. You respect her freedom and she will respect yours. I call it Aquarian equality love.

AQUARIUS FATHER FIGURE

Victor, a triple Aquarian, is a lighting specialist who tours internationally with well-known rock bands. He started out as an electrician but loved music so much that he eventually grew into becoming a deejay. It was then an easy leap for him to design the lighting for huge shows. Victor is married with three children, but travels so much that he's not there all the time, like other fathers. When he is home, he's in his lighting studio, creating new looks for the next show. Luckily, his kids all love music and also love the thought that their dad is cool and hangs out with rock stars.

Victor is an unconventional Aquarian with long, streaked hair, tattoos, and piercings, and fits in perfectly with his outrageous rock star clients. Actually, over the years they've changed from being his clients to being his friends. They have to count on each other as they travel, so they got very close on the road. Victor is their genius lighting guru who changes the look of each show drastically with his creative designs. All the lighting cues are part of his computer programming, which he's incorporated into the stage as well as into the entire arena. He has developed a technique by which each member of the audience feels the music in their individual seat. Victor has created an intimately shared experience for the twenty thousand people in his grasp. He has an adoring audience and wows them with his magical use of group sensory perception. Leave it to a triple Aquarian to electrify each member of the audience.

Aquarius is an air sign and sometimes they seem like airheads to the uninformed observer. This sign is hard to understand because it is both the genius and the mad scientist. Scatter is the biggest challenge for Aquarians and it sure shows in Victor. He stays up most of the night in his lighting studio/theater, playing loud music, smoking weed, and often just sleeping on his couch in the studio. His music friends come over and party with him as he experiments with new tunes and matching lighting. I've had the pleasure of testing some of his music light shows and I felt like I was in a cozy concert hall. His studio is actually an indoor amphitheater or a scaled-down version of the huge stages he lights up throughout the world. The high-tech equipment, lasers, holographic images, and electronic smoke and mirrors he works with boggle the mind. Oftentimes, the actual performing artist was there to work on the show. Quite fantastic. I was watching a genius at work.

Oh, yes, his children. Where are they? As you can tell, Aquarians are also unconventional parents. Victor is more of a friend than a father figure to his children. He invites them into his studio/theater, including them in his world. An Aquarian father treats his children as equals. This sign understands and lives his life by relating equally to others, even his children. Loving independence himself, there is no way he imposes discipline on them. Their home is more like a dormitory than a homey home. The kids can basically do what they want. In fact, Victor happens to be much more radical than the conservative generation of his children. He's always trying to talk them into some crazy, exciting project. But they want no part of it and almost see him as the child. Aquarius is the wild child of the zodiac.

If your father is an Aquarian, you are one of the lucky ones. No micromanager, like a Virgo dad, or a control freak, like a Scorpio dad. You have an easygoing, lively, exciting, and altogether odd father. Yes, Aquarians are odd and unusual and he'll get more eccentric as he ages, so you're in for a wild ride. An Aquarian father is very supportive of his children and wants them to be free and happy. He's kind, fun, and will always introduce creative excitement to the family. You have to love your father, even love his quirky, embarrassing, and weird antics. He can't help it—he's an Aquarian!

AQUARIUS MOTHER FIGURE

Nicole is a mega-Aquarian; in fact, she's part of a group called the Aquarian Kids. In February and March of 1962, a huge lineup of planets occurred all in Aquarius, which is the sign of social revolution and global connectivity. (Remember the song from the musical *Hair*, "The Age of Aquarius"?) Will this group of babies change the world? I think so. It was such a rare alignment of planets that astrologers all over the world started doing research on this group, anticipating the grand contributions these babies would be making to the world. Some astrologers heralded that moment as the beginning of the Aquarian Age. I tend to agree with them, now that I've gotten to know the quintessential Aquarian Kid, Nicole.

The Aquarian mission is to bring change to the world, so what do you think an Aquarian Kid would do? Nicole was always interested in spiritual development and meditation as a way of calming the mind and becoming more connected with the universe. She got a chance to explore the spiritual world personally because she was also the mother of four beautiful children with incredibly busy lives. The built-in Aquarian restlessness always drove her to try to discover her mission in life. She knew it was more than only being a mother, even though she adored motherhood and has well-balanced and successful children. She felt that the universe had something bigger in mind for her. So she started hosting circles in her home—meditation circles. Her friends would come over every Tuesday morning and she would lead a one-hour meditation for the group. Through word of mouth only, new and very powerful people were attracted to her meditation groups. It grew and grew and became too big for her living room. What now?

Because of her pure intention of helping humanity, Nicole now has a holistic center of higher consciousness where she is a magnet for the highest of the high. The most famous healers, spiritual gurus, inspirational speakers, and musicians in the world just walk through her door and want to be involved. Most of these stars are used to outsize venues like concert halls or huge conference spaces and yet they're speaking in Nicole's gong/yoga room. They are doing it to be around the fresh, Aquarian energy that surrounds her. She has the aura of an angel with a soft, lilting voice and an ever-present smile. Yet Nicole is an angel with a purpose. She leads her circle meditations in a much larger room now, for many more people. She meets with new speakers and presenters and handles the media for interviews or TV. Nicole is a star in her own right.

If your mother is an Aquarius, you are indeed lucky. She will give you plenty of space to be yourself without interfering in your business. An Aquarian mother values you as an independent person, not just as her child. Respect her freedom and she'll respect yours. If she wants to spend some time in her room alone, don't bother her. I hope you didn't want a mother who coddles you, holds your hand at every turn, doesn't want to let you go, and bakes cookies. You were standing in the wrong line for mothers, if you do. Your Aquarian mother is more like a friend or mentor than the domestic, homey type of mother. She has a detached attitude toward your personal dramas. So if you feel as if she's not always listening to you, you're right. She can't relate to reliving the past and thinks in the present or the future. No whiners, please.

Nicole is the perfect example of an Aquarian mother, since she considers the entire world of spiritual seekers as her children. This type of mother gives to a wider community beyond her family. So you might have to share her love with the world, but isn't your mother worth it? You have almost total freedom to be yourself. She will always support you in whatever you plan for your life, instead of imposing her agenda on you. If you chose an Aquarian mother, you must have wanted to be yourself without any restrictions. It is true that you are more on your own, but that is the freedom and independence that you wanted, right?

AQUARIUS CHILD

Alexander is nine years old and is showing signs of being a genius already. He is a double Aquarius and fits his sign well. Even though he's brilliant, he gets in trouble at school for not paying attention. His teachers say he's always got a distant look on his face, as if he's in another world. He *is* in another world—his own world. Alexander understood what the teacher was saying the first time and he gets totally bored when the teacher has to go over it again for the other kids. He got it instantly and has moved on to something new.

Your Aquarius child came to you to teach you to look toward the future. Your little one truly is gifted and it's not just because he is your beautiful child and you like to brag about him. Just like Alexander, he really is special and not like the other kids. Your little Aquarius will always be ahead of his time and will keep you young as parents. The most important gift you can give to your Aquarius is the gift of independence. Try not to confine or control your little one or else you will have a rebel in your household instead of a progressive free spirit.

The baby Aquarius is a real bundle of energy. Remember Aquarians' planet, Uranus—the planet of surprises? The energy of Uranus comes through the baby like waves of electricity. Not a lot of cuddling with this independent spirit. Aquarius is just too busy experiencing the world and doesn't want to be held or held down.

Guess what's the first word uttered by your Aquarian toddler? *No!* It doesn't matter what you are asking or telling him, the answer is still an emphatic *No!* You will easily see the unpredictable nature of Aquarius in your little one's actions. One minute he's happy and the next he'll be restless and fidgety. When you see that restless look on this face, introduce something new to him. He's bored. Aquarians have very short attention spans and need lots of mental stimulation to keep them entertained.

School is easy for Aquarians, except for abiding by the rules. They are so bright that they might not see the necessity of learning about a subject that they think they will never use. Aquarians are the radical thinkers and don't see the reason for restrictions. "How can my teacher tell me what I need to know?" So if you can, try enrolling him in schools that promote independent thinking and learning. Your Aquarian will rebel against too much structure.

The teenage Aquarian can be the biggest challenge of all. Remember, this is the sign of the free spirit or the rebel. You always want to promote the free spirit, which means relinquishing control of your teenager. By this age they know right from wrong, so it's in their hands now. I know that might be difficult for Virgo parents, but you'd be fighting a losing battle. The more you control them, the more out of control they become. So just trust that they know what is best for them, because they do.

What is the most important thing you can do to help your Aquarian child? Gently, without them knowing it, try to keep them on track. Aquarians are involved with so many activities that they can easily get scattered or distracted. They need to know that they are in charge of their own lives and that you are supporting their interests, not yours. You are raising a free spirit and must have a light hand or you will suffer the consequences.

AQUARIUS PET

If you have a very active family and want a dog that can keep up, choose one born under the sign of Aquarius. I might have to explain why I picked my example of an Aquarian dog. I chose a mutt. Aquarius is friendly and very tolerant of other dogs. They are not prima donnas, are easy to get along with, and don't get bothered by much. An Aquarian puppy will be full of almost-uncontrollable energy and will need a doggie training class to learn basic commands. Once your dog knows the language, he will be much more responsive. Only one caveat for an Aquarian dog: They need space to run. So please don't get a dog born under this sign if you live in an apartment and don't have much activity in your household. This dog needs lots of action and movement. No doggie run or enclosed areas, please, or else you will have an inveterate barker on your hands.

ANIMALS FOR AQUARIUS
Camel
Dolphin
Hippopotamus
Ostrich
Reindeer
Seagull

AQUARIUS CELEBRITIES AND THEIR BIRTH DATES

Geena Davis	January 21
Christian Dior	January 21
Diane Lane	January 22
Alicia Keys	January 25
Ellen DeGeneres	January 26
Eddie Van Halen	January 26
Paul Newman	January 26
Bridget Fonda	January 27
Elijah Wood	January 28
Sarah McLachlan	January 28
Edward Burns	January 29
Oprah Winfrey	January 29
Vanessa Redgrave	January 30
Franklin D. Roosevelt	January 30
Justin Timberlake	January 31
Minnie Driver	January 31
Lisa Marie Presley	February 1
Christie Brinkley	February 2
Morgan Fairchild	February 3
Ashton Kutcher	February 7
Chris Rock	February 7
Charles Dickens	February 7
Mia Farrow	February 9
Emma Roberts	February 10
Jennifer Aniston	February 11
Sheryl Crow	February 11
Jane Seymour	February 15
Michael Jordan	February 17
Rene Russo	February 17
Matt Dillon	February 18

PERFECT GIFTS FOR AQUARIUS

Aquarians are fun to buy presents for because of their unusual hobbies and interests. Their main areas are computers, books, and things that are futuristic and quirky.

Computers

- The smallest travel computer
- Cool computer accessories
- Music gadget with unlimited tunes
- Portable DVD player
- Astrology software

Books

- Online gift card for books
- Science fiction, fantasy, astrology, or metaphysical titles
- Brain teasers or puzzles

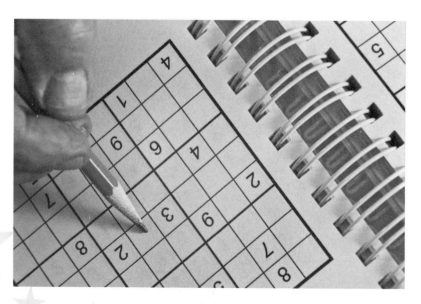

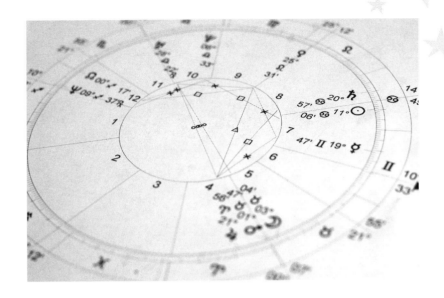

Futuristic and Quirky

- Chemistry or electronics set
- Basket of unusual socks (ankles are the Aquarian body part)
- Skydiving tickets
- Astrology software
- Mylar balloons
- CDs of electronic music

PISCES

February 20–March 20

KEYWORDS
POSITIVE KEYWORDS
Mystical

Spiritual

Intuitive

Soft

Poetic

Visionary

CAUTION KEYWORDS
Spacey

Insecure

Victim

INFORMATION
TWELFTH SIGN OF THE ZODIAC

Glyph: ♓

Planet: Neptune

Symbol: The Fishes

Element: Water

Mode: Mutable

Colors: Lavender, Purple

Gemstones: Amethyst, Quartz

Metal: Strontium

Body Part: Feet

PISCES: THE DREAMER

Pat is a double Pisces and works as a professional clairvoyant. She can do readings over the phone as well as in person. As a child, she always saw things and knew what was going to happen before it happened. But she soon realized that others didn't want to hear about her insights, so she shut this part of herself down. As an adult, she became interested in the spiritual world again, and her gift came back. When she read me, she told me things that no one knew. How did she know?

Pisces came here to connect with the unknown. I've named them the dreamers of the zodiac, and they do live in a dream world. As a professional clairvoyant, Pat does psychic readings for people all day long. It's fascinating to watch her during a reading. She asks your name and birthday and writes it down on a pad of paper. She then starts drawing circles over circles until they form a vortex. As soon as she gets the shape on the paper, the vortex opens in her mind and the information just starts pouring out. She gives names and dates, and describes entire stories about events that are going to happen. She's comfortable to be with because she looks like your neighbor instead of a woo-woo lady in a turban with a crystal dangling from her forehead. She gives what I would call a "meat and potatoes" psychic reading. Her suggestions concerning your life are practical and down to earth. Pat is a Pisces who is using her gift of intuition to help the world.

The symbol for Pisces is the well-known fishes swimming in circles in the sea of emotions. Fittingly, Pisces' planet, Neptune, is well-suited for the fish. Neptune is the planet of healing, compassion, and inner wisdom. With all these fish and Neptune images, it's not surprising that Pisces is the last of the water signs. Remember that Cancer's water is a babbling brook in front of a cottage and Scorpio's water is twelve thousand leagues under the sea. Pisces is too nebulous to have water in liquid form, so I'm assigning Pisces mist and fog. A vivid Pisces image is a shimmering rainbow through light rain or mist. If you turn around, it might disappear as you realize it was only an illusion anyway.

IF YOU'RE A PISCES, READ THIS!

You, dear heart, are the last sign of the zodiac. That makes you extra special because you have the accumulated knowledge of all the previous signs tucked away in your intuitive mind. All that wisdom can be completely illuminating or quite confusing to your psyche. So you are either the guru or the psychotic. Pisces are often misunderstood, because you do live in your own dream world, which is very difficult, sometimes even impossible, for anyone else to truly comprehend. You are the visionary of the zodiac and have the most vivid imagination of all the signs. Your purpose is to realize your power and seize your confidence that comes from inner knowing. You have a gigantic heart and will always help your fellow beings, but make sure you don't give everyone the shirt off your back. Pisces can easily oversacrifice themselves for the sake of humanity. Be as tough as you can!

WHAT MAKES YOU HAPPY?

Serenity

Your lifestyle must give you a feeling of peace of mind. You are a sensitive little bunny and need comforting surroundings with not many bright lights or loud noises. Pisces like a waterfall in the background for ambient sound instead of loud rock music, like Aquarians. You need a private refuge where you can escape to regularly. I call that the Pisces sanctuary. Don't think getting away into your own world is an indulgence—for you it's a necessity. Go to a tear-jerking matinee movie by yourself and cry. Get away to water or the beach often or at least wash your hands and face several times throughout the day. Baths are wonderful Pisces escapes and will give your psyche an amazingly refreshed feeling. My moon is in Pisces, so I totally understand your deep emotions. Don't feel bad if you cry at inopportune times; it shows your humanity and loving vulnerability. You're a softie and need to be proud of it.

The Ideal Pisces Lifestyle

You are a musician and a poet and are working on your third CD. Each day you get up and walk along the beach and take a swim in the ocean before you head back to your studio. Your amazing studio overlooks the ocean, giving you all the inspiration you need for your next song. Your music is soft, romantic, and perfect for your sentimental poetry. Your family life is contented and you feel loved and wanted by your spouse and your children. Work and success come to you so easily that you are never hurried or stressed. You love your gentle life and wouldn't trade it for any jet-setter's in Paris. Calm and sweet is perfect for this Pisces.

Your Ultimate Dream

To feel peaceful inside because you are respected for your creative ideas. You are surrounded by people who love you and appreciate your gentle strength and compassion. Part of your life is volunteering for your favorite charity, which gives you a warm sense of fulfillment deep in your soul.

PISCES STRENGTH

Pisces are fabulous at connecting two worlds together. They are the intermediaries between the dream world and reality. Staring off into space and daydreaming are their fortes, not weaknesses. Some people would say, "They don't pay attention!" But they *are* paying attention—to another reality, not this one. Pisces usually see auras, hear voices, or at least have strong hunches. Pisces have unconditional love for their fellow beings. Often they take in stray dogs and cats or even stray people who are lost and in need of help. They can relate to lost souls, because they have a deep well of emotions and deal with that every day. This sign has a talent for finding troubled souls, and knows how to coax them into redemption or rehabilitation. Meditation, prayer, and spiritual inspiration belong to the evolved Pisces. I call it the Pisces peace of mind.

PISCES CHALLENGE

Addiction is Pisces' biggest challenge. Although drugs and alcohol are common addictions among Pisces, they may also obsess over food, TV, sugar, emotions, video games, love, or many other seductive pleasures of the senses. Pisces like to enter altered states of consciousness, and their mission is to choose the safest method of getting high. Meditation and drugs could get you to almost the same place, but with different ultimate outcomes. But I think an even bigger challenge is the innate Pisces tendency toward self-pity, confusion, and lack of direction. They play the guilt game better than anyone else. This is ironic because they help more than anyone, but it's never quite enough. You'll never catch an Aquarian with a guilty conscience. But a Pisces will worry about hurting someone's feelings when that person didn't even give it a thought. The poor Pisces is losing sleep over nothing.

MENTAL CHARACTERISTICS

Pisces lives in the heart and not in the mind. People with this water sign sense their way through life using intuition only—with no plan and definitely no logic. Logic or left-brain thinking belongs to Virgos and Capricorns. But the creative, intuitive, right-brain thinking style belongs to Pisces. They don't have the quick, photographic memory of the air signs, but instead they recall images, colors, and impressions. That's why Pisces are much better off playing with art than working with statistics. Please save that type of mental gymnastics for Virgo! Pisces may feel insecure, so please don't compare yourself to other signs. Hear this: Pisces is just as smart as Virgo or any other sign; they just think differently. Pisces understand the concept but get lost in the details. Virgo is the opposite sign from Pisces and thinks in numbers and graphs. Not better, just different.

EMOTIONAL MAKEUP

Pisces are most comfortable in the world of emotions. They are psychic, intuitive, and dream their way through life, so the emotional place is their home. Pisces is at ease with sensitive issues and they make great healers, counselors, and spiritual advisors. My moon is in the sign of Pisces, so I'm an expert at this placement. Sensitive Pisces can cry easily at the slightest drama. It doesn't have to be sad because happiness can bring on the same heartfelt reaction. I cry when I listen to a song when the singer touches my heart and I also cry at a dancer when she is in the zone and dances like an angel defying gravity. One of the challenges of a Pisces is to be proud of those emotional outbursts instead of seeing them as moments of weakness. I finally understand that the power of Pisces is to open up the heart in a passionate way and truly feel deeply. It's really a precious gift of inner knowing and trust.

PHYSICAL CHARACTERISTICS

Appearance

Pisces has a gentleness of spirit that is easily recognizable in their bodies as well as their mannerisms. The typical Pisces body is of average height, with rounded shoulders, a short neck, soft and fine hair, and a broad head. The coloring, depending on background, of course, is usually pale with light-colored, large, and liquid eyes. When a Pisces looks at you, it seems as though she is in a dream and you can see right into her soul. Pisces usually have delicate or dainty hands and their body movements are graceful and flowing.

Fashion Sense

The watery Pisces likes flowing colors and soft fabrics. Often they are attracted to ocean-inspired blues, sea greens, aquamarines, and violet. Pisces will chose nebulous patterns that resemble waves, clouds, or gentle abstract images, made out of soft fabric or fine silk. They also like patterns that are repeated in nature, like light bouncing off leaves. Since Pisces is the spiritual guru, many wear white, flowing, gauzy clothing with healing crystals around their necks. Yes, Pisces is the sign that wears tunics or caftans with incense and candles in the background and represents the new age. A Virgo sure wouldn't do that.

Health Type

We started at the head with Aries and now Pisces completes the body by being associated with the feet. This sign needs to be pampered with regular pedicures and comfortable shoes. But I think the most important thing for Pisces to understand is their tendency to addiction. If they let themselves get out of control, they could end up struggling with alcohol, drugs, or other addictive habits. Some are addicted to food, TV, shopping, sex, or whatever makes them feel better. Let's face it: Pisces like to enter altered states of consciousness, and their health will be affected by their drug of choice.

Exercise Approach

The Pisces fish is perfect for swimming or water aerobics. Even getting into a pool and splashing around is enough exercise for many relaxed

Pisces. This not the sign of the marathon runner, but they can try to stretch or take a yoga class once in a while. While Aries need to exercise to burn off excess energy, Pisces need to exercise to build up their stores of energy because they are on the lethargic side. If they could, the tender Pisces would stay in bed all day reading, sleeping, or dreaming. Pisces might want to try a tai chi class so they can meditate and work out at the same time.

PROFESSIONAL LIFE

A perfect career for Pisces is one in which they use their gift of compassion to serve humanity, so many are doctors, nurses, massage therapists, healers, psychics, or counselors. Their natural creativity also shines as artists, photographers, musicians, or poets. I have a couple of Pisces clients who are clothing designers and two who actually design shoes. Since drugs and alcohol are major draws for Pisces, many are very good pharmacists, chemists, and drug counselors. Winemakers, winery owners, and bartenders fall under this sign in a healthy way, as long as alcohol is not their addiction. The yachting business, as well as working on cruise ships, as fishermen, and as sailors are all favored Pisces careers. A good percentage of Pisces choose a spiritual path and become clergy or at least active devotees.

Pisces Employer

There aren't many Pisces executives, because their sympathetic nature isn't aggressive enough for the driven ambition needed to succeed in the corporate world. Some Scorpio would eat them and spit them out. All Pisces have the heart of a woman, even if he is a manly looking man. He will have a kind, gentle voice and a compassionate manner. The best arenas for Pisces are nonprofit organizations, charities, art galleries, dance studios, and houses of worship. Your Pisces boss is very psychic and will always know your intentions, and you will feel as if he can see right into your soul—and he can. Organization is definitely not the Pisces' forte and Virgos or Capricorns make great assistants or managers to help. Your Pisces boss wants to be the creative source and only needs you to implement his dreams. And, yes, you will occasionally see the lost fish swimming around aimlessly, in need of guidance and direction.

PISCES IN THE BEDROOM

Pisces is one of the most romantic lovers of them all, so you can pull out all the schmaltzy tricks with this sign. Create the ambience for love with rose petals on the bed, dozens of candles flickering, romantic music, aromatherapy, flowers, and more flowers. Pisces have sensitive skin and would absolutely love silk sheets and a soft comforter. Throw your Pisces over the edge by giving her a romantic blank card with your very own handwritten poem. Read it in a slow, soft voice and watch your Pisces merge with you. Remember the Pointer Sisters' song lyric: *I want a lover with a slow hand*? Well, that could easily be the Pisces love anthem. They live in Pisces dreamland anyway, so Pisces love land is a promise—that is, if you have enough candles and soft kisses.

PISCES MALE PARTNER

Sean is a Pisces and he always wanted to be an artist. He took art and photography in college, but his family talked him into getting a "real" job." So he became a chiropractor and put his dream of being an artist on hold. Although his Pisces compassion made him a good doctor, he wasn't happy. Then an odd thing happened that ended his career as a doctor. He hurt his hand on the job and could no longer adjust his patients. It was a perfect accident because he earns great disability and could pursue his photography. Sean is now a world-class photographer and is living his Pisces dream. Is he happy? He's on cloud nine!

Pisces is the dreamer and absolutely needs to follow his chosen path in life to be happy. Sean is a great example of a sweet Pisces who let his family talk him out of his dream, but not for long. He was an artist as a child and all the way through college, and even invented some new photographic techniques. This water sign is naturally artistic and creative, and sees in shapes and colors. Pisces have an abstract way of looking at the world. They visualize swirls of water or ripples in the atmosphere and most of them are always trying to put down on paper what they see with their vivid imagination. Neptune, the planet of the unknown, inspires Pisces to look inward to find even more inspiration. They have a bottomless well of wisdom and imagination to tap into, and love spending time in their private sanctuary to discover what's in their well.

If you have come across a Pisces and want to know more about him, good luck. Those born under this sign are very elusive and vague when it comes to revealing personal or intimate details about themselves. They're not trying to be evasive or sneaky—save that for Scorpios—but they don't know which way they are headed currently. They will honestly tell you when they know. The Pisces fishes often find themselves swimming around in circles, looking for their next adventure. They swim toward whatever sparkly treasure lights up at the moment without a thought of deliberate planning. It's totally intuitive for the fish. So if you want a man who checks his portfolio online daily and faithfully puts a preplanned percentage of each paycheck in his retirement account, you are knocking on the wrong door. The nebulous Pisces goes with the flow and can't do it any other way—he's a fish.

This sign does come with some pretty good challenges that you need to know about. He needs time alone to reflect on his inner, private issues. Even though he's a man, he feels like a woman, so his emotions could rival any female's, any day. He is easily hurt and will pull into himself to heal his wounds. Believe me, you don't want to be with him when he's in that Pisces moody mood. If you try to draw him out of it before he's ready, he'll become confused, spacey, quiet, and ultrasensitive. Here's an important point: Choose a Pisces after he's found his mission in life. Until then, he might be searching restlessly and can't quite focus on a relationship when he feels unstable. In this mode, he's disorganized, procrastinates, and could feel sorry for himself. Guilt belongs to Pisces and your fish might not be able to commit yet because he's guilty about not being successful by now. The unhappy fish is a sad fish. But watch out, because if he feels too lost, that's when he could reach for a drink or something else to soothe himself. Substance abuse is the way the unhappy fish medicates himself against the harsh reality of life.

If you have good timing and have found your Pisces partner after he's discovered his purpose in life, you're lucky. A happy and satisfied Pisces is one of the most loving partners of them all. This sign often feels insecure in love and needs romance to feel protected. To keep your Pisces man secure, he needs to be appreciated. It's not enough for him to know that you love him; he needs to be reassured all the time. He's very receptive to tender words and tender touches, so shower your Pisces with affection. He's very affectionate and loves to hold hands, kiss, and snuggle. If he knows that you really love him, he'll return that love with total unconditional love, like a happy fish.

PISCES FEMALE PARTNER

Tina, a double Pisces, is a shoe designer. How perfect, since Pisces is associated with the feet. She is so clever and not only with her designs, but also in how she named them. She gave each pair of shoes the name of a city in the world. So you can order the Hawaiian yellow sandals or the Parisian purple pumps. She travels all over the globe to get inspiration for next year's styles. Tina creates her designs out of her beach home on the ocean. She's soft-spoken, gentle, and very feminine, with the palest of steel-blue eyes and long, fine blond hair that falls into natural ringlets. She looks like a Pisces angel.

Tina is a romantic, loving Pisces and she glides across the floor instead of just walking. But she looks like she hasn't quite landed totally in her body yet. Either that or she's sleepwalking, which could happen with the dreamy Pisces. This is the last and, I think, the most watery of all the three water signs. The sign of Cancer has to pay attention to his family responsibilities, so that keeps him a bit grounded. Scorpio is so intensely focused on his money or manipulations that it keeps him on track. But the Pisces fish must go inward, so there is nothing to distract her except herself. So Pisces often feel isolated and out of touch with reality. Let's see, reality belongs to Saturn and Capricorn. Pisces got stuck with Neptune, the daydreamer and wimp of all the planets. Neptune whispers instead of talking, so Pisces have to really listen or else they miss out on all that infinite wisdom.

Like many Pisces, Tina is very spiritual and actively practices her various meditations. For her entire adult life, she has traveled all over the world searching for her mystical inner self. She's meditated with gurus from India, sitting on a mat in the Himalayas. She's climbed Machu Picchu in Peru with a shaman. That was the time she went on a guided trip using the sacred herb Ayahuesca. She told me that she threw up for hours and then saw the most enlightened visions all night. Tina said that she could see the energy being emitted by every living plant and creature. Was she seeing auras? It reminded her of halos that she sees in holy paintings. She could see the molecules in the air moving when she breathed in and out. It took her quite a while to come down from that trip. Pisces love to enter states of altered consciousness and if they can combine that with spirit, they're in heaven.

So, have you fallen for a Pisces angel? If you have, put on your soft kid gloves, because you have to be extra gentle with her. Sweet Pisces are very sensitive and get their feelings hurt incredibly easily. They take everything literally and, unlike Scorpio, are not very streetwise. Pisces is shy, gullible, and always trusting. She will always see the best in people, even if they are of questionable character. Her innocence protects her, but she needs to be treated like a delicate flower. Abrupt movements or a loud voice will scare her off. Think soft little bunny. Would you yell or surprise a little bunny? No! Your Pisces angel is just as pure and delicate. Honor her quiet time when she's reflecting or just resting. Pisces need more sleep than any other sign of the zodiac. Even catnaps through the day help the ethereal Pisces. My theory is that Pisces are mostly in dreamland and occasionally descend to earth, but not often.

If you treated your Pisces angel well enough that she also fell in love with you, what a loving relationship you will have with her! Pisces and Libra are the two romantics of the zodiac, so you are in luck. Your Pisces partner is compassionate, kind, tenderhearted, and very loving. She needs to be told and shown that you love her often. You couldn't say "I love you" and "You look beautiful" enough for a Pisces, who needs constant reassurance. Like the little bunny, confidence is not her strength, so you will have to pay particular attention to her feelings. If you see her withdraw and get quiet, reach out and give her a hug because she's feeling insecure for some reason. Is your Pisces worth a little extra attention? Of course she is. Few of us have our very own angel.

PISCES FATHER FIGURE

Benoit (Ben-wa), a double Pisces, was born in France to a well-known winemaking family. He is the fifth generation to continue his family's winemaking business and they have some of the best land and grape stock in all of France. He's married to a beautiful, aristocratic French woman and they have three lovely children. Benoit and his family live on an estate with their vast acreage of grapes nearby. Their extensive formal gardens are graced with huge white statues that reminded me of Greek gods and goddesses. If wine is the nectar of the gods, this Pisces knows how to celebrate in fine style.

Benoit has a fantasy life, even for a Pisces. I've been lucky enough to visit my clients all over the world and have seen some of the most elaborate and expensive estates on this planet. Benoit's scene is one of the best I've ever seen.

The view from his personal chateau is almost 360 degrees, and it is truly breathtaking. He also has a farm and I sat there for hours watching the different animals migrate to new fields throughout the day. He raises cows, goats, and chickens, as well as a totally organic vegetable and herb garden. They have a French chef who cooks exclusively from their bounty. As I sat there, the light danced on the hills as the sun made its daily arch along the ecliptic, or that planetary highway in the sky. It was so easy to meditate on the grassy deck overlooking the valley. It was truly one of the most beautiful and relaxing places I've ever visited—and that was without a glass of wine!

Pisces love serenity, so Benoit had little sanctuaries built all over his estate. I took a long walk and found numerous meditation havens along the path. He's traveled all over the world collecting holy statues from many different religions and has given them each their own sanctuary. So I sat with Buddha for a while and then moved to Saint Francis in the bird aviary. After that I walked over to a huge Ganesh, which was by his petting zoo, where I spent some time with that amazing sacred elephant from India. I think Ganesh comfortably living in his zoo was my favorite. Benoit spends a lot of time meditating in his different spots of sacred shelter. Pisces need to get away from reality often, and meditation and prayer are positive avenues of escape for them. Of course, right at 5:00 p.m. each day, Benoit goes to his underground wine cellar and chooses a new bottle of wine for the evening. Oh, my, what a wine cellar!

Benoit is mild-tempered, gentle, kind, and charming. He is a wonderful host and made me feel completely at home. But I did notice the other side of Pisces, even with his charm. He never left his estate. I think he's more shy and introverted than I had realized before I stayed there. He has a fragile look to him, even though he's a strong man. I had the feeling that he missed his calling, that he had been a monk for lifetimes, and that part of him yearned for that old familiar, meditative solitude. It's almost as though life is a distraction to the more important mission of devotion. His family seemed used to his need for privacy and left him alone when he needed it. Pisces is the recluse and Benoit enjoyed his seclusion. I have to admit that the thought did run through my mind that he was lucky to be born into a wealthy family without much responsibility. Of course, he had a Virgo personal assistant taking care of his every need—thank goodness.

Pisces require a serene life and when they have that, the love just pours out from them. Benoit is very affectionate and loving with his children. So if you have a loving Pisces father, count your lucky stars. He's very kind and trusting and, if anything, is on the lenient side of discipline. No yelling, like an Aries dad, or control, like a Scorpio father. In fact, your dad is a pushover and will let you do pretty much whatever you want. But he is so trusting; please don't take advantage of him. Mean or tricky kids could manipulate this kind dad for selfish purposes. He doesn't deserve that because a Pisces really is pure, with no hidden motives. Your Pisces father will give you unconditional love, so give it back to him and everyone will have that Pisces peace-of-mind grin.

PISCES MOTHER FIGURE

Mary is a sweet Pisces and made her living as a social worker specializing in abused children. She is a devout Catholic and basically fell in love with her priest, whose name is Arthur. After years of working together on parish projects, he also fell in love with her. For the sake of true love, he quit the church and they got married. Soon after, they had a son, named Adam, and are very happy as a family. Mary wanted more children but couldn't have any more, so they became foster parents. Their family has now had over thirty children come through their loving home on the way to an adoptive family. Now that's an inspirational Pisces mother who helps children in need!

Mary is the most perfect Pisces mother I know, plus she has a wonderful love story to tell. She went to Catholic schools growing up and always wanted to be a nun, but went into social work instead. Mary even looks like a nun, with a kind face and a genuine smile, and volunteers for a variety of children's programs. Pisces have a need to help charities and the underprivileged, just to make them feel good about themselves. Those born under this sign work tirelessly to help the world and feel guilty at night because they aren't doing enough. Neptune, the planet for Pisces, encourages compassion and a deep concern for others. Mary's focus is on the children who have had a rough start. Her role model is Mother Teresa and I think she does an incredible job of dedicating herself to humanity, starting with the little ones.

Now comes the part of the story where love enters her life. By the way, the ex-priest she married is also a Pisces. Mary and Arthur are so natural as a family that it seems like they've been working together for lifetimes. No religion was going to keep them apart in this lifetime, either. Arthur now works with a nonprofit organization that does fundraising for charities. After Mary had their son, Adam, she's stayed at home with him as a full-time mother. When Adam was around five years old, they were approved as an official foster family. Since then, approximately three children a year have lived with them as the young ones are processed into permanent families. Mary, Arthur, and Adam love each and every one of the foster children, and see them all as siblings.

I think Mary is more stable emotionally than many Pisces because she has found her purpose in life. Pisces fish can swim around in a confused daze until they find the right path. Many are late bloomers and discover their life's work after going down a few dead ends looking for the right street. But once they find their purpose, they are on a mission and won't be satisfied until it's completed. Other Pisces often grapple with lack of direction, insecurity, confusion, or procrastination. But the main challenge I see for Mary is her habit of sacrifice. She takes absolutely no time for herself and dedicates her life totally to her family, including her foster children. The nun in her takes her work so seriously that she always has a look of sad concern in her eyes. It makes me want to give her a hug whenever I see her.

If your mother is a Pisces, you have one of the kindest mothers of all. She will always be there for you with unconditional love when you need her. Her Pisces sense of compassion and true love comes through everything that she does for you. But be sure to remember her emotional needs, too. When she's tired, give her some space to rest and recuperate. Rubbing her Pisces feet will always bring a smile to her face. She's not very materialistic, but she would love a handmade card or present showing your love. But the best thing you could do to make your mom happy is to have a peaceful Pisces home.

PISCES CHILD

Anna is a double Pisces who is delicate and shy, but she's quite a little swimmer. Even as a baby, they couldn't get her out of her bath, so they enrolled her in an infant swimming class. She's only eight years old now, but is already on the swim team. She's not on a racing team, but prefers the more creative and flowing synchronized swimming and water gymnastics. They're all amazed at her naturally elegant movements in the water. She really swims like a fish. Luckily, her family has a swimming pool in the backyard, so she gets lots of practice. Anna is now taking ballet, so she can even be more graceful in the water. I call her the Pisces mermaid.

Your Pisces child is the most fragile sign of them all. This child came to you to be treated with gentle kindness and emotional respect. Pisces get their feelings hurt very easily, so unless you want them in therapy about their parents when they are adults, treat them kindly as children. Never yell or intimidate your little Pisces, because that will scar them for life. Instead, you will need to help them build their confidence, as Pisces tend to be insecure. You have a delicate flower and need to treat it accordingly or else it will wither in your hand. You have been given the precious gift of caring for a dear sweetheart and need to learn how to treat her with a soft touch.

As a baby, Pisces is one of the love bugs. Pisces babies are among the most affectionate of all the signs. In fact, the Pisces baby wants to be held and needs a lot of attention because he could easily feel abandoned if he is left alone very much. No loud noises or bright lights, please.

Pisces toddlers will be quite easy to care for in comparison to other more rambunctious signs. The little water baby is gentle, sweet, and sensitive. Make sure Pisces clothes and bedding are extra-soft for their extra-tender skin. The Pisces young child isn't going to be running around, out of control, and is more comfortable with creative activities. Have art supplies galore for the emerging artist. Quiet music in the background is also soothing for the soft Pisces.

School can be a challenge for the shy Pisces, until she makes friends and settles into this new, safe environment. Since Pisces have such strong and vivid imaginations, often they need to learn the difference between truth and what is imagined. This is the perfect child for an imaginary friend, but try gently to bring into her world a bit of reality. Pisces are born psychic and need parents who appreciate and are not afraid of that talent.

Pisces need to realize that their style of learning is different from that of other signs. This water sign is much more intuitive and creative and probably won't be the captain of the debate team or fall in love with statistics. Their mind works with images and concepts, and they are not very good at details and organization. Look the other way and don't fret about the mess they call their bedroom. Does it really matter in the larger scheme of things? I do feel sorry for the Virgo moms, though.

One more important thing to understand about Pisces—they daydream. I know the teachers will say that they aren't paying attention and seem to be in another world. They *are* in another world—their own world of genius. Maybe they're trying to remember their dream this morning when they solved the mystery of time. They see that daydream as being much more important than listening to the silly teacher. I think I agree with the Pisces genius. Now that you understand this delicate sign, I'm sure you will be wonderful, loving parents to your little Pisces. Not all parents are blessed with a real angel.

PISCES PET

Pisces pets, as well as Pisces humans, are very sensitive. If your home is calm, fairly quiet, and full of gentle people, then you can choose a pet born under the sign of gentle Pisces. If you have three rough little Aries boys running around, please pick an Aries, Leo, or Sagittarian pet. The sweet little Pisces will hide under the bed with all that noise and ruckus. But if you have one teenage daughter who wants to groom and pamper your Pisces pet, go for it. I've chosen a gracious, but nervous Afghan as an example of a Pisces dog. Those born under this sign need gentle, loving care or they will turn neurotic on you. The last thing you need is a neurotic doggie in your house. But if you have a quiet, placid home life, a Pisces pet will offer you years of sweet, unconditional love. If that seems too much, just buy an aquarium with fish.

ANIMALS FOR PISCES
Condor
Elephant
Fish
Hyena
Mink
Panther
Parasite
Rhinoceros
Walrus
Whale
Wildcat

PERFECT GIFTS FOR PISCES

Pisces love to receive gifts and will be very responsive in thanking you for them. Their main areas of interest are fantasy, music, and escape. Choose gifts from this list to make any Pisces happy!

Fantasy
- Incense
- Candles
- Bath bubbles
- Flowers

Music
- Romantic CDs
- Concert tickets for two
- MP3 player with playlists included

Escape
- Aquarium with lots of fish
- Silk bedding
- Water feature or fountain
- Favorite wine or spirit
- Alaskan cruise holiday

PISCES CELEBRITIES AND THEIR BIRTH DATES

Smokey Robinson	February 19
Prince Andrew	February 19
Cindy Crawford	February 20
Jennifer Love Hewitt	February 21
Drew Barrymore	February 22
Edward Kennedy	February 22
Peter Fonda	February 23
Dakota Fanning	February 23
George Harrison	February 24
Ann McCrea	February 25
Pierre Renoir	February 25
Johnny Cash	February 26
Joanne Woodward	February27
Elizabeth Taylor	February 27
Ron Howard	March 1
Jon Bon Jovi	March 2
Jessica Biel	March 3
Kevin Connolly	March 5
Michelangelo	March 6
Freddie James Prinze Jr.	March 8
Juliette Binoche	March 9
Billy Crystal	March 14
Eva Longoria	March 15
Lauren Graham	March 16
Kurt Russell	March 17
Queen Latifah	March 18
Bruce Willis	March 19
Glenn Close	March 19

BIBLIOGRAPHY

Hall, Manley Palmer. *Astrological Keywords*. Savage, MD: Littlefield Adams Quality Paperbacks, 1958.

Lineman, Rose, and Jan Popelka. *Compendium of Astrology*. Gloucester, MA: Para Research, Inc., 1984.

Lynch, John. *The Coffee Table Book of Astrology*. New York, NY: Viking Press, 1967.

Munkasey, Michael. *The Astrological Thesaurus*. St. Paul, MN: Llewellyn Worldwide, Ltd., 1992.

Parker, Julia and Derek. *Parkers' Astrology*. London, England: Penguin Group, UK, 1991.

PHOTO CREDITS

ABOUT THE AUTHOR

Susie Cox has been a professional astrologer since 1971 and has interpreted approximately 43,000 charts. Since 1981, she has been employed as an astrologer at the highly acclaimed Tucson, Arizona, location of the Canyon Ranch Spa and Health Resort chain. She has spearheaded the growth of their popular Metaphysics department and was appointed Master Astrologer in 2006. Her clients include an A-list of celebrities, business leaders, royalty, self-help gurus, and politicians from around the world.

Susie is the author of numerous astrological columns, articles, and books. In the late 1970s, she co-owned and operated The White Light Book Shop and Metaphysical Learning Center. Soon after, she became co-owner of The Aquarian Angels, a media company that published the wildly popular *Aquarian Almanac*. Much later, in 1992, Susie developed FISA, the Foundation for the International Study of Astrology, and published the first of two editions of *The International Directory of Astrologers*, which sold in 57 countries.

Susie is a leader in the international astrological community and a member of the ISAR (International Society of Astrological Research), AFAN (Astrological Federation of Astrological Networking), and a founder of TAG, the Tucson Astrologers Guild. An accomplished speaker in her field, she lectures regularly at national and international conferences and presents workshops and does readings throughout the United States and Europe. One of her European locations is Alchemy, a popular New Age center in London. Susie also writes an astrology column for *Holistic Health, a bimonthly magazine published in Dublin.*

Although she travels extensively, Susie was born and raised in Tucson, Arizona, where she now lives. Susie's boundless energy and enthusiasm, as well as her positive outlook on life, bring hope, joy and inspiration to her clients.

31901051654079